rumours

OF ANOTHER WORLD

Resources by Philip Yancey

The Jesus I Never Knew
What's So Amazing About Grace?
What's So Amazing About Grace? Visual Edition
The Bible Jesus Read
Reaching for the Invisible God
Where Is God When It Hurts?
Disappointment with God
The Student Bible (with Tim Stafford)
Meet the Bible (with Brenda Quinn)
Church: Why Bother?
Finding God in Unexpected Places
I Was Just Wondering
Soul Survivor

Books by Philip Yancey and Dr. Paul Brand

Fearfully and Wonderfully Made
In His Image
The Gift of Pain

PHILIP YANCEY

rumours

OF ANOTHER WORLD

WHAT
ON
EARTH
ARE
WE
MISSING?

ZONDERVAN™

GRAND RAPIDS, MICHIGAN 49530 USA

ZONDERVAN™

for those who live in the borderlands of belief

contents

a note from the author

I wrote this book for people who live in the borderlands of belief, a phrase first suggested to me by the writer Mark Buchanan. In regions of conflict, such as the Korean peninsula, armies on both sides patrol their respective borders, leaving a disputed territory in between as a buffer zone. Wander into that middle area and you'll find yourself in a "no-man's-land" belonging to neither side.

In matters of faith, many people occupy the borderlands. Some give church and Christians a wide berth yet still linger in the borderlands because they cannot set aside the feeling that there must be a spiritual reality out there. Maybe an epiphany of beauty or a sense of longing gives a nudge toward something that must exist beyond the everyday routine of life—but what? Big issues—career change, the birth of a child, the death of a loved one—raise questions with no easy answers. Is there a God? A life after death? Is religious faith only a crutch, or a path to something authentic?

I also meet Christians who would find it difficult to articulate why they believe as they do. Perhaps they absorbed faith as part of their upbringing, or perhaps they simply find church an uplifting place to visit on weekends. But if asked to explain their faith to a Muslim or an atheist, they would not know what to say.

What would I say? That question prompted this book. I wrote it not so much to convince anyone else as to think out loud in hopes of coming to terms with my own faith. Does religious faith make sense in a world of the Hubble telescope and the Internet? Have we figured out the basics of life, or is some important ingredient missing?

To me, the great divide separating belief and unbelief reduces down to one simple question: Is the visible world around us all there is? Those unsure of the answer to that question—whether they approach it from the regions of belief or unbelief—live in the borderlands. They wonder whether faith in an unseen world is wishful thinking. Does faith delude us into seeing a world that doesn't exist, or does it reveal the existence of a world we cannot see without it?

I "think out loud" by putting words on paper, and out of that process this book emerged. I begin with the visible world around us, the world all of us inhabit. What rumours of another world might it convey? From there, I look at the apparent contradictions. If this is God's world, why doesn't it look more like it? Why is this planet so messed up? Finally, I consider how two worlds—visible and invisible, natural and supernatural—might interact and affect our daily lives. Does the Christian way represent the best life on this earth or a kind of holding pattern for eternity?

I am at times a reluctant Christian, buffeted by doubts and "in recovery" from bad church encounters. I have explored these experiences in other books, and so I determined not to mine my past yet again in this one. I am fully aware of all the reasons not to believe. So then, why do I believe? Read on.

PART ONE

what are we missing?

Every ant knows the formula of its ant-hill,
every bee knows the formula of its beehive.
They know it in their own way, not in our way.
Only humankind does not know its formula.

FYODOR DOSTOYEVSKY

life in part

The most beautiful thing we can experience is the mysterious. It is the source of all true art and science. He to whom this emotion is a stranger, who can no longer pause to wonder and stand rapt in awe, is as good as dead: his eyes are closed.

ALBERT EINSTEIN

More than ten million people in Europe and Asia have viewed a remarkable exhibition known as Body Worlds. A German professor invented a vacuum process called *plastination*, which replaces individual cells of the human body with brightly coloured resins and epoxies, much as minerals replace the cells of trees in a petrified forest. As a result, he can preserve a human body, whole or stripped away to reveal its inner parts, and display the cadaver in an eerily lifelike pose.

I visited Body Worlds in a warehouse art gallery in London after an overnight flight from my home in Colorado. I was feeling the effects of jet lag until, on entering the gallery, I encountered the exhibition's signature piece: a man all muscles, tendons, and ligaments, his face peeled like a grape, with the entire rubbery organ of skin, flayed and intact, draped over his arm like a raincoat. Sleepiness immediately gave way to a morbid fascination.

For the next two hours I shuffled past the sixty preserved bodies art-fully arranged among palm trees and educational displays. I saw a woman eight months pregnant, reclining as if on a couch, her insides opened to reveal the foetus resting head-down inside. Skinned athletes—a runner, swordsman, swimmer, and basketball player—assumed their normal poses to demonstrate the wonders of the skeletal and muscular systems. A chess player sat intently at a chessboard, his back stripped to the nerves of his spinal cord and his skull removed to reveal the brain.

One display hung the pink organs of the digestive system on a wire frame, descending from the tongue down to the stomach, liver, pancreas, intestines, and colon. A placard mentioned five million glands employed for digestion, and I could not help thinking of the combination of cured salmon, cinnamon rolls, yogurt, and fish and chips—sloshed together with at least a quart of airline coffee—challenging those glands inside me at that moment. Moving on, I learned that babies have no kneecaps at birth, that the body's total volume of blood filters through the kidneys every four minutes, that brain cells die if deprived of oxygen for even ten sec-onds. I viewed a liver shrunken from alcohol abuse, a tiny spot of cancer in a breast, globs of plaque clinging to the walls of arteries, lungs black from cigarette smoke, a urethra squeezed by an enlarged prostate gland.

When not observing the plastinated bodies, I observed the people observing the plastinated bodies. A young girl wearing all black, her midriff bare, with orange hair and a lip ring, roses tattooed on her arm, alert to all live bodies but barely noticing the preserved ones. A Japanese woman in a flowered silk dress and straw hat with matching straw plat-form shoes, very proper, staring impassively at each exhibit. A doctor ostentatiously showing off his knowledge to a beautiful young compan-ion twenty years his junior. A know-it-all college student in a jogging suit explaining wrongly to his girlfriend that "of course, the right brain controls speech." Silent people pressing plastic audio wands to their ears, marching on cue like zombies from one display to the next.

The sharp scent of curry drifted in from outdoors, along with the throb of hip-hop music. Local merchants, sponsoring a curry festival, had blocked off several streets for bands and dancing. I moved to a window and watched the impromptu block party. Outside the gallery, life; inside, the plastinated residue of life.

Wherever Body Worlds had opened, in places like Switzerland and Korea, organized protests had followed, and the exhibition had papered one wall with news accounts of the demonstrations. Protesters believed that it affronted human dignity to take someone like a grandmother, with a family and home and name and maybe even an eternal destiny, and dissect and plastinate her, then put her on display for gawking tourists.

In response, Professor Gunther von Hagens had posted a vigorous statement defending his exhibition. He explained that the cadavers/persons had before death voluntarily signed over their bodies for precisely this purpose. Indeed, he had a waiting list of thousands of prospective donors. He credited Christianity as being the religion most tolerant of this line of scientific research and included a brief history of the church and medicine. Bizarrely, the exhibition ended with two splayed corpses, all muscles and bones and bulging eyes, kneeling before a cross.

———

That groggy afternoon at Body Worlds highlighted for me two distinct ways of looking at the world. One takes apart while the other seeks to connect and put together. We live in an age that excels at the first and falters at the second.

The cadavers, dissected to expose bones, nerves, muscles, tendons, ligaments, blood vessels, and internal organs, demonstrate our ability to break something down—in this case, the human being—into its constituent parts. We are *reductionistic,* say the scientists, and therein lies the secret to advances in learning. We can reduce complex systems like the solar system, global weather patterns, and the human body into simpler parts in order to understand how things work.*

---

*René Descartes stated the motto for reductionism: "If anyone could know perfectly what are the small parts composing all bodies, he would know perfectly the whole of nature." Francis Crick, codiscoverer of the structure of DNA, applies the formula to human beings: "You are nothing but a pack of neurones. . . . You are . . . no more than the behaviour of a vast assembly of nerve cells and their associated molecules."

The recent digital revolution is a triumph of the reducers, for computers work by reducing information all the way down to a 1 or a 0. Nearly every day a friend sends me jokes by email. Today, I got a list of questions to ponder, including these: Why is "abbreviated" such a long word? Why is the time of day with the slowest traffic called rush hour? Why isn't there mouse-flavoured cat food? People with too much time on their hands come up with these jokes, type them into a computer, and post them electronically for the amusement of the rest of the world.

I think of all the steps involved. The jokester's computer registers a series of keystrokes, translates them into binary bits of data, and records them magnetically as a file on a hard disk. Later, communications software retrieves that file and translates it into a sequential code, which it sends over a modem or broadband line to a computer server sitting in an isolated room. Some user plucks the joke for the day from the server, imports it to a home computer, and forwards it to a list of email contacts. The cycle goes on and on, with bits of joke data streaming over phone lines and wireless signals, even bouncing off satellites, until at last I log onto the Internet and download my friend's attempt to bring a smile to my face.

Masters of the art, we can reduce not just jokes but literature and music and photographs and movies into digital bits and broadcast them around the world in seconds. On the ski slopes of Colorado I meet Australians who email snapshots of their ski vacation back to friends and family every night. A few minutes on an Internet site will let me search and locate any word in Shakespeare or view the artwork hanging in the Louvre museum.

Have we, though, progressed in creating content that others will someday want to store and retrieve? Does our art match that of the Impressionists, our literature compare with the Elizabethans', our music improve on Bach or Beethoven? In most cases, taking apart what exists proves easier than creating what does not yet exist. Think of the best artificial hands, built with state-of-the-art technology, yet clumsy and mechanical in their motion compared to the human body's.

School textbooks used to report that the chemicals constituting the human body could be bought by catalogue for eighty-nine cents, which of course does nothing to explain the magnificence of an athlete like Michael Jordan or Serena Williams. A junior high sex-education study of fallopian tubes and the vas deferens hardly captures the wonder, mystery, and anxiety of marital sex. And the impressive displays at Body Worlds in London pale in comparison to the ordinary people chewing gum, sipping Starbucks coffee, and chatting on cellphones as they file past.

We reduce into parts, but can we fit together the whole? We can replace the cells of a human body with coloured plastic or slice it into a thousand parts. We have a much harder time agreeing on what a human person is. Where did we come from? Why are we here? Will any part of us survive death? The people on display at Body Worlds—do they endure as immortal souls somewhere in another dimension, perhaps peering whimsically at the line of tourists filing past their plastinated bodies? And what of an invisible world rumoured by the mystics, a world that cannot be dissected and put on display in a gallery? Knowing the parts doesn't necessarily help us understand the whole.

I once heard the missionary author Elisabeth Elliot tell of accompanying the Auca woman Dayuma from her jungle home in Ecuador to New York City. As they walked the streets, Elliot explained cars, fire hydrants, sidewalks, and red lights. Dayuma's eyes took in the scene, but she said nothing. Elliot next led her to the observation platform atop the Empire State Building, where she pointed out the tiny taxi cabs and people on the streets below. Again, Dayuma said nothing. Elliot could not help wondering what kind of impression modern civilization was making. Finally, Dayuma pointed to a large white spot on the concrete wall and asked, "What bird did that?" At last she had found something she could relate to.

I have visited the tip of Argentina, the region named Tierra del Fuego ("land of fire") by Magellan's explorers, who noticed fires burning on shore. The natives tending the fires, however, paid no attention to the great ships as they sailed through the straits. Later, they explained that they had considered the ships an apparition, so different were they from anything seen before. They lacked the experience, even the imagination, to decode evidence passing right before their eyes.

And we who built the skyscrapers in New York, who build today not just galleons but space stations and Hubble telescopes that peer to the very edge of the universe, what about us? What are we missing? What do we not see, for lack of imagination or faith?

———

Søren Kierkegaard told a parable about a rich man riding in a lighted carriage driven by a peasant who sat behind the horse in the cold and dark outside. Precisely because he sat near the artificial light inside, the rich man missed the panorama of stars outside, a view gloriously manifest to the peasant. In modern times, it seems, as science casts more light on the created world, its shadows further obscure the invisible world beyond.

I am no Luddite who opposes technological change. My laptop computer allows me to access the text of every book I have written in the past twenty years, as well as thousands of notes I have made during that time. Though I am holed up in a mountain retreat, using this same computer I have sent messages to friends in Europe and Asia. I pay my monthly bills electronically. In these and other ways I gratefully enjoy the benefits of the reducers' approach to technology and science.

Yet I also see dangers in our modern point of view. For one thing, reductionism, the spirit of our age, has the unfortunate effect of, well, reducing things. Science offers a map of the world, something like a topographical map, with colours marking the vegetation zones and squiggly lines tracing the contours of cliffs and hills. When I hike the mountains of Colorado, I rely on such topographical maps. Yet no map of two dimensions, or even three dimensions, can give the full picture. And none can possibly capture the experience of the hike: thin mountain air, a carpet of wildflowers, a ptarmigan's nest, rivulets of frothy water, a triumphant lunch at the summit. Encounter trumps reduction.

More importantly, the reducers' approach allows no place for an invisible world. It takes for granted that the world of matter is the sum total of existence. We can measure and photograph and catalogue it; we can use nuclear accelerators to break it down into its smallest particles. Looking at the parts, we judge them the whole of reality.

Of course, an invisible God cannot be examined or tested. Most definitely, God cannot be quantified or reduced. As a result, many people in societies advanced in technology go about their daily lives assuming God does not exist. They stop short at the world that can be reduced and analysed, their ears sealed against rumours of another world. As Tolstoy said, materialists mistake what limits life for life itself.

I have a neighbour who is obsessively neat. He lives on ten forested acres, and every time he drove up his long, winding driveway, the disorderly dead branches on the Ponderosa pine trees bothered him. One day he called a tree-trimming service and learned it would cost him five thousand dollars to trim all those trees. Appalled at the price, he rented a chain saw and spent several weekends perched precariously on a ladder cutting back all the branches he could reach. He called the service for a new estimate and got an unwelcome surprise. "Mr Rodrigues, it will probably cost you twice as much. You see, we were planning to use those lower branches to reach the higher ones. Now we have to bring in an expensive truck and work from a bucket."

In some ways, modern society reminds me of that story. We have sawed off the lower branches on which Western civilization was built, and the higher branches now seem dangerously out of reach. "We have drained the light from the boughs in the sacred grove and snuffed it in the high places and along the banks of sacred streams," writes Annie Dillard.

No society in history has attempted to live without a belief in the sacred, not until the modern West. Such a leap has consequences that we are only beginning to recognize. We now live in a state of confusion about the big questions that have always engaged the human race, questions of meaning, purpose, and morality. A sceptical friend of mine used to ask himself the question, "What would an atheist do?" in deliberate mockery of the What Would Jesus Do (WWJD) slogan. He finally stopped asking because he found no reliable answers.

Eliminating the sacred changes the story of our lives. In times of greater faith, people saw themselves as individual creations of a loving God who, regardless of how it may look at any given moment, has final control over a world destined for restoration. Now, people with no faith find themselves lost and alone, with no overarching story, or meta-narrative, to give promise to the future and meaning to the present. To regard nature as beautiful, humans as uniquely valuable, morality as necessary—these are mere "constructs," we are told, invented to soften the harsh reality that humans play an infinitesimal role in a universe governed by chance.

Most people in history have experienced this world with its pleasures and pains, its births and deaths and loves and passages, as linked to the sacred, invisible world. No longer, or not for many, at least. Now we are born, play, work, accumulate possessions, relate to one another, and die with no consolation that what we do matters ultimately or has any meaning beyond what we assign it.

Jacques Monod bluntly states the modern plight: "Man must learn to live in an alien world that is deaf to his music and is as indifferent to his hopes as it is to his sufferings or his crimes.... Man at last knows that he is alone in the unfeeling immensity of the universe, out of which he emerged only by chance."

Einstein remarked that the modern age has perfect means but confused ends. Physicists have reduced matter to subatomic particles and software engineers have reduced most of what we know about the world to bits of information. We know how things work, but not why. We seem bewildered, actually, about why anyone makes any given choice—whether to love their kids or beat them, whether to study for a test or binge-drink. Why do we act the way we do and make the choices we do?

The new science of evolutionary psychology has arisen to assert that we simply act out the script of our DNA. Advocates propose a single principle, the "selfish gene," to explain behaviour, and evolutionary theorists herald this insight as the most important advance since Darwin. I do what I do, always, to perpetuate my genetic material. Even individual acts that do not benefit me personally will benefit my gene pool.

In a sour twist, these thinkers view all goodness as a form of self-ishness. Altruism, proclaims Edward O. Wilson, is purely selfish: a person acts in an apparently noble way toward the goal of getting some reward. Goodness depends, he says, on "lying, pretence, and deceit, including self-deceit, because the actor is most convincing who believes that his performance is real." Challenged to explain Mother Teresa's behaviour, Wilson pointed out that, believing she would get her reward from Christ, she acted on that selfish basis.

Although specialists may believe this selfish-motive theory, for most people it does not ring true. Therapists who spend all day listening to people's stories know that the choices we make do not easily reduce to a single explanation. Parents learn by hard experience that no reward-and-punishment scheme can guarantee the results they want.

What drives us, any of us, to become the persons we are? What makes some students responsible and conscientious while others drop out of school? What drives some people to become millionaires, others to become missionary nurses, and others to watch television all day, leeching off their parents? No single explanation of purpose or motive tells the full story.

The reducers face their greatest challenge in trying to find a stable ground for morality. Not long ago, two evolutionary psychologists roused the ire of feminists by presenting rape as a normal part of natural selection, a technique males use to spread their seed as widely as possible. Given their selfish-gene assumptions, this distasteful theory made good sense.

Another leading evolutionary theorist, Frans de Waal, says, "We seem to be reaching a point at which science can wrest morality from the hands of the philosophers." He looks to nature for examples of "ethical" behaviour, and they abound: whales and dolphins risking their lives to save injured companions, chimpanzees coming to the aid of the wounded, elephants refusing to abandon slain comrades.

21

Well, yes, but it all depends on where you aim your field binoculars. Where do you learn about proper behaviour between the sexes, for example? Each autumn outside my Rocky Mountain home, a bull elk bugles together sixty to a hundred cows, bullies them into a herd, and uses his magnificent rack of antlers to gore all male pretenders. Nature offers relatively few examples of monogamy and fewer still of egalitarianism. Should our females, like the praying mantises, devour the males who are mating with them? Should our neighbourhoods resolve their disputes as do the bonobo chimpanzees, by engaging in a quick orgy in which all the neighbours mate with one another? Why not, if we learn our morality from other species?

Or consider violence. Zoologists once thought murder a peculiarly human practice, but no longer. Ground squirrels routinely eat their babies; mallards gang-rape and drown other ducks; a species of African fish, the cichlid, feeds on the eyes of other cichlids. Hyenas get the prize for ruthless cannibalism: within an hour, the stronger of newborn twins will fight its baby sibling to the death. Some evolutionary psychologists concede that humans are genetically scripted to further this cycle of violence.

We feel outrage when we hear of a middle-class couple "dumping" an Alzheimer's-afflicted parent, or when kids push a five-year-old out the window of a high-rise building, or a sniper opens fire on strangers, or a ten-year-old is raped in a hallway, or a mother drowns her two children because they interfere with her lifestyle. Why? On what grounds do we feel outrage if we truly believe that morality is self-determined or scripted in our genes? And if morality is not self-determined, then who determines it? How do we decide?

In a widely publicized case a year before the famous "Scopes Monkey Trial," attorney Clarence Darrow successfully defended two university students against the capital offence of murdering a boy for the intellectual experience of it. Argued Darrow, "Is there any blame attached because somebody took Nietzsche's philosophy seriously and fashioned his life on it? . . . Your Honour, it is hardly fair to hang a nineteen-year-old boy for the philosophy that was taught him at the university."

In short, the reducers offer little compelling reason why we humans should rise above the behaviour of beasts rather than mimic it. Adolf Hitler said it well: "Nature is cruel, therefore we too can be cruel."

———

Not always, but often, the act of reducing the world around us also dilutes pleasure. I would guess that an uneducated Masai warrior, standing on one leg, leaning on a staff, gazes at a lunar eclipse with a greater sense of wonder than I do after studying the scientific explanation in the day's newspaper.

Some famous reductionists readily admit the atrophy of a pleasure sense.* Charles Darwin poignantly describes the process:

> Up to the age of thirty or beyond it, poetry of many kinds ... gave me great pleasure, and even as a schoolboy I took intense delight in Shakespeare.... Formerly pictures gave me considerable, and music very great, delight. But now for many years I cannot endure to read a line of poetry: I have tried to read Shakespeare, and found it so intolerably dull that it nauseated me. I have also almost lost any taste for pictures or music.... I retain some taste for fine scenery, but it does not cause me the exquisite delight which it formerly did.... My mind seems to have become a kind of machine for grinding general laws out of large collections of facts.... The loss of these tastes is a loss of happiness, and may possibly be injurious to the intellect, and more probably to the moral character, by enfeebling the emotional part of our nature.

Uneducated, "primitive" people intuit something mysterious and sacred behind the world of buffaloes, scarlet macaws, orangutans, and giraffes. Often they even make nature an object of worship. In contrast, those who reduce the world to matter risk withering the sense of wonder.

23

---

*A reducer of an altogether different sort, Vladimir Lenin, could not tolerate a flower in his room. "I cannot listen to music too often," he confessed after attending a performance of Beethoven's "Apassionata" sonata. "It makes me want to say kind, stupid things, and pat the heads of people. But now you have to beat them on the head, beat them without mercy."

I stood once in a field in Finland, shivering in the cold, and watched a brilliant display of aurora borealis, the northern lights. Waves of luminous green arced across the heavens, covering perhaps one-seventh of the dark dome above. Tendrils of green light assumed the shapes of puffy clouds, then split into segments, then pulsed and slid together like the interlocking teeth of a giant comb. They floated in the heavens, defying gravity, blocking stars. It amazed me that a marvel so magnificent and vast proceeded in utter silence; no roar of volcano or growl of thunder accompanied this celestial fireworks show. I found myself wondering how such a spectacle would have struck the ancient Norsemen, who knew nothing of sunspots, solar wind, and electromagnetic disturbances.

The biblical psalms celebrate the created world as the expression of a Person, a masterpiece of artistic creation worthy of praise. But how can we ascribe beauty to a world assumed to be an accidental by-product of collisions of matter—especially when our sense organs also result from random collisions?

For years I have been receiving the magazines that come with membership in the Sierra Club, Wilderness Society, and National Audubon Society. Reading them usually leaves me depressed because most issues devote many pages to accounts of how we are fouling our water and air, bulldozing wilderness, and consigning animal species to extinction. I find it surprising, though, how often the authors of these articles use words like "sacred," "hallowed," and "immortal" in their impassioned pleas for corrective action. As one environmentalist said about saving a stretch of river in Montana: "It's ours to preserve for progeny. It would be sacrilegious not to."

The Sierra Club was founded by John Muir, an eccentric naturalist who had a well-developed theology of nature. To him, it showed God's handiwork. Hiking through the Cumberland forests of the southeastern U.S., he wrote,

> Oh, these forest gardens of our Father! What perfection, what divinity
> in their architecture! What simplicity and mysterious complexity of

detail! Who shall read the teaching of these sylvan pages, the glad brotherhood of rills that sing in the valleys, and all the happy creatures that dwell in them under the tender keeping of a Father's care?

Most of Muir's heirs as leaders of the Sierra Club have abandoned his theology. Yet just as the founders of the United States appealed to "unalienable rights . . . endowed by their Creator," environmentalists still grope for some transcendent authority, a Higher Power, to sanction our reverence for creation. Hence they borrow the musty metaphor of "sacred," even after rejecting the reality, and continue to draw on the biblical concept of stewardship. Otherwise, what inherent value can we assign to a snail darter or a redwood forest?

Vaclav Havel, former president of the Czech Republic, a survivor of a communist culture that earnestly tried to live without God, stated the problem:

> I believe that with the loss of God, man has lost a kind of absolute and universal system of coordinates, to which he could always relate everything, chiefly himself. His world and his personality gradually began to break up into separate, incoherent fragments corresponding to different, relative, coordinates.

Havel saw the Marxist rape of his land as a direct outgrowth of atheism. "I come from a country where forests are dying, where rivers look like sewers, and where in some places the citizens are sometimes recommended not to open their windows," he said, tracing the cause to the "arrogance of new age human beings who enthroned themselves as lords of all nature and of all the world." Such people lack a metaphysical anchor: "I mean, a humble respect for the whole of creation and awareness of our obligations to it. . . . If the parents believe in God, their children will not have to wear gas masks on their way to school and their eyes will not be blinded with pus."

We live in dangerous times and face urgent questions not only about the environment but also about terrorism, war, sexuality, world poverty, and definitions of life and death. Society badly needs a moral tether, or "system of coordinates," in Havel's phrase. We need to know our place in the universe and our obligations to each other and to the earth. Can we answer those questions without God?

Modern literature exalts as a hero the rebel who defiantly stands his ground in a meaningless universe. Evolutionary philosophy holds up *Homo sapiens,* a species much like any other, destined to live out the script of selfish genes. What if both views of the world are missing something large, important, and portentous for our future—like the natives of Tierra del Fuego who simply ignored Magellan's ships sailing past?

———————

> Endless invention, endless experiment,
> Brings knowledge of motion, but not of stillness ...
> Where is the Life we have lost in living?
> Where is the wisdom we have lost in knowledge?
>
> T. S. ELIOT

rumours

Behind the corpse in the reservoir, behind the ghost on the links,
Behind the lady who dances and the man who madly drinks,
Under the look of fatigue, the attack of migraine and the sigh
There is always another story, there is more than meets the eye.

W. H. AUDEN

My wife and I stayed once in a bed and breakfast in rural Tasmania, the rugged island off the southern coast of Australia. A sheep rancher had built a guest cottage in the middle of his fields, and for an extra fee lodgers could take a meal in the ranch house. Aware that we would probably never eat fresher lamb, we signed on.

Over dinner I innocently asked about the odd colouring—orange, red, blue, and green blotches—we had seen on the rumps of his sheep. "Ah, that's how we tell when the ewes mated," he explained with a chuckle. "I hang a container of coloured chalk in a rather strategic place on my ram. He leaves his mark when he does his duty, and that way I know that all the ewes with orange rumps, say, were serviced on the twenty-first. When the due date rolls around—sheep are almost always fertile, you see, and they deliver right on schedule—I can herd the orange ewes into the barn and give them special care."

In the next few minutes I learned much more about the reproductive habits of sheep. Each ewe has only a six-hour window of receptivity to mating. This poses no problem to the ram, who can infallibly sense which ewe might welcome him at any given moment. The rancher relied on ten rams to "service" four thousand female sheep, which meant that the rams worked themselves to exhaustion over several weeks, losing much of their body weight in the process. All work, no romance. When I saw a scrawny, bedraggled ram, his chores done, his strength dissipated, good for nothing but the slaughterhouse and even then unfit for human consumption, I breathed a prayer of thanks for human sexual arrangements. (Zoologists note that very few species—humans, dolphins, some primates, and the large cats—engage in sex as a form of pleasure.)

The next morning as I went jogging through the fields, taking care where I stepped, I tried to imagine life from the sheep's point of view. Ninety percent of waking hours they spend wandering around, heads down, looking for lush green grass. Every so often a pesky dog barks and nips at their heels, and to humour him and shut him up they move in the direction he wants. Lo, better grass often awaits them there. As weather changes, they learn to huddle together against the rain and wind.

Once a year a rambunctious cousin appears among them and dashes from sheep to sheep, leaving the ewes marked with strange colours on their rumps. Bellies swell, lambs emerge, and attention turns to weaning these small, frisky creatures and watching them gambol through the grass. Brothers and sisters may disappear, sometimes attacked by a Tasmanian devil—these carnivorous marsupials, nastier than any cartoon stereotype, really do exist!—and sometimes ushered away by the two-legged one. The same upright creature periodically drives them into a barn where he shaves off their coats, leaving them cold and embarrassed (sheepish) for a time.

As I jogged, it occurred to me that sheep, to the degree they think at all, may well presume they order their own destiny. They chew cud, roam the fields, make choices, and live out their lot with only a few rude interruptions from dogs, devils, rams, and humans. Little do they know that the entire scenario, from birth to death and every stage in between, is being orchestrated according to a rational plan by the humans who live in the ranch house.

C. S. Lewis conjectured, "There may be Natures piled upon Natures, each supernatural to the one beneath it." Do we stand in relation to God as sheep stand in relation to us? The Bible suggests that in some ways we do. "It is [God] who made us, and we are his; we are his people, the sheep of his pasture," wrote a psalmist. Note the possessives: *his* people, *his* pasture. According to this point of view, we live out our days in a world owned by another. We may insist on autonomy—"We all, like sheep, have gone astray"—but in the end that autonomy is no more impressive, or effective, than the autonomy of a Tasmanian ewe.

If God exists, and if our planet represents God's work of art, we will never grasp why we are here without taking that reality into account.

———

Rumours of another world sneak in even among those who restrict their view to the world of matter. Scientists who dare not mention God or a Designer speak instead of an "anthropic principle" evident in creation. Nature is exquisitely tuned for the possibility of life on planet Earth: adjust the laws of gravity up or down by one percent, and the universe would not form; a tiny change in electromagnetic force, and organic molecules will not adhere. It appears that, in physicist Freeman Dyson's words, "The universe knew we were coming." To those who know it best, the universe does not seem like a random crapshoot. It seems downright purposeful—but what purpose, and whose?

I find more of a spirit of reverence among secular science writers than in some theologians. The wisest among them admit that all our widening knowledge merely exposes our more-widening pool of ignorance. Things that used to seem clear and rational, such as Newtonian physics, have given way to gigantic puzzles. In my lifetime, astronomers have "discovered" seventy billion more galaxies, admitted they may have overlooked 96 percent of the makeup of the universe ("dark energy" and "dark matter"), and adjusted the time of the Big Bang by four to five billion years. Biologists who gaze through microscopes rather than telescopes have discovered unfathomable complexity in the simplest cells.

The process of reducing has, ironically, made the world more complex, not less. The DNA molecule inside each cell contains a three-billion-letter software code capable of overseeing and regulating all the anatomy on display in Body Worlds. Increasingly, we are learning to read the code. But who wrote it? And why? Can anyone guide us in reading not only the microcode inside each cell but the macrocode governing the entire planet, the universe?

Rumours of another world seep into art as well. Poets, painters, novelists, and playwrights—those who know a little about creating a universe—feel stirrings even when they cannot detect their source. Virginia Woolf described "moments of being" that hit her with the force of an electric shock:

> Perhaps this is the strongest pleasure known to me. It is the rapture I get when in writing I seem to be discovering what belongs to what: making a scene come right, making a character come together.... At any rate, it is a constant idea of mine that behind the cotton wall is hidden a pattern, that we—I mean all human beings—are connected with this, that the whole world is a work of art, that we are parts of the work of art. Hamlet, or a Beethoven quartet, is the truth about this vast mass that we call the world. But there is no Shakespeare, there is no Beethoven. Certainly and emphatically, there is no God. We are the words. We are the music. We are the thing itself. And I see this when I have a shock.

To an artist, the world presents itself as a creation, akin to Beethoven's quartets and Shakespeare's *Hamlet*. What if Woolf is wrong and there is a personal/creator? If we are in fact God's music and God's words, what tune should we be playing, what words reciting? Milton's question echoes across time: "What if earth be but the shadow of heaven?"

Sometimes the shock hits not one person but a community, a whole nation even, a shock so great that, unlike Virginia Woolf's, it does turn thoughts to God. That happened to the United States on September 11, 2001. As a side effect, an act of monstrous evil exposed the shallowness of an entire society. Professional sports ground to a halt, television comedians went off the air, as did all commercials. In a flash we saw the comparative meaninglessness of much of our lives. That three thousand people could go to work as part of their daily routine and never come home made us all aware of our fragile mortality. Married couples cancelled divorce plans; mothers and fathers trimmed work hours to spend more time with their children. We found a new kind of hero: firefighters and police officers who, contra the principles of sociobiology, gave their lives for people they never knew.

Over the next months, the *New York Times* ran a separate article commemorating every single person who died, not just the famous or the newsworthy, as if each person killed on that day had a life of value and meaning, a life that mattered. And for a time attendance at churches swelled. The shock conveyed good and evil, death and life, meaning and absurdity in such stark terms that we turned for answers to the people—pastors, priests, rabbis—who have always warned us not to build our houses, let alone our skyscrapers, on shifting sand.

What Americans learned on that day, and are learning still, is that sophisticated moderns have not renounced transcendence but rather replaced it with weak substitutes. Unlike past generations, many are unsure about God and an invisible world. Even so, we feel the longings for something more.

———

A society that denies the supernatural usually ends up elevating the natural to supernatural status. Annie Dillard tells of experiments in which entomologists entice male butterflies with a painted cardboard replica larger and more enticing than the females of their species. Excited, the male butterfly mounts the piece of cardboard; again and again he mounts it. "Nearby, the real, living female butterfly opens and closes her wings in vain."

C. S. Lewis uses the phrase "sweet poison of the false infinite" to describe this same tendency in the human species. We allow substitute sacreds, or false infinites, to fill the vacuum of our disenchanted world. Politics offers one dangerous example.

"I am warning you in all seriousness. I tell you that communism is sacred," said Nikita Krushchev in 1961, hailing a massive political experiment. Ten years later his successor Leonid Brezhnev reiterated, "Everything which bears on the life, activities, and name of Lenin is sacred"; the idolatry found its expression in thousands of statues and in Lenin's corpse macabrely displayed in Red Square. For all but a few diehards, however, the promise of communism vaporized as it joined the fate of other substitute sacreds. In the words of A. N. Wilson, "Dethroning God, that generation found it impossible to leave the sanctuary empty. They put man in His place, which had the paradoxical effect, not of elevating human nature but of demeaning it to depths of cruelty, depravity and stupidity unparalleled in human history."

Sex seems the most blatant of the false infinites today. I remember with a start the first glimpse I got of a *Playboy* centrefold, just a few years into its publication. The sight pulled back a veil of mystery and beckoned me, an adolescent, to a new, unexplored world charged with seduction and promise. Now *Playboy* is something of a relic, long since overtaken (outstripped?) in its audacity. This morning when I checked my email, I had an invitation to watch an eighteen-year-old named Brandi, naked, on her webcam. Kathleen promised to do *anything* for me while her husband was away. No matter how many filters I sign up for, such invitations still leak through.

I do not mean to pick on sex nor flinch like a middle-aged moralist. I am merely suggesting that the modern West has raised it almost to divine status. Tellingly, *Sports Illustrated* refers to its bathing beauties as "goddesses" and Victoria's Secret dresses its supermodels in angel outfits. Previous generations honoured virginity and celibacy. Now we present sex as the highest good, the magical lure that advertisers use to sell us convertibles, Coke, and toothpaste. In the documentary film on AIDS,

Longtime Companion, one man is nursing his lover on his deathbed. "What do you think happens when we die?" the narrator asks. "We get to have sex again," they reply. Compare that eternal ideal to what most medievals would have said: We get to enjoy the presence of God.

A priest I know mentioned that he has come to suspect the transcendent power of sex as portrayed in ads and rock music videos. According to the surveys, one out of three or four of the people he sees on the commuter train each day has had sex the previous night. But he can't see any difference as he studies their faces. They look no happier, no more fulfilled, no more transformed. "Shouldn't something as powerful as sex is promised to be—I speak as a celibate priest—have a more lasting effect?" he asks.

In the Old Testament, God complained that "my people ... have forsaken me, the spring of living water, and have dug their own cisterns, broken cisterns that cannot hold water." An idolater chooses things that may be good in themselves and grants to them a power they were never meant to have. What once was called "idolatry," enlightened Westerners call "addictions."

Eventually an idol, or addiction, begins to control the devotee, rather than vice versa. Woody Allen, a cultured and brilliant filmmaker, explained his affair with his twenty-one-year-old adopted daughter this way: "The heart wants what it wants. There's no logic to those things. You meet someone and you fall in love and that's that." The poet Michael Ryan, in his memoir *Secret Life: An Autobiography,* openly admitted that his own sex addiction became a form of idolatry: "It determined what I thought and what I felt. My personality was formed around it. All of my talents, all my good qualities as a human being, were devoted to serving it, and I was willing to sacrifice anything to it. Although I could perform practical tasks perfectly well, it was running my life."

Virtually anything can become an idol. Ancient Egyptians worshipped dung beetles, and some Hindus in India still worship cobras and the smallpox virus. In Melanesia, followers of the cargo cult pray for airplanes and ships to descend on them with containers of Spam and crackers, as they

33

did during World War II. Each false infinite indicates a disorder of values and reveals much about the society that honours such idols.

Sportswriters calculate that the year after Michael Jordan retired (the second time), he earned from his endorsements more than twice as much as all U.S. presidents earned for all of their terms combined. He earned more endorsing Nike shoes than all the workers in Malaysia who made the shoes. He may pay $200 for a round of golf, but earns $33,390 while playing that round. I like Michael Jordan and wish him all the best, but a society that pays him more in one year—for *not* playing basketball—than it pays all their presidents combined seems to me a society out of balance.

Alone of all the beasts, the human animal has the power and freedom to centre life in one impulse. We have not, it seems, the power to abstain from worship.* Instead, we swallow the sweet poison, substituting lesser gods for God. "Nearby, the real, living female butterfly opens and closes her wings in vain."

———

R obert Barron writes:

> [God] delights, it seems, in using trees, flowers, rivers, automobiles, friends, enemies, church buildings, paintings in order to announce his presence or to work out his purposes. . . . There is something crude in the depiction of God intervening directly in the play, the clumsy *deus ex machina* interrupting the speeches of the other actors and upsetting the stage. How much more tantalizing the God who hints and lurks and cajoles hiddenly *through and around* the actors, even unbeknownst to them. It is the humble God who chooses so to act.

---

*Dostoyevsky had predicted this in his novel *The Possessed:* "The one essential condition of human existence is that man should always be able to bow down before something infinitely great. If men are deprived of the infinitely great they will not go on living and die of despair. The Infinite and the Eternal are as essential for man as the little planet on which he dwells." Simone Weil adds, "One has only the choice between God and idolatry. There is no other possibility. For the faculty of worship is in us, and it is either directed somewhere into this world, or into another."

The ordinary, natural world contains the supernatural, a necessary step since we do not have the capacity to apprehend God directly. We see God best in the same way we see a solar eclipse: not by staring at the sun, which would cause blindness, but through something on which the sun is projected.

Nevertheless, all too often the church has given the impression of opposing natural desires, judging them, in a word, "unspiritual." Mystics have fled into deserts and caves in a self-denying quest for the supernatural. Whole denominations have taken refuge in legalism, labelling as sinful any expression of natural desire.

I have certainly gone through odd phases of desire-quenching, even after moving away from Southern fundamentalism and its long list of forbidden activities. After reading stories of believers in concentration camps—Alexander Solzhenitsyn in the Soviet Gulag, Dietrich Bonhoeffer and Corrie ten Boom in Nazi prisons, Ernest Gordon in a Japanese work camp—I tried to adjust my lifestyle accordingly (whether in solidarity with the prisoners or in paranoid expectation, I cannot recall). Every alternate day I drank no coffee, for whoever heard of a prison serving good coffee? I stopped using Visine drops for dry eyes and hand lotion for dry skin. I gave away two-thirds of my income, wore the same dull clothes day after day, and tried to dispose of all unneeded possessions.

Simple lifestyle became, for me, boring lifestyle. I resigned myself to an attitude of enduring life on earth—better yet, suffering here—in anticipation of a better life to come. One day a question occurred to me, or perhaps to my friends: Why should anyone look forward to a better life without experiencing at least clues of it here? I realized that natural desire was not an enemy of the supernatural and repressing desire not the solution. Rather, to find the path of joy I needed to connect desire to its other-worldly source.

I learned a healthier approach from C. S. Lewis, who had awakened to the reality of another world through such pleasures as Nordic myths, nature, and Wagnerian music. He sensed in our longings not just rumours but "advance echoes" of that world. Flashes of beauty and pangs of aching sweetness, he said, "are not the thing itself; they are only the scent of a flower we have not found, the echo of a tune we have not heard."

I realized I needed to smell some flowers and listen to some melodies in order to recognize what clues I might be missing on earth. My attention turned from dividing life into natural and supernatural, or spiritual and unspiritual, and instead I sought a way to combine the two, to bring about the unity that, as I increasingly believed, God intended.

What pleasures do I enjoy? I asked myself. I find a strange thrill in wildness. Dashing down to the safety of timberline over slippery mountain rock as the thunder clouds roll in and lightning bolts strike closer. Coming face to face with a grizzly bear on a trail and realizing that not a single decision I make matters; the bear controls the options. Visiting exotic cultures where I can identify nothing that I eat, smell, or hear. Oh, I enjoy domesticated pleasures also: gourmet coffee, high-fat ice cream, peaches and blueberries picked at the orchards. And now that I live in the country, I miss the cultural fare of the city: foreign movies, fine music, theatre productions that stay with me for days.

I began to listen to my own longings as rumours of another world, a bright clue to the nature of the Creator. Somehow I had fallen for the deception of judging the natural world as unspiritual and God as antipleasure. But God invented matter, after all, including all the sensors in the body through which I feel pleasure. Nature and supernature are not two separate worlds, but different expressions of the same reality.

I discovered in St Augustine, a connoisseur of women, art, food, and philosophy, a guide to the goodness of created things. "The whole life of the good Christian is holy desire," he wrote. The Latin phrase *dona bona,* or "good gifts," appears throughout his writings. "The world is a smiling place," he insisted, and God its *largitor,* or lavisher of gifts. He likened these gifts to a wedding ring fashioned by a fiancé for his betrothed. What bride would decide, "The ring is enough. I need not see his face again"? No, the ring, a token from the groom, underscores the real message, his pledge of love.

Augustine knew well the seductions of desire that might tempt him away from the giver of good gifts. For this reason he prayed for God to gather together his "scattered longings" and keep them in their proper place. "I had my back to the light and my face turned towards the things upon which the light fell," he said of the desires he felt during his days as a pagan. Only as he turned to face the light could he see the generous source of all good things.

Others, too, followed a similar path of tracing rays of light to their source. Thomas Merton credits the religious art of Rome as instrumental in his conversion. "After all the vapid, boring, semi-pornographic statuary of the Empire, what a thing it was to come upon the genius of an art full of spiritual vitality and earnestness and power—an art that was tremendously serious and alive and eloquent and urgent in all that it had to say." Gradually, almost by accident, he became a pilgrim—appropriately, he notes, for the artwork was originally intended for the instruction of people incapable of understanding anything higher.

The Jewish scholar and revolutionary Simone Weil memorized George Herbert's poetry, especially the poem "Love," to repeat to herself as a way of fighting off migraine headaches. She recited it both for aesthetic and anaesthetic value, and to her own surprise the poem became a prayer: "Christ himself came down and took possession of me." She felt at that moment of intense physical pain "a presence more personal, more certain, and more real than that of any human being."

The poet Herbert himself foresaw a day when God "shalt recover all thy goods in kinde / Who wert disseized by usurping lust," when redeemed creation will reclaim beauty, art, nature, and culture for its original intent. Until then, we must content ourselves with a process of decoding. Like rescuers who sift through pieces of stained glass shattered by a bomb, we trace dispersed clues to their original source and significance.

My natural desires, I now see, are pointers to the supernatural, not obstacles. In a world fallen far from its original design, God wants us to receive them as gifts and not possessions, tokens of love and not loves in themselves. I have learned to pray, following Augustine, not that my desires be quenched or taken away, rather that my scattered longings be gathered together in their Source, who alone can order them.

When the email invitation came, uninvited, to tune in to a webcam pointed toward a naked eighteen-year-old named Brandi, I recognized it immediately as a symptom of this disordered, reductionistic world. My computer offered pixels of nude flesh from a digital camera, not a living person. God has more, far more, in mind for my scattered longings than disembodied deception.

———

No doubt we will always feel a tug between two worlds, for human beings comprise an odd combination of the two. We find ourselves stuck in the middle: angels wallowing in mud, mammals attempting to fly. Plato pictured two horses pulling in opposite directions, with our immortal parts pursuing the divine Good while beastliness strains against it. We have "eternity in our hearts," said the Teacher of Ecclesiastes, and yet bend under the "burden of the gods." We stumble from cradle to grave, tipping sometimes toward eternity and sometimes toward base earth, the humus from which we got our name.

C. S. Lewis once made the observation that the tug of two worlds in humans could be inferred from two phenomena: coarse jokes and our attitudes toward death. Comedians tell us something about reality, for many of their jokes revolve around excretion and reproduction, two of the most natural processes on earth. (Not once did the sheep in Tasmania look for shelter before using the bathroom, and the rams certainly didn't blush at sex.) Yet we humans, in our smirks and double entendres, treat these biological functions as unnatural, even comical.

As for death, man responds to it even less like an animal. Nature treats death as a normal occurrence, the foundation of the all-important food chain. Only we humans react with shock and elaboration, as though we can't get used to the fact. We dress up our corpses in new clothes, embalm them, and bury them in airtight coffins and concrete vaults to slow natural decay. We act out a stubborn reluctance to yield to this most powerful of life experiences.

These two "unnatural" reactions hint at another world. In a way unique to our species, we are not fully at home here. As a symptom of that fact, we feel stirrings toward something higher and more lasting. Although our cells may carry traces of stardust, we also bear the image of the God who made those stars.

I sense the tug in two different directions. On the one hand, for reasons I have been explaining, I have come to doubt the reducers' explanation of the world. Rumours of transcendence awaken my spiritual intuition, and as I follow them I find a way of solving at least part of the mystery of existence. Why are we here? We are God's creation, an unfinished work in which we play a decisive role.

On the other hand, I stumble over the absurdity of flawed human beings expressing anything of supernatural reality. After all, we who are made in God's image are also subject to baldness, hemorrhoids, presbyopia, osteoporosis, and every other ailment in the medical encyclopedia, not to mention our moral defects. And the human body, a dollar's worth of chemicals, becomes, according to the apostle Paul, the temple of God's own Spirit. Can the supernatural world really find a home in such earthy containers?

Because we are material beings, God must deal with us on that level. Every spiritual experience depends on the cooperation of our very mundane bodies. A stroke can put an end to a saint's prayer life. Stop all intake of food and water, and a mystical state will soon come to an end. Nearly everything we know about the supernatural world comes filtered through the ordinary, natural world—which makes it easy for sceptics to dismiss or disbelieve.

That very fact frustrated my belief for several years. I kept running into frauds, people who practiced the "natural" behaviour of faith with no real connection to any reality beyond.

As a journalist, I encountered a woman who by using forty different aliases had conned scores of churches in a dozen states out of thousands of dollars. Having studied the behaviour and language of evangelical churches, she then learned to mimic it convincingly. She would appear at a Calvary Chapel, Baptist, or Assemblies of God church and testify that she was ready to renounce her Mormon beliefs. In every case the churches welcomed her, "protected" her from Mormon officials supposedly on her trail, and showered her with cash, food, housing, and medical care. By every measure, her behaviour convinced them she was a soul mate. In the next city, this amateur actress would reverse the con, appearing at a Mormon church to renounce her evangelical convictions. More than fifty Mormon churches baptized her, as did scores of evangelical churches. She was last spotted in Birmingham, Alabama, claiming to be a former Jehovah's Witness.

Years earlier, I had followed the exploits of Marjoe Gortner, a child evangelist who began his career at the age of four. I watched films of him as a child, standing on a chair to preach, screaming at the devil, gesturing with his hands like a preschool Billy Sunday. When he reached adolescence, Marjoe began making his living as a tent evangelist, converting thousands and raking in millions of dollars. Finally, at the age of twenty-eight he admitted to himself he didn't believe a word of it and decided to quit—but not before inviting a documentary film crew to record his last evangelistic crusade. The film footage shows him speaking in tongues, shedding crocodile tears, pleading for funds, preaching fire and brimstone, giving invitations, and leading new converts in "the sinner's prayer"; then it shows him backstage laughing, counting the offering, and explaining to the camera each of the "tricks" he had used in the service.

I suppose these frauds disturbed me so much because they hit close to home. As a teenager, I began attending prayer meetings and imitating whatever respected Christians did. I learned the key to acceptance was a ritual called "giving your testimony" in which your voice took on a soft, sincere tone and you told of some way the Lord had blessed you or "spoken to you." After a few weeks I had become one of the best testimony-givers of the bunch. I could incite prayers of thanksgiving or beckon tears from those around me.

In my mind, I had exposed others' faith as unfounded. If I could pass for a veritable saint just by following the prescribed formula, how could

Christian experience possibly be genuine? I look back on those days with shame and regret because I have since experienced God's grace and mercy, even to one who sought to discredit faith. That agnostic phase did, however, give me sympathy for those who want to believe yet find no unshakeable proof of the supernatural. Today, I get letters from doubters, sceptical of the church, asking for such ironclad proof. I have to tell them there is none.

You need eyes to see and ears to hear, Jesus said to those who doubted him. It takes the mystery of faith, always, to believe, for God has no apparent interest in compelling belief. (If he had, the resurrected Jesus would have appeared to Herod and Pilate, not to his disciples.)

Because rumours of another world are just that, rumours and not proofs, a thin membrane of belief separates the natural from the supernatural. Prayers may sometimes seem like hollow, sleepy words that bounce off walls and rise no higher than the ceiling. Kneeling may on occasion give a sharper sense of sore knees than of God's presence. We experience the highest realities through the lowest, and we must learn to pay attention to notice the difference.

I thought of a rather cruel trick I once played on a wasp. He was sucking jam on my plate, and I cut him in half. He paid no attention, merely went on with his meal, while a tiny stream of jam trickled out of his severed oesophagus. Only when he tried to fly away did he grasp the dreadful thing that had happened to him. It is the same with modern man. The thing that has been cut away is his soul.

GEORGE ORWELL

paying attention

Master of beauty, craftsman of the snowflake, inimitable contriver,
endower of Earth so gorgeous & different from the boring Moon,
thank you for such as it is my gift.

JOHN BERRYMAN

A short story by the Spanish writer Carmen Corde tells of a young woman who gives birth to a blind son. "I do not want my child to know that he is blind!" she informs family and neighbours, forbidding anyone to use telltale words such as "light," "colour," and "sight." The boy grows up unaware of his disability until one day a strange girl jumps over the fence of the garden and spoils everything by using all the forbidden words. His world shatters in the face of this unimagined new reality.

In modern times, Christians resemble the strange girl who brings a message from outside. To a sceptical audience they bring rumours of another world beyond the fence, of an afterlife beyond death, of a loving God who is somehow working out his will in the chaotic history of this planet. As in Carmen Corde's story, the news may not be welcome. "We forget that what is to us an extension of sight is to the rest of the world a peculiar and arrogant blindness," the Catholic novelist Flannery O'Connor admitted.

I have found that living with faith in an unseen world requires constant effort. After all, the "garden" in which we live, the natural world, conceals as much about God as it reveals. The Westminster Catechism teaches that the primary purpose of life is "to glorify God, and to enjoy him forever." But how does that well-honed answer translate into actual day-to-day living, especially when the God we are supposed to enjoy and glorify remains elusive and hidden from view?

As a start, I can aim to make daily life *sacramental*, which means literally to keep the sacred *(sacra)* in mind *(mental)*. In other words, I seek a mindfulness—a mind full—of God's presence in the world. I have no desire to escape the natural world, the pattern of gnostics, desert monks, and fundamentalists who flee "worldliness." Nor do I deny the supernatural, the error of the reducers. Rather, I want to bring the two together, to reconnect life into the whole that God intended.

This world, all of it, either belongs to God or it does not. As Meister Eckhart said, "If the soul could have known God without the world, the world would never have been created." If I take seriously the sacred origin of this world, at the very least I must learn to treat it as God's work of art, something that gave God enormous pleasure. "God saw all that he had made, and it was very good," Genesis reports.

I think of a piece of art, a sculpture, given to me by a friend this year. I made a shelf to display it prominently, in the best light. Often I stop to admire it and point it out to guests. Clearly, modern society is not treating creation as God's work of art. We pave over fertile land for parking lots, pump toxins into the sky and rivers, and mindlessly cast species into extinction. Our treatment of human beings follows suit: we allow 24,000 children to die each day of preventable diseases and abort 126,000 more, house families in cardboard shacks and under bridges, and manufacture weapons capable of exterminating most of humanity. And as the Body Worlds exhibit made clear, the way some people abuse their own bodies also shows deep disrespect for God's masterpiece.

At the same time, we tend to confine the sacred to a fenced-in area, the "spiritual," reserved for church activities. Many people rarely give

God a thought apart from an hour on Sunday morning, when they sing songs of praise, listen to a sermon, and then re-enter the secular world as if passing through an air lock. My pastor tells me that church members tell off colour jokes in the parking lot that they would never repeat in the sanctuary. When the doors close behind them, they believe they leave sacred space, as if the world neatly divides between secular and sacred.

Blaise Pascal, who achieved renown both for his mathematics and his devotional writings, suggests another approach, of seeing the natural world as a foreshadowing of the supernatural. "He has done in the boun-ties of nature what He would do in those of grace, in order that we might judge that He could make the invisible, since He made the visible excel-lently." Beauty abounds in nature: a collection of seashells, the castoff excretions of lowly mollusks, is probably the most beautiful artwork in my home. And I need only read the Psalms to realize that God wants us to love and honour him through the creation, not apart from it.

Celtic spirituality speaks of "thin places" where the natural and supernatural worlds come together at their narrowest, with only a thin veil between them. I have visited places where nature's works speak loudly of their Creator: bald eagles and beluga whales in Alaska, coral and tropical fish on the Great Barrier Reef off Australia, exotic birds and butterflies at Angel Falls in Venezuela, seashells on the beaches of Kenya. Each of these memories stands out as a highlight of a year, each involved a major logistical effort, and periodically I review the memories in thick photo albums that hardly do justice to what I experienced. One day I real-ized with a start that God "sees" all the wonders of the earth at all times. Not only does God see them, God is their source, and each reveals some-thing of the Creator.

A year ago a friend stopped by Colorado on a farewell tour. She was going blind, doctors had told her, and in preparation she was revisiting her favourite places so that when the darkness descended they would live on in her mind. For her, as for me, beauty is a strong pointer to God. She was, in effect, storing away a memory bank of grace.

The first step in being mindful is to accept my creaturely state. Frankly, I find that process much easier now that I live in Colorado. When I climb a mountain, I sense my status as creature immediately. My self-importance recedes. In Chicago, surrounded by high-rise buildings, I could look out my window and see people dining in restaurants, standing in line at cash machines, jogging or roller-blading, commuting to work, shopping, walking their babies in strollers. We humans design cities for our own convenience, and while living there it was easy to assume the world was about *us*. City lights dimmed the stars, and manmade structures shut out my view of the natural world. Climbing a mountain, everything changes.

A few years ago, hikers in the Rocky Mountains found a herd of two hundred elk killed by a freak ball of lightning. Photos from a helicopter show their swollen bodies arranged in a random pattern among thousands of trees blown over by the explosive force. I think of that scene sometimes when I scramble down a trail above timberline, glancing every few seconds at an angry thunderhead closing in. An old climber once observed that mountains are neither fair nor unfair, they just simply sit there. Perhaps, but when I am standing on an exposed ledge, enveloped in immensity, vulnerable to hail, blizzards, lightning, and other dangers, I feel very small and very fragile. Any hubris I picked up living in a city melts away. Nature reminds me how dependent and frail I am, how mortal.

———

Too late I have loved you, O beauty so ancient and so new," Augustine laments in *The Confessions*. He proceeds to describe a time in his life when he allowed things of beauty to seduce him away from God their maker. Later, he returned to "those fair things" and at last traced the sunbeams to their source. I find that I too must consciously track that source, must "hallow" the world around me.

One night in Costa Rica I joined a guided expedition to a government reserve in order to observe a natural phenomenon: giant leatherback turtles laying their eggs. The guide used a red-filtered flashlight so as not to disorient the turtles, and at midnight we trudged for almost a mile along the beach, its sand still warm from the day's sun, until we found a female preparing her nest.

The turtle reached down in soft sand, one muscular flipper at a time, to scoop out and then fling the sand behind her. As she worked her way down, each scoop required more and more effort. The sand got wet and heavy, and she had to fling it above the rim of the hole she was digging. Eventually she reached a depth of three feet, her body fully submerged in sand. Now, each flinging of sand thrust her whole body to the side, and despite her best efforts much of the sand still fell back in the trench. She scooped it up again and slung it toward the surface.

We tourists, from Germany, Holland, Costa Rica, and the U.S., stood in silence late into the night, spellbound, watching this primordial drama. The crashing surf made a rhythmic soundtrack, and silvery clouds drifted over the moon. The mother turtle heaved and gasped, her mouth opening and closing like a fish labouring to breathe. Finally, after an hour's hard work, the trench satisfied her and she began to drop shiny white eggs the size of billiard balls. They glistened in the moonlight, gelatinous. We counted at least sixty. The last few eggs were smaller—also infertile, said the guide, so that if predators uncovered her nest, these would go first.

Her task accomplished, the leatherback clambered slowly out of the nest and began a forty-five-minute process of filling it in with sand. Her powerful front flippers, made dexterous by separate "fingers," could toss sand ten feet behind her. She filled the trench, tamped the sand delicately, as with loving care, added more on top, packed it too, then made a wide circle of disturbed sand to confuse any predators. Exhausted, she lumbered off, dragging herself on the sand and resting after every three to four strokes, toward the sea. We watched as the smallest waves, their foam glowing in the moonlight, repeatedly pushed her back toward shore. At last she gained the strength to lunge past the waves, dipped her head beneath the surface, and disappeared.

The guide informed us that the mother turtle weighed almost a ton and was probably a hundred years old. (Many used to live past two hundred, before deep dragnets on the shrimp boats started entangling them and the population dwindled.) The largest reptiles on earth, leatherbacks don't even breed for the first sixty years, and of course the mother never sees the results of her efforts. When the babies hatch, they burrow to the surface and make a mad dash to the sea, with only a third surviving the onslaught of coyotes, raccoons, and seagulls. The sea poses many more dangers, and few of the baby turtles live to lay eggs themselves. Those who do will unfailingly return in sixty years to the same beach in Costa Rica, one of only three beaches frequented by leatherbacks.

Revisiting the site the following morning, I could barely make out the camouflaged nest. Tracks like those made by a large-wheeled all-terrain vehicle (ATV) led from the nest to the sea. The mother turtle's flippers had made the rounded furrows, and between them I noticed a much more shallow one made by her dragging tail.

I sat on a piece of driftwood and thought of the immensity of the world within the sea. How little of creation do we humans understand, much less control: the wonders of instinctual behaviour, the rhythms of nature that go on whether any humans observe them or not, the comparative smallness of human beings. I made a conscious choice to turn the memory of the previous night into an act of gratitude, even worship. It had put me in my place.

Five hundred years ago the Renaissance scholar Pico della Mirandola delivered an oration that defined the role of humanity in creation. After God had created the animals, all the essential roles had been filled, but "the Divine Artificer still longed for some creature which might comprehend the meaning of so vast an achievement, which might be moved with love at its beauty and smitten with awe at its grandeur." To contemplate and appreciate all the rest, to revere and to hallow, to give mute creation a voice of praise—these were the roles reserved for the species made in God's image.

The great French entomologist Jean Henri Fabre climbed the same six-thousand-foot mountain more than forty times because of the perspective it gave him on his work and on humanity. He said, "Life has unfathomable secrets. Human knowledge will be erased from the archives of the world before we possess the last word that the Gnat has to say to us." Not to mention the turtle.

———

Along with many Christians, I have undergone two conversions: first from the natural world to discover the supernatural, and later to rediscover the natural from a new viewpoint. For some, the second conversion comes almost without effort. Gerard Manley Hopkins lived in a world "charged with the grandeur of God," and St Francis treated not just birds and beasts but the sun and moon as his beloved siblings. As the Egyptian saint Pachomius, leader of seven thousand monks in the fourth century, observed, "The place in the monastery which is closest to God is not the church, but the garden. There the monks are at their happiest."

In his writings, naturalist John Muir made virtually no division between the natural and supernatural. He named as one of his life's two greatest moments the time he found the rare Calypso orchid blooming in a Canadian swamp (the other was when he camped with Ralph Waldo Emerson at Yosemite). Muir loved God's creation so fiercely that he said with remorse, "It is a great comfort ... that vast multitudes of creatures, great and small and infinite in number, lived and had a good time in God's love before man was created."

For me, though, the second conversion has not come without struggle. I have sampled the glories of the natural world, yes—even finding the rare Calypso orchid blooming among ferns on the hill behind my home—and have also tasted of the grace and goodness of God. How, though, do I bring the two worlds together? The mixed messages in nature confuse me, its beauties so often commingled with brutality and pain.

"Are not two sparrows sold for a penny? Yet not one of them will fall to the ground apart from the will of your Father," promised Jesus. "And even the very hairs of your head are all numbered. So don't be afraid; you are worth more than many sparrows." Yet sparrows still fall to the ground, as do the hairs from chemotherapied human heads; and of sixty leatherback turtles born, only two or three survive. A sovereign God who wills against his ultimate will, who superintends a universe of a hundred billion galaxies and yet lavishes intimate attention on its tiny creatures—how do I comprehend such a God?

Sometimes I rail against the mysteries and sometimes I accept them. As a starting point, I take for granted that a creature's proper response to God is humility. Accepting creatureliness may require that I, like Job, bow before a master plan that makes no apparent sense.

In the face of doubt, I have learned the simple response of considering the alternatives. If there is no Creator, what then? I would have to view the world with all its suffering as well as all its beauty as a random product of a meaningless universe, the briefest flare of a match in cosmic darkness. Perhaps the very sense that *something is wrong* is itself a rumour of transcendence, an inbuilt longing for a healed planet on which God's will is done "on earth as it is in heaven."

"Remember your Creator in the days of your youth, before the days of trouble come," warned the Teacher of Ecclesiastes in the pangs of foreboding over old age and death. His book chronicles a systematic search for an alternative, a life apart from a Creator. In the end, he found that both hedonism and despair lead to a vexing sense of meaninglessness. "Fear God and keep his commandments, for this is the whole duty of man," the Teacher concluded, in words reminiscent of the Westminster Shorter Catechism.

Astonishingly, the Creator seldom imposes himself on his creatures. It requires attention and effort on our part to "remember your Creator," because the Creator slips quietly backstage. God does not force his presence on us. When lesser gods attract, God withdraws, honouring our fatal freedom to ignore him.

———

Isaac Luria, a Hasidic mystic of the eighteenth century, proposed a system known as *zimsum* to explain the existence of suffering and evil as well as how God relates to his creation. To make room for the material world, God had to pull himself back and concede space, the space necessary for something other than God to exist. God poured his own essence in the form of light into holy vessels, which in turn would pour it down on the creation.

God's voluntary withdrawal, however, made possible the emergence of opposing forces, including evil. A cosmic catastrophe occurred, introducing confusion into creation. Some of the sparks of God's light returned to their source; what remained within the broken vessels, or "husks," fell onto every animal, vegetable, and mineral part of the world.

The resulting creation, said Luria, now shields God's holy light, hiding it from view. Or, in another metaphor, creation retains the "smell" of God as a wineskin retains the smell of wine. Sceptical, unseeing people can even deny that God exists. Believers have the task of releasing the holy sparks from the husks. We do so through a process of "hallowing," and all of us have a part to play in this process.

Other theologians have refined Luria's thoughts, and from them I learn that hallowing is a deliberate, ongoing process. I do not gain a new set of supernatural eyes that enable me suddenly to see the world with perfected vision. Every day, every hour, every moment, I must exercise my calling to hallow God's creation, whether it be leatherback turtles in Costa Rica or the irritating kid next door who peppers my yard with golf balls. Holy sparks are potentially trapped in every moment of my day, and as God's agent I am called to release them.

John Calvin urged his followers to heed a "universal rule, not to pass over, with ungrateful inattention or oblivion, those glorious perfections which God manifests in his creatures."* To abide by that rule requires a training of spiritual senses akin to how naturalists develop their physical senses.

In the town where I live, an elderly couple leads the local chapter of the National Audubon Society. Bill eats too much, has had numerous

---

*In *The Imitation of Christ* Thomas à Kempis says, "If your heart were right, then every created thing would be a mirror of life, and a book of sacred doctrine. There is no creature so small and worthless that it does not show forth the goodness of God." He adds one caution about the natural world, that we not cling "to anything created with unmeasured affection."

surgeries, and walks with a cane. Sylvia strikes you as a kindly soul who spends the day knitting and baking cookies for Bill and the grandchildren. Yet when I accompany them on birding expeditions, their trained ears and eyes put mine to shame. Within three notes they identify a bird call and can usually point to the bird in question in seconds. I can walk through a wetland area and see nothing; they peer behind the twigs and leaves to the wildlife hidden inside.

I am working on improving my senses in both the natural world and the more artificial world we human beings have constructed around us. From my home in Colorado, a parade of God's creation marks the passing of the day. I begin the day reading and sipping coffee in a solarium. In the summer, broad-tailed hummingbirds appear first, zooming in like Harrier jets only to brake, hover, and extend their long tongues to slurp sugar-water from their feeder. Out another window hangs a bird feeder full of sunflower seeds. (It more resembles a miniature space ship because of all the squirrel deterrents I've added to it.) Small birds that nest in neighbouring trees stop by first: three varieties of nuthatches, chickadees, pine siskins, an occasional goldfinch bright as the morning sun. Then larger birds home in for a snack: black-headed and evening grosbeaks, Stellar jays, Cassin's finches, hairy and downy woodpeckers.

The woodpeckers have beaks designed for drilling wood, not for plucking sunflower seeds out of a container, and as a result they scatter seeds like small hailstones on the ground below. That attracts the squirrels. First come the common brown squirrels, and soon their mountain cousins pay a visit. These, the Abert squirrels, are solid black with reddish eyes and tufted ears that give them a diabolical look. They spend half an hour or so chasing the brown squirrels away before finally settling down to feast on the fallen seeds. Next a red fox shows up. He stalks behind the same rock every morning, a routine the Abert squirrels know well. After a few feints and a futile charge, he usually gives up and trots away, with the squirrels loudly clucking their disdain.

Eight times I have watched the fox catch a squirrel. Once I saw a hawk dive out of the sky and pluck a pygmy nuthatch off the feeder. It then sat on a woodpile and turned its head from side to side, glaring, as its talons squeezed out the tiny bird's life. I've watched a doe and her two spotted fawns take halting, stiff-legged steps toward the bird bath for a drink. Herds of elk wander through the yard to feast on our carefully tended shrubs and flowers. A bear once climbed the deck and pawed for the feeder until I shouted him away. Skunks and raccoons make nighttime appearances. Some years, a marmot takes up residence in a culvert at the end of the driveway.

Sitting behind glass in a heated house, I have a daily sense that I am the impostor on this scene. I have little trouble believing that this is God's world in which I am blessed to live. "Beauty and grace are performed whether or not we will sense them," writes Annie Dillard. "The least we can do is try to be there."

In downtown Chicago my day proceeded very differently. Most mornings began with a run through the park. I saw few animals, other than squirrels and pigeons, unless I chose a route through the Lincoln Park Zoo. I saw instead winos and homeless people sleeping under newspapers and smelly blankets; prostitutes sleeping in doorways next to discarded condoms; well-dressed yuppies standing in neat lines at the bus stops; foreign-born nannies pushing the carriages of those yuppies' children; garbage collectors, janitors, street sweepers, sewer workers, and others who perform the undesirable jobs that keep a city running.

These too are God's holy sparks, I had to remind myself. More, these creations harbour not just God's sparks but his very own image. He created them in order to reflect back something of himself, a privilege assigned to no other part of creation. And what did I do then, what do I do now, to release those holy sparks, to polish the mirror that reflects back God's image?

When I moved to Chicago, it took a while for me to adjust to the background noise of Clark Street. Lying in bed in the summer with windows open, I heard buses growling and wheezing down the street, sirens in the distance, the crash of bottles being thrown into a dumpster behind a late-night bar, the throbbing bass from speakers in a car stopped at a red light. I thought I would never adjust, until one night I barely noticed. The sounds had dissolved into a kind of white noise.

When I moved to Colorado, I had to adjust to silence. The slightest noise jerked me awake. I started when the refrigerator kicked on and when steam made the heating pipes clank. I began to wonder what else I had become deaf to during my time in Chicago.

I learned a lesson about paying attention from an eccentric orchestra conductor, a year when the Romanian musician Sergiu Celibidache paid a visit to Chicago with his Munich Philharmonic. Few orchestras would work with Celibidache because he demands twelve to eighteen rehearsals before every performance, compared with four for most orchestras. He insists on an Eastern approach to music: striving not so much to recapitulate an "ideal" performance by some other conductor and orchestra, but rather to create an engrossing encounter with music at the moment. He refuses to listen to recordings or even to allow taping of his own performances: How can you reproduce on a flat disk something heard in a concert hall with walls and cushioned seats and human bodies modifying the sound? "Like peas, music cannot be canned," he says.

Celibidache made his first trip to the U.S. at age seventy-one, and when I heard him, five years later, he needed assistance mounting the podium. He chose familiar pieces for the concert, but, oh, what a difference. He ignored the tempo markings by the composer, stretching out Mussorgsky's *Pictures at an Exhibition* to twice its normal length. Considering one phrase and the next, he seemed far more interested in drawing out the tonal quality of a given passage than incorporating that passage in the onward march of the piece. He approached the music more like meditation than performance.

I missed the precision of the Chicago Symphony yet heard the music as a revelation, or series of revelations, with individual moments more important than the whole. At the end the audience rose to their feet and applauded for twelve minutes. Celibidache had every soloist, duet, and orchestral section stand, and bowed to them.

A concertmaster who played under Celibidache said, "His whole concept is that every phrase has a shape and it comes from one phrase and leads to another. He feels that there is a truth in music, and it should be discovered." A critic likened his concerts to religious rites over which the conductor presides as a high priest. Celibidache himself says, "How does this piece go? No idea. We'll have to find out. Emptiness is the highest form of concentration."

Our very bodies react when we pay attention. At Orchestra Hall I leaned forward, moved my head from one side to the other, cupped my hands behind my ears, closed my eyes. Simone Weil says, a poet encounters beauty by intensely fixing attention on something real. So does a lover. Can I do something similar in the inner life, with God? I need not always search for new insights, new truths: "The most commonplace truth when it floods the *whole soul,* is like a revelation."

I realized, on reflection, that I tend to approach life as a sequence rather than as a series of moments. I schedule my time, set goals, and march onward toward their achievement. Phone calls, or any unscheduled event, I view as a jarring interruption. How different from the style of Jesus, who often let other people—interruptions—determine his daily schedule. He gave full attention to the person before him, whether it be a Roman officer or a nameless woman with a hemorrhage of blood. And he drew lasting spiritual lessons from the most ordinary things: wildflowers, wheat crops, vineyards, sheep, weddings, families.

———

In the movie *Awakenings,* Robert DeNiro portrays one of the patients of Dr Oliver Sacks, who discovered the near-miraculous powers of the drug L-DOPA on patients suffering from severe Parkinsonism and an encephalitic sleeping-sickness disease. Some of these patients had lived in a rigid, almost frozen state for years, even decades, unable to speak or communicate. The new drug acted on their brains in such a way that their bodies loosened up, and instead of sitting immobile like statues all day they "awakened" to new life.

DeNiro delighted in the simplest actions. He could rise from his wheelchair and take a walk, deciding on a whim whether to turn to the left or the right. He could speak and respond in ways that others could notice. He could touch another person. In a poignant scene, the whole ward came to life, going out on the town, dancing together, listening to music, then returned to the ward as the drug wore off to resume their catatonic states.

Sacks's case studies give detailed reports of individual patients. Some could not cope with the new realities; Rose R., "frozen" for forty-three years, felt herself in a dizzying time warp. Others, such as Leonard L., embraced the new world joyfully. "I feel saved," he said, with tears of joy on his face—"resurrected, reborn. I feel a sense of health amounting to Grace." He read Dante's *Paradiso*, visited Manhattan at night, touched flowers and leaves with astonished delight, typed a 50,000-word autobiography in three weeks. Tragically, as happened with most of the patients, the effects of L-DOPA faded and after five months Leonard regressed to his former condition.

Reading the heartrending accounts of Sacks's patients, I understood the secret of the mystics, those we know as saints. They live one moment at a time. Perhaps that is why so many head into the desert or wilderness: it facilitates extreme attention.

If you can live through a moment, you can live through a day, and how you live a day is eventually how you live your life. I spend so much energy on the correct way to live in general that I miss the specific moments that are actually the only way I can live. Joan Chittister, a modern Benedictine, gives the corrective I need:

[We must] hold every isolated thing in high regard whatever their use, to treat them gently, to take care of them well whatever their age. It leads us to become part of the holiness of the universe by recognizing each and every element of it as a spark of the Divine....

We are part of a holy universe, not its creators and not its rulers. God has done the creating, God does the judging, and God waits for us to realize that....

Everything we are, everything that is said to us, everything that happens to us is some kind of call from God. In fact, everything that happens is God's call to us either to accept what we should not change or to change what we should not accept so that the Presence of God can flourish where we are. . . .

Finding God is a matter of living every minute of life to its ultimate.

The goal of contemplation is to see life as God sees it, a unity of two worlds and not a division. That encompasses both a lifetime of practice and rare, single flashes of revelation.

———

There is nothing unclean of itself," said the apostle Paul; and again, "So whether you eat or drink or whatever you do, do it all for the glory of God." To him, a sacramental view of life had everything to do with *direction*. Nature, people, eating, work, worship—everything in daily life points up the chain of a reordered world toward God. To ignore sexual, personal, social, professional, even political concerns would diminish the reality of God's presence in the world. When Paul touched on each area, he placed it in the order ordained by its Creator.

The reducer looks down for his or her instructions: Edward Wilson standing over an anthill with his magnifying glass scouting clues to human behaviour. From that perspective, we use other people in order to enhance ourselves, because only the fittest survive. We follow the instinct of lust to perpetuate our genes. We exploit nature for our own use. We act altruistically with calculation, as a strategy.

A seeker of the sacred looks up, tracing the rays of sun back to their source. For Dante, the power of adolescent sexuality awakened in him awe and fear, and he looked to God, not his own body, for guidance on how to respond. For John Muir, nature expressed the brilliance of a master Artist, to whom he responded with gratitude and worship. For Mother Teresa, the dying beggars in the streets of Calcutta shrouded holy light, and though it helped the least fit to survive, she served them as if she were serving Christ himself. The Celtic saint Columba learned to experience God's presence everywhere: "At times plucking crabs from the rocks; at times fishing; at times giving food to the poor; at times in a solitary cell."

Biology is destiny, concludes the one who looks down. The prospects are bleak, for according to psychologists our impulses include a natural urge to murder our fathers and mothers, at least an occasional tendency to laziness and idleness, a penchant for cruelty and vulgarity.

Eternity is destiny, concludes the one who looks up. Our genes may indeed contain predispositions toward bestial instincts, but we hear a call to rise above them. You could stare at an anthill a long time before coming up with this list of qualities: love, joy, peace, patience, kindness, goodness, faithfulness, gentleness, and self-control. Yet Paul holds these up as proof of the presence of God in a person's life, the "fruit of the Spirit." Where God lives, those qualities flourish.

All of life involves a clash between impulse and inhibition, between our fallen nature and the image of God. A sacred view of life calls for simple trust that the One who created the human creature has our ultimate good in mind.

We are all of us more mystics than we believe or choose to believe.... We have seen more than we let on, even to ourselves. Through some moment of beauty or pain, some subtle turning of our lives, we catch glimmers at least of what the saints are blinded by; only then, unlike the saints, we go on as though nothing has happened. To go on as though something has happened, even though we are not sure what it was or just where we are supposed to go with it, is to enter the dimension of life that religion is a word for.

FREDERICK BUECHNER

CHAPTER FOUR

God loveth adverbs

For three things I thank God every day of my life: thanks that he has vouchsafed me knowledge of his works; deep thanks that he has set in my darkness the lamp of faith; deep, deepest thanks that I have another life to look forward to—a life joyous with light and flowers and heavenly song.

HELEN KELLER

Last Sunday, after I spoke in my church about a recent trip, two strangers from the congregation came to greet me. One, a middle-aged man wearing a flannel shirt, with an incongruous cowlick sticking up from his grey hair and a generally dishevelled look about him, discussed my report with great animation. Obviously it had made an impression, and I felt pleased that he took my words so seriously. Then his companion, who had been guiding him by the elbow, interrupted.

"Jason is sincere. He liked your report very much. I should tell you, though, that I work with people who have had traumatic brain injuries. Jason lost his wife in a car accident twelve years ago, and his own injuries caused him to lose all short-term memory. By the time I drive him home, he'll have forgotten everything you said, including the fact that we had this conversation." Jason smiled and nodded agreement. "That's right," he said with a foolish grin, "I won't even remember you."

Living for the moment has its limitations. Unless I put together the parts of my life into some meaningful whole, they will have no more lasting impact than the scenes and thoughts that flit through poor Jason's brain. While I learned from the Romanian orchestra conductor about paying attention and attending to the moment, the segments must somehow connect, or otherwise the concert would sound like the orchestra warming up: a French horn blasting out Bruckner, a violinist limbering up with a Bach partita, a drummer annoying his colleagues with a U2 imitation.

Our lives form some sort of pattern whether or not we consciously arrange it. I have friends whose lives centre on material possessions. They scour the stock market pages each day, maintain houses in several countries, and buy new luxury cars every year. I have other friends who work at minimum-wage jobs in deliberate rebellion against parents who pressed them relentlessly to achieve. I have friends who boast about their seventy-to-eighty-hour work weeks, and others who boast about sleeping till noon each day. Some women I know spend several hours each day keeping fit and making themselves beautiful; others have greasy hair, wear no make-up, and disdain standards of beauty. I know a wine connoisseur who stores ten thousand bottles of vintage wine in humidity-controlled coolers; I know an alcoholic who can't keep a single unopened bottle in his house. One neighbour practices two hours every day, using a homemade lectern and reaction-monitoring device, toward his goal of becoming a contestant on the TV show *Jeopardy*. A girl down the street lives for weekend rave parties at nightclubs.

These life patterns grow out of natural desires and longings. Our bodies desire food, drink, stimulation, pleasure, sex. At another level, we also long for beauty, love, security, worth, meaning, belonging. Everyone has such longings, and how we respond to them depends largely on what we believe about why we're here.

If I see myself as one more species of animal, with no life beyond this one and no accountability to a Higher Power, then why not follow the pleasure instinct to the end? On the other hand, if I see this planet as God's world, and my longings as rumours of another world, then I want to connect those clues to God's overall plan. I want to bring the two worlds together, and I do so by accepting that we human beings must look beyond ourselves—above ourselves—for direction in ordering our desires.

———

God lavished good gifts on the world, and how we use those gifts determines whether or not they remain good and satisfying. Living a balanced life is like riding a horse, in that falling poses equal dangers on the left side or the right. Only if you stay in the saddle can you experience the thrill of riding.

As a member of the Woodstock generation who grew up in a repressive church background, I know about falling off horses in both directions, metaphorically at least. The late 1960s were heady years, in which the young questioned everything the previous generation had told us. We believed we were building a new kind of society based on freedom, peace, and love.

The sexual revolution freed sex from the strictures of marriage. Revolutionaries assured us "people's governments" in Cuba and elsewhere could impose justice from the top down. Harvey Cox and others celebrated religion without church and spirituality without religion. Magazines proclaimed, "Lust Is Back!" and "Greed Is Good." College professors praised the merits of mind-altering drugs.

I now look back on those promises, so glossy and alluring at the time, with a different perspective. Political revolutions may have redistributed wealth (though most proved better at redistributing poverty), but at a horrific cost in violence and death. The sexual revolution left in its wake broken families, teenage pregnancies, epidemics in sexually transmitted diseases, and arguably even more exploitation of women. Greed drove major companies into bankruptcy and wiped out employees' life savings. Spirituality without religion left people disconnected from community. Drugs altered not only minds but also bodies, fatally in such cases as Janis Joplin, Jimi Hendrix, and Jim Morrison.

We humans struggle to find a balance between expressing our desires without inhibition and squelching them altogether. Even as the West lived through a period of great permissiveness, other parts of the world were tightening controls over behaviour. Some Muslim societies passed laws against women driving cars, showing their faces, or even speaking in public lest their voices prove too alluring. Communist governments, though atheistic, were almost as repressive and warned their citizens against the loose morals and rock music of the decadent West.

I came back to Christianity because it made the most sense of the world around me, in part by achieving the necessary balance. It exalts every person as a creature made in the image of God and yet warns that the image has been marred—something I found true of everyone I met. It honours sex, money, and power as good things, God's own gifts, while also recognizing them as powerful forces that must be handled with care, like radioactive material. In short, it applies a dose of realism to the chaos of human longings.

Yes, I came back, though not without resistance, for the churches I knew showed no such balance. They looked upon pleasure and desire with a frowning face. It took years for me to trust God as the smiling source of every good thing on this planet. "The thief comes only to steal and kill and destroy; I have come that they may have life, and have it to the full," said Jesus (pointedly, he was addressing the religious establishment). From another world, he came to show us how best to live in this one.

Despite Jesus' stated goal, his followers often tilt away from pleasure. Early Christians would travel hundreds of miles to gaze upon spiritual athletes who sat atop poles for thirty years, or who sealed themselves up in cisterns, or who ate only a hunk of bread or a patch of grass each day and lived in cages too small to allow standing. James Agee once described a human being as "a furious angel nailed to the ground by his wings," and some of that fury shows up in the Christian ascetics. They wanted to escape humanity and fly away.*

---

*To be fair, though, the wisest among the ascetics knew very well what they were relinquishing. They did not denounce sex, food, and comfort as evils but esteemed them as God's good gifts. That is what made their sacrifice a valuable offering. They forfeited natural pleasures for one supernatural pleasure, and most of them seemed to think it a fair trade.

Over time, Christians got the reputation of being anti-pleasure. According to the stereotype, we grimace our way through this life toward an afterlife. The more we deny natural desires, the more "spiritual" we are. The apostle Paul had stern words against such purveyors of super-spirituality who, in effect, were slandering God's good gifts. "Hypocritical liars," he called them: "They forbid people to marry and order them to abstain from certain foods, which God created to be received with thanksgiving by those who believe and who know the truth. For everything God created is good, and nothing is to be rejected if it is received with thanksgiving."

Clearly, God did not create us with desires simply so that we would renounce them. As Paul insisted, this world is God's creation. Like a loving parent, the God who created us wants for us the best, most satisfying life possible.

Christianity does not promise the ultimate in personal pleasure, a life oriented around hedonism. Rather, it promises an ordering of life—a putting together, not a reduction—so that we realize pleasures as they were intended by our Creator. Otherwise, we risk indulging to our own destruction, like an alcoholic who determines how much to drink. Abuses arise from regarding pleasure as an end in itself rather than a pointer to something more. "Perfect are the good desires you have given me," prayed Pascal; "Be their End, as you have been their Beginning."

———

The Puritans had a saying, "God loveth adverbs," implying that God cares more about the spirit in which we live than the concrete results. They sought to connect all of life to its source in God, bringing the two worlds together rather than dividing them into sacred and secular.

Pleasing God does not mean that we must busy ourselves with a new set of "spiritual" activities. As the Puritans said, whether cleaning house or preaching sermons, shoeing horses or translating the Bible for the Indians, any human activity may constitute an offering to God. In that spirit, Thomas Merton would later remark, "You can tell more about a monk by the way he uses a broom than by anything he says."

I find it relatively easy to "hallow" God in nature and much harder to hallow the ordinary events of my life. How can I see the mundane tasks that comprise my day as forming any sort of meaningful pattern? How can I bring the two worlds together, reading God into the course of my day?

I heard one clue from the Lutheran professor and author Martin Marty who described his professional life this way: "I go to work because I have a job that's part of a career, which is part of a profession that I do because of my vocation that is the shape of my life." Marty had grasped the big picture, his calling, which put everything else in place. Somehow the daily tasks required—in his case, grading papers, lectures, committee meetings, writing, and research—fit together as rungs of a ladder leading all the way up to a *vocation,* a word taken from the Latin for "calling." Marty went on to say that a sense of calling may be the most important step for any who seek fulfilment and meaning.

Marty was following the pattern of Martin Luther himself, who saw a potential calling in any kind of work. "Even dirty and unpleasant work, such as shovelling manure or washing diapers, is pure and holy work if it comes from a pure heart," he said. Luther urged ordinary folk—farmers, milkmaids, butchers, and cobblers—to perform their work as if God himself was watching.*

Luther was, in effect, bringing two worlds together, reading God into everyday life. A thousand years before Luther, Saint Benedict had founded the Benedictines in order to break down the artificial wall between spiritual and secular activities. To pray is to work and to work is to pray, he told his followers. While studying theology and producing astonishing illuminated manuscripts, Benedictine monks also worked outdoors, draining swamps and cultivating fields. They laid the foundation for modern

---

*Some took Luther's advice quite literally. In Oxford, England, I have seen exquisitely carved statues hidden behind walls and visible only by reaching in with a mirror through holes in the plaster. Medieval artists walled up some of their best work because they believed God himself saw it, and left it for God's eyes only. The art remained hidden until uncovered by modern restoration projects.

Europe, and even today, a millennium and a half later, Benedict's Rule attracts a devoted following.

One such Benedictine, Joan Chittister, summarizes spirituality as "living the ordinary life extraordinarily well ... if we are not spiritual where we are and as we are, we are not spiritual at all." The Benedictines value God's good gifts. If a tool or machine breaks, they repair it rather than buy a new one. They grow their own food and hire no servants. No work is beneath them, Chittister observes, and from common tasks they can learn spiritual lessons, like humility: "The rich do not sweep faster or better than the poor; the educated do not wash clothes better than the illiterate; the professional does not shovel snow more easily than the farm labourer; the cleric does not change automobile oil with more delicacy than the mechanic."

Modern, high-tech society makes it difficult for most of us to see work as connected to anything else, to learn from it spiritual lessons. We commute from home to attend meetings and shuffle papers, or to hammer nails or string wires, and then return home to resume life, only to find that very little energy remains for living.

I think of my own career in light of Martin Marty's formula for absorbing daily tasks into a calling. Like Marty, I have the privilege of spending hours each day dealing directly with the things of God. I do not sell cars or process insurance claims or clean carpets or work in a busy office; I write books about God. Yet daily I encounter the difficulty of reading God into that very task. It requires a trained set of eyes to see God in the details.

Today I fiddled with adjustments to the computer software I use. I sat and fidgeted, listening to canned music through a telephone receiver, while waiting for an airline ticketing agent. Then I drank coffee. I cleared a paper jam in a printer. I signed for a delivery from the UPS driver. I searched the Internet to check details about Martin Luther and Benedict of Nursia. I drank more coffee. I went over and over the same sentences, trying to get the words right (thus successfully avoiding writing new words). I checked a thesaurus. I answered a few letters from readers. I paid some bills. I drove to Starbucks.

How do I make these mundane tasks sacred? In part, I do so by trusting that the details serve a role in the overall scheme of writing, which I accept as my calling. I see them as necessary steps in arriving at the final product, a book that one day I will hold in my hand. (Some, I admit, are stalling tactics that may in fact delay the final product.) Because I have been through this process before, I can trust that an accumulation of such days, with little productivity to show for many of them, will eventually result in that book.

My friend the late Lew Smedes tells in his memoir of being introduced, in a class in English Composition at Calvin College, "to a God the likes of whom I had never even heard about." This God, says Smedes,

> liked elegant sentences and was offended by dangling modifiers. Once you believe this, where can you stop? If the Maker of the Universe admired words well put together, think of how he must love sound thought well put together, and if he loved sound thinking, how he must love a Bach concerto and if he loved a Bach concerto think of how he prized any human effort to bring a foretaste, be it ever so small, of his Kingdom of Justice and peace and happiness to the victimized people of the world. In short, I met the Maker of the Universe who loved the world he made and was dedicated to its redemption. I found the joy of the Lord, not at a prayer meeting, but in English Composition 101.

I too have learned that my work, in all its tedium, matters to the Maker of the Universe. God loveth adverbs.

Far more difficult, I find, is the faith required in the other direction: to recognize something of lasting value in each of the mundane tasks. Did I treat the airline ticketing agent, the UPS driver, my readers, with the attention they deserve? In my tightly controlled day, did I remain open to the possibility of the extraordinary breaking in on the ordinary? Did I hallow my day with the same enthusiasm—the same faith—with which I hallow nature? Did I incorporate the small details of my life into its overall pattern?

Caring for an elderly parent. Cleaning up after a child. Sitting on a porch with a neighbour. Fielding a customer's complaint. Laying fiber-optic cable. Filling out charts at a nurses station. Sitting in traffic. Sawing lumber. Reporting waitress tips. Shopping for groceries. We spend much of our time, if not most, immersed in the mundane. It takes faith to believe that these things matter, that somehow they contribute to anything like a vocation.

And yet, I remind myself, did not the apostle Paul write the grand letter to the Romans while on a fund-raising trip for the poor of Jerusalem? Do not almost all his letters begin with soaring prayers and lofty theology and then descend abruptly to practical advice and requests to greet his friends? After the stirring doxology of Romans 11, the next few chapters cover such topics as hospitality, sex, taxes, debt, holidays, and eating vegetables.

"We have the mind of Christ," Paul says at one point, and he is writing to the Corinthian church, which of all his churches shows least evidence of that mind. What does it mean to exercise "the mind of Christ" in the midst of the mundane?

I have a clue, thanks to a book I wrote called *Soul Survivor*. In it, I profiled thirteen people who have had a formative influence on me. I reflected on how I changed because of those thirteen people, and as I wrote it they lived large in my mind. When I felt cheated or ripped off, I asked myself how Martin Luther King Jr would respond. When shopping for a new car, I wondered what kind of car, if any, Gandhi might drive. When I got impatient with a waitress in a restaurant, I remembered hearing psychiatrist Robert Coles tell of his hypocrisy in treating the servant class. When I felt too lazy to recycle office paper, I thought of Dr Paul Brand and the allergic reaction to wastefulness he learned in India.

Perhaps the mind of Christ should operate on me in a similar way. Surely that spirit would affect my attitude toward those who criticize and wrong me. Surely the mind of Christ will also affect the people I spend my time among, for I know what kind of people Jesus singled out.

67

"You did not choose me, but I chose you," Jesus told his disciples. Perhaps that statement applies not only to his disciples but also to me and to all the people who touch my life in some way: the woman I married, the colleagues I work with, the neighbours I live by, the telephone solicitors who interrupt me. I cannot be sure, and perhaps that too is a good thing to contemplate—consciously to accept every relationship as a potential revelation of Jesus.

I read a book on marriage that advises we should stop looking to marriage as a place in which to fulfil our romantic and ego needs and look on it instead as God's great tool for character formation. Whenever I can keep that principle in mind—admittedly, about 5 percent of the time—my outlook changes dramatically. Losing an argument becomes an opportunity to learn humility; sexual frustration becomes a chance to exercise patience and hope. One day it occurred to me that perhaps I should look at every human relationship as a tool for character formation, including every encounter with a surly clerk or selfish neighbour or demanding relative. In that way the values of another world could penetrate this one. Could Paul have been thinking along these lines when he wrote, "Regard no one from a human point of view"?

———

When I worked as a young journalist for *Campus Life* magazine, my assistant kept a plaque on her desk with this two-line poem:

> Only one life, 'twill soon be past
> Only what's done for Christ will last.

Reading that plaque brought me up short every time. Although I believed its truth, how could I put it into practise? Getting the oil changed in my car, watching the Chicago Bears football game on television, swapping funny stories at coffee break downstairs, planning an outing on Lake Michigan, marking up a manuscript with typesetting codes—were these acts done for Christ? How *should* my faith in the invisible world affect day-to-day life in the visible world?

According to Jesus, what other people think of me matters very little. What God thinks, matters far more. Pray in a closed room, Jesus said, where no one but your Father can see you, rather than in a public place where you might get credit for being spiritual. In other words, live for God and not other people. I keep clamouring for attention and achievement. Jesus invites me to let go of that competitive struggle, to trust that God's opinion of me is the only one that counts, ultimately.

"There are but two principles of moral life in the universe," said the mystic Madame Guyon: "one which makes ourselves, or the most limited private good, the centre; the other, which makes God, who may be called the universal good, the centre." I could summarize my entire spiritual pilgrimage as an effort to move the operating centre from myself to God.

I ask myself how my life would differ if I truly played to an audience of One, if I continually asked not "What do I want to do?" or "What would bring me approval from others?" but "What would God have me do?" Certainly my sense of ego and rivalry would fade because I would no longer need to worry about proving myself to other people. I could concentrate instead on pleasing God, by living in such a way that would attract people to Jesus' style of life.

My standards of success would also change. Our celebrity culture measures success with great precision, broadcasting the gross revenue of each current movie, details of the latest multimillion dollar signing by a sports star, the rise and fall of stock markets and mutual funds. Yet Jesus made the sweeping statement that nothing is more important than loving God and loving our neighbours. He said we serve *him* by offering water to the thirsty, caring for the sick, and visiting those in prison. Rarely do I see that kind of success celebrated in the media. Nor should we expect anything else, for the kingdom of heaven has different rewards in place. It takes faith to believe that the rewards promised by God matter more than the immediate rewards of a success-driven culture.

"We are not trying to please men but God," the apostle Paul said about his own work, which brought him so much adversity. "For none of us lives to himself alone and none of us dies to himself alone. If we live, we live to the Lord; and if we die, we die to the Lord. So, whether we live or die, we belong to the Lord."

The theologian Urs von Balthasar suggests that we think of ourselves as being engaged in a "theo-drama." We accept that we are but actors in the play, not the director, and in fact we must listen carefully to the whispered stage directions. In a good play, even the most minor characters serve a purpose essential to the plot, and in the drama on this planet the unique role that is mine only becomes clear as my life unfolds. We succeed by following the counsel of the director, who alone knows how each part fits into the whole.

This morning, knowing I had a difficult day of writing ahead, I went to a local restaurant, and instead of my normal fare of Fiber One cereal, I feasted on eggs, bacon, home-fried potatoes, and pancakes. I hoped that the act of eating high-energy food might help clarify my mind to focus on spiritual issues in the same way it might prepare an athlete to run a race.

I prayed, pacing the floor, for a friend who this very day is undergoing a double mastectomy. On Sunday, I will attend church. If the usual pattern holds, I'll find my mind wandering at times and will read the fine print in the bulletin when I should be paying attention. One or two of the praise choruses will probably grate on me. I will walk forward to receive a pinch of bread dipped in wine, and leave the service with that taste souring on my tongue.

Each one of these spiritual acts involves my body interacting with the natural world. So does serving the poor, building houses for the homeless, searching for the best words to express my faith, loving my family and neighbours, and walking the hills behind my home with a spirit of gratitude and praise. These ordinary acts, fuelled by faith, may push me away from my constant self-obsession so that life becomes something of a reflection back to the Giver.

The prize-winning Irish poet Evangeline Paterson sums up her life: "I was brought up in a Christian environment where, because God had to be given pre-eminence, nothing else was allowed to be important. I have broken through to the position that because God exists, everything has significance."

Do not forget that the value and interest of life is not so much to do conspicuous things ... as to do ordinary things with the perception of their enormous value.

PIERRE TEILHARD DE CHARDIN

designer sex

Perhaps, I thought, while her words still hung in the air between us like a wisp of tobacco smoke—a thought to fade and vanish like smoke without a trace—perhaps all our loves are merely hints and symbols; a hill of many invisible crests; doors that open as in a dream to reveal only a further stretch of carpet and another door; perhaps you and I are types and this sadness which sometimes falls between us springs from disappointment in our search, each straining through and beyond the other, snatching a glimpse now and then of the shadow which turns the corner always a pace or two ahead of us.

EVELYN WAUGH

A physician friend of mine spent two months in a remote part of the African nation Benin. The airplane on which he travelled home was showing current movies, and after two months away from all media he found them jarring. Each movie centred on sex, as though this were the only significant topic in the world, whereas David had just been dealing with weighty matters—disease, poverty, hunger, religion, death—while relating to colleagues in a way that had nothing to do with sexual intercourse. When the plane stopped for re-fuelling at the Brussels airport, David saw rows of magazines for sale featuring women's breasts in various stages of exposure. That too seemed odd, for he had been working in an area where women commonly uncovered their breasts in public, not for sexual arousal but to feed their children. *Welcome back to Western civilization,* he thought to himself.

Back in 1873 John Stuart Mill predicted a lessening of the sex drive as civilization advanced. "I think it most probable that this particular passion will become with men, as it is already with a larger number of women, completely under the control of the reason." Oh, how wrong he was! A visitor could, with few exceptions, mark a country's progress toward technological sophistication by counting its pornography outlets. Societies that have abandoned the sacred, such as in the secular West, exalt sexuality to a new and lofty status.

I know no clearer example of the modern, reductionistic approach to life than human sexuality. We survey people about their private sex lives and write manuals based on data gained by watching people perform sex in a laboratory setting. To junior high students we teach details of sexuality forbidden to previous generations.

At the same time, I know of no greater failure among Christians than in presenting a persuasive point of view on sexuality. Outside the church, people think of God as the great spoilsport of human sexuality, not its inventor. In a sex-saturated society, even true believers find it hard to accept that traditional Christian morality offers the fullest, most satisfying life. The pope utters pronouncements, denominations issue position papers, and many Christians ignore them and follow the lead of the rest of society. Surveys reveal little difference between church attenders and non-attenders in the rates of premarital intercourse and cohabitation. Surveys also show that millions of people have left the church in disgust over its hypocrisy about sex, especially when priests and ministers fail to practise what they preach.

Sex, then, deserves a closer look, as a conspicuous case study of the difference between a one-world and two-world approach to life. I am fully aware of the challenge involved in tackling this subject in today's permissive atmosphere. Yet, if Christianity makes sense, it must make sense here.

———

Nothing intrinsic in human sexuality keeps a person from experimenting with multiple partners, both genders, even children, close relatives, or animals. Yet every tribe studied by anthropologists has taboos that fence off some of these practices. As if by instinct, the most "primitive" of humans recognize in sex something beyond a merely physical act.

Only in technologically advanced cultures do people reduce sex to an act of pleasure we perform like any other animal. Music gives us away. Tina Turner still belts out, "What's love got to do with it?" A contemporary Swedish rock group sings "In Lust We Trust." And a popular song by Bloodhound Gang urges, "You and me, baby, ain't nothin' but mammals, so let's do it like they do it on the Discovery Channel." Why not? The Discovery television channel portrays close-up detail of sex in the animal kingdom every night in prime time.

The attempt to reduce human sex to a merely animal act, however, runs into unexpected problems. The more we learn about human sexuality, the more it apparently differs from how the animals do it. Most obviously, humans come vastly overequipped for sex. The human male has the largest penis of any primate, and the female is the only mammal whose breasts develop before her first pregnancy. Virtually all other mammals have a specified time in which the female is receptive, or in heat, whereas the human female can be receptive anytime, not just once or twice a year. In addition, the human species is one of very few in which females experience orgasm, and humans continue to have sex long after their childbearing years have passed. Why are we so oversexed?

Relationship is the key. Human beings experience sex as a personal encounter, not just a biological act. We are the only species that commonly copulates face to face, so that partners look at each other as they mate, and have full-body contact. Unlike other social animals, humans prefer privacy for the act. In many species, females openly advertise their receptivity with swollen, colourful genitals, and the male and female mate in full view of the group. (Imagine how such behaviour among humans might disrupt a work environment.)

I have referred to the hornets' nest stirred up when two evolutionary theorists released *A Natural History of Rape*. They observed quite accurately that male animals use rape as one more strategy for spreading their seed. Interestingly, in their rebuttals feminists defended sex as an expression of intimacy and relationship. In fact, such expression is a most *unnatural* state of affairs in the animal kingdom, part of what makes us distinctively human.

Zoologists puzzle over the oddities of human sexuality, unable to find any evolutionary advantage in sex apart from reproduction. Some conclude that for humans sex represents a huge waste of time—certainly true if the point is fertilization rather than relationship.

We humans make love not to a body but to a person. Sex partners negotiate a contract, one as simple as a tourist paying for an hour of a prostitute's time or as complicated as a Shakespearean love triangle. Unlike the Tasmanian ram who services every receptive female within sniffing distance, mating humans demand some sort of mutual consent. When none exists, we call that rape and punish it.

Some people (usually men) try to treat sex as an animal act. In a scene from the movie *A Beautiful Mind*, the brilliant but socially inept mathematician John Nash approaches an attractive woman in a bar: "Listen, I don't have the words to say whatever it is that's necessary to get you into bed, so can we just pretend I said those things and skip to the part where we exchange bodily fluids?" He learns quickly, from the imprint of her palm on his face, that reductionism does not work well as a pickup line.

Schizophrenic is the best way to describe modern society's view of sexuality. On the one hand, scientists insist that we are organisms like any other animal, and that sex is a natural expression of that animal nature. The pornography industry (which in the U.S. grosses more money than all professional sports combined) happily complies, supplying sexual images of the famous and the anonymous to anyone willing to pay. On the Internet, any high school kid can find videos of Pamela Anderson's honeymoon and nude photos of famous celebrities like Britney Spears and Jennifer Lopez. Never has sex been so disconnected from personal relationship.

On the other hand, when people truly act out their animal natures, society frowns in disapproval. The mathematician John Nash gets slapped for telling the truth. Sheriff's deputies arrest members of the Spur Posse in a California high school for competing to "conquer" girls, with some victims as young as ten years old. A few states in the U.S. allow legalized prostitution, but no parents encourage their daughters to pursue such a career. Hollywood may glamourize adultery onscreen, but in real life it provokes pain and a rage sometimes strong enough to drive the wounded party to murder the rival or jump off a bridge.

Society's schizophrenia develops from an attempt to reduce sex between humans to a purely physical act. For humans, unlike sheep or chimpanzees, sex involves more than bodies. *A Natural History of Rape* reports that only 22 percent of rapes involve "gratuitous" violence beyond what is necessary to subdue the victim, yet any rape counselor knows that the real violence occurs on the inside and may lead to years of depression, nightmares, memory loss, and sexual dysfunction. Victims of abusive relatives and paedophiliac priests testify that something far more than a body gets hurt when a trusted adult abuses a child sexually. Decades later, suffering persists.

In 2002 the U.S. Supreme Court ruled that Congress cannot outlaw "virtual child porn," consisting of computer-generated images on the Internet, since no one gets harmed in its manufacture. Their decision neglects the harm done to the people feeding on such images, for the real damage in sexuality occurs inside. Sex may engage our bodies, but unlike such bodily functions as excretion, sneezing, and burping, it also touches our souls—as tenderly, and as precariously, as they can be touched.

I might feel more attraction toward a reductionistic approach to sex if I saw that it addressed these deeper needs, if I sensed that the sexual revolution had increased respect between genders, created a more loving environment for children, relieved the ache of personal loneliness, and fostered intimacy. I have seen no such evidence.

_____

C. S. Lewis drew a short parable to make a point about sex:

> Now suppose you came to a country where you could fill a theatre by
> simply bringing a covered plate on to the stage and then slowly lift-
> ing the cover so as to let every one see, just before the lights went out,
> that it contained a mutton chop or a bit of bacon, would you not think
> that in that country something had gone wrong with the appetite for
> food? And would not anyone who had grown up in a different world
> think there was something equally queer about the state of the sex
> instinct among us?

Why does sex play so much larger in modern cities than, say, in the
villages of the Amazon? Clothing fashions, billboards, and ads on the sides
of city buses give human sexuality a prominence it never attains in the
naked jungle. The French sociologist Jacques Ellul sees our modern fixation with sex as the symptom of a breakdown in intimacy. Having detached
the physical act of sex from relationship, we can only work at perfecting
the "technique"—hence the proliferation of sex studies, sex manuals, and
sex videos, none of which address the real source of our pain.

I would suggest that the rumour of another world also enters in.
Many sophisticated moderns have little transcendence in their lives. They
avoid church and believe science has figured out most of the mysteries of
the universe. Sex, though, poses a mystery to which normal principles of
reductionism do not apply. Feed it, and the appetite increases. No amount
of knowledge diminishes its magic: even a nudist gets turned on when his
wife greets him in Victoria's Secret underwear.

When a society loses faith in its gods, or God, lesser powers arise to
take their place. Blocked longings seek new routes. "Every man who
knocks on the door of a brothel is looking for God," said G. K. Chesterton.
In modern Europe and the U.S., sex has a near-sacred quality of mythic,
numinous power. We select our sexiest individuals and accord them the
status of gods and goddesses, fawning over the details of their lives,

broadcasting their bodily statistics, surrounding them with paparazzi, rewarding them with money and status. Sex no longer points to something beyond; it becomes the thing itself, the substitute sacred.

While writing this chapter, sequestered in the mountains, I turned on *The Today Show* and saw a report from Rio de Janeiro on the Carnival celebration. Cameras gave close-up views of women wearing thong bikinis on the beach and men and women in provocative costumes strutting in the street. Somehow all this erotica is connected with a religious holiday, said the commentator with a sly grin. The only transcendent force evident was a visceral pull toward those nameless, faceless bodies parading across the screen: sex as an act of worship.

The very word *sex* comes from a Latin verb that means to cut off or sever, and sexual impulses drive us to unite, to restore somehow the union that has been severed. Freud diagnosed the deep pain within as a longing for union with a parent; Jung diagnosed a longing for union with the opposite sex. The Christian sees a deeper longing, for union with the God who created us. Sex prefigures that union by bringing together body and soul in a kind of wholeness not otherwise known.

Unfortunately, few people look to the church for perspective on the true meaning of human sexuality, since they view the church as an implacable enemy of sex. It should be obvious why the church so often falls on the side of repression, rather than celebration, of sexuality: no human longing is more powerful, more difficult to rein in. "The strongest oaths are straw to the fire i' the blood," said Shakespeare. Surveys showing that 70 percent of evangelical Christians engage in premarital sex give strong evidence of that fire. Sex has enough combustive force to incinerate conscience, vows, family commitments, religious devotion, and anything else in its path.

How the church got its reputation as an enemy of sex is a long story, in some ways understandable and in some ways shameful. As I have mentioned, every society sets boundaries, or taboos, around sexuality, and in Western civilization Christianity was the main force to set those boundaries. Against the background of pagan Greek and Roman culture, which incorporated temple prostitutes into worship activities, the early church went through a period of purging.

Saint Augustine, converted out of that pagan background and tormented by his own guilty past, connected the transmission of sin with the act of intercourse and proclaimed that sex for any purpose other than conceiving is a sin. He came to regret that God had created sex in the first place.

Augustine's contemporary Jerome went even further. Plagued by sexual fantasies—"I often found myself surrounded by bands of dancing girls"—he fasted to the point of starving in an attempt to control the temptations. "My face was pale with fasting; but though my limbs were cold as ice my mind was burning with desire, and the fires of lust kept bubbling up before me when my flesh was as good as dead."

Finally Jerome turned to studying Hebrew as form of sublimation. His scholarship resulted in the Latin Vulgate translation of the Bible used by the church for a thousand years, but did little for Jerome's attitude toward sex. He assigned spiritual values to women: a hundred for virgins, sixty for widows, and thirty for married women, ranking marriage just above fornication. "I praise wedlock, I praise marriage; but it is because they produce me virgins," he said, and proceeded to give prison-like rules to the mothers who raised these virgins. To husbands he declared, "Anyone who is too passionate a lover with his own wife is himself an adulterer."

In the succeeding centuries church authorities issued edicts forbidding sex on Thursdays, the day of Christ's arrest; on Fridays, the day of his death; on Saturdays, in honour of the blessed Virgin; and on Sundays in honour of the departed saints. Wednesdays sometimes made the list too, as did the forty-day fast periods before Easter, Christmas, and Pentecost, and also feast days and days of the apostles, as well as the days of female impurity. The list escalated until, as John Boswell has estimated, only forty-four days a year remained available for marital sex. Human nature being what it is, the average churchgoer ignored these rules, and after Martin Luther most of them were abandoned.

One pope assigned a painter, "Daniel the Trouserer," to clothe the nudes of the Sistine Chapel. Another ruled that all priests must be celibate. Even so, for most of its history the church had no trouble recruiting priests and nuns to take a vow of chastity. And when women were banned from singing in church, legions of *castrati* volunteered to forgo a normal sexual future for the sake of the higher octaves. (One was still singing in the Sistine Chapel at the beginning of the twentieth century.)

The Protestant Reformation brought about a shift in attitudes toward sex. Luther scorned the church's rule against marital sex for the sake of pleasure and transferred to the home much of the respect that had been accorded the nunnery. When secular revolutions swept across Europe in the eighteenth and nineteenth centuries, the church's position as guardian of sexuality faded. Yet in England and America, Victorians brought back an ethic of repression, even to the extent of covering the legs of furniture lest they arouse impure thoughts.

I dwell on the church's severe attitude toward sex because I believe we Christians bear heavy responsibility for the counter-reaction so evident in modern society. Jesus treated those who had fallen into sexual sins with compassion and forgiveness, and reserved his harshest words for the hidden sins of hypocrisy, pride, greed, and legalism. How is it that we who follow him use the word "immoral" to signify sexual sins almost exclusively* and reserve church discipline for those who fail sexually?

Perhaps worse, though, the church in its prudery has silenced a powerful rumour of transcendence that could point to the Creator and originator of human sexuality, who invested in it far more meaning than most modern people can imagine. We have desacralized it, in effect, by suppression and denial, and along the way our clumsy attempts at repression helped empower a false infinite. Sexual power lives on, but few see in that power a pointer to the One who designed it.

Few Christians "hallow" sex in the way that we hallow nature. I know many hymns that celebrate natural creation, but none that celebrate

81

*Acknowledging this trend, Dorothy Sayers wrote an essay entitled "The Other Six Deadly Sins."

sexuality in the way that Song of Solomon or the book of Proverbs does. In the old Anglican marriage ceremony, a husband used to declare to his bride, "with my body I thee worship," acknowledging sex as a gift of God that could become a form of homage, even praise.

"The nakedness of woman is the work of God," said William Blake, as he gave a Job-like list of natural wonders, "portions of eternity too great for the eye of man." Blake had it nearly right: in a truly Christian view, the naked body is indeed a portion of eternity, but designed exquisitely for the eyes of man and woman.

———

I want to try to recover, as best I can, a view of sex that corresponds to God's original design. I want to tune my ears to this most intriguing rumour of another world, a rumour that the church has so often ignored or hushed.

Before doing so, I must say a word of compassion for those who already have failed to meet that design—through promiscuity, adultery, divorce. Jesus set the example for the rest of us by responding with great tenderness to those who had failed sexually. Recognizing the depth of their pain, he offered forgiveness and not judgement. The pain that lingers after sexual failure is, oddly, an indirect proof of sexuality's original design. Those who test that design, and fail, in the process gain some haunting sense of what we are missing. We want desperately to connect, to grow in personal intimacy even as we progress in sexual intimacy. We want to be fully known, and fully loved. When that does not happen, or when the fragile link snaps, it simply proves that in sex, as in every area of life, fallen humanity gets in the way and keeps us from realizing the ideal.

The Stoics of ancient Greece and thought police of Maoist China prove that religion is not the only force that struggles to restrain sex.*

---

*To extinguish any residue of Christian morality, Lenin espoused a Glass of Water theory about sex. Sexual desire is no more sacrosanct than desire for food or water, he declared, and rewrote the Soviet lawbook accordingly. That theory led to sexual chaos and Soviet society became—on the surface at least—almost puritanical about sexual morality.

Sex has an explosive power that can easily get out of control and turn destructive. Most authorities, religious or not, put sex "in its place" by encouraging repression in some form or other. There may, however, be another way to put sex in its place, and that is to *find* its place as God intended: to look at sex not with a voyeur's leer but with a probing aim toward learning what lies behind it.

Uptight Christians forget the fundamental fact that God *created* sex. Having studied some anatomy, I marvel at God labouring over the physiology of sex: the soft parts, the moist parts, the millions of nerve cells sensitive to pressure and pain yet also capable of producing pleasure, the intricacies of erectile tissue, the economical and ironical combination of organs for excretion and reproduction, the blending of visual appeal and mechanical design. As the zoologists remind us, in comparison with every other species the human is bountifully endowed.

A connected view of life assumes this is God's world, and that despite its fractured state clues of its original design remain. When I experience desire, I need not flinch in guilt, as if something unnatural has happened. Rather, I should follow the desire to its source, in search of God's original intent.

Desire. "You have heard that it was said, 'Do not commit adultery.' But I tell you that anyone who looks at a woman lustfully has already committed adultery with her in his heart." In this, the Bible's strongest statement about sexual desire, Jesus cuts to the heart of the matter. He affirms that sexual desire affects the inside of a person ("in his heart") whether or not anything takes place externally. He also connects sexual desire with relationship, startlingly, by linking lust and adultery. The voyeur wants to keep his desires both discreet and discrete, disconnected from any actual personal contact; Jesus exposes the deception.

Recently I came across Martin Luther's pastoral advice about lust:

But some might say, "Waiting for marriage is unbearable and aggravating!" They're right. It's very similar to other difficulties requiring patience that believers must face, such as fasting, imprisonment, cold,

sickness, and persecution. Lust is a serious burden. You must resist it
and fight against it. But after you have overcome it through prayer,
lust will have caused you to pray more and grow in faith.

It struck me that most of the difficulties Luther mentions—fasting,
imprisonment, cold, persecution, even most sicknesses—no longer confront Christians in prosperous democracies. We have eliminated many of
the burdens common to our forebears. Lust, however, we have not eliminated but perfected. In Luther's day, a teenage boy might get a glimpse
of a girl's bare legs as she stomped on grapes or bent over to draw water
from a well. He did not face the temptation of MTV reports on coeds who
flash their breasts on the beach during spring break; he did not have photos of Britney and J-Lo and Anna Kournikova streaming digitally over
his DSL line in the privacy of his bedroom.

Technology has allowed modern society to cleave sexual desire from
personal relationship. In connected sex, physical desire grows in concert
with personal intimacy. In modern lust, people sit in living rooms or even
office cubicles watching strangers undress and make love. Yielding to
such unattached desire can become addictive and often damages true relationship. A wife who discovers her husband fawning over pornography
may well feel rejected and devalued, her feelings of intimacy betrayed.

Luther correctly identified lust as a spiritual battle, not merely a
physical one. Lust entices us away from sex-as-God-intended, replacing
it with a shortcut, illusory world of self-gratification. (I say illusory
because if I ever ran into Anna Kournikova in public she wouldn't give
me the time of day; any "relationship" is an illusion.) For a cure, I need
help in reordering my desires so that they indeed reflect the reality of
relationship.

In his "Eleven Addresses to the Lord," John Berryman prayed,

> Sole watchman of the flying stars, guard me
> against my flicker of impulse lust: teach me
> to see them as sisters & daughters. Sustain
> my grand endeavours: husbandship & crafting.

Berryman was asking, in effect, for a reordering of desire. He wanted to view other females as sisters and daughters, not bodies inciting him to misplaced desire. He wanted God to sustain his vocation both as husband and as poet, with desires lining up to serve that vocation and not detract from it. By naming lust for what it was, a flicker of impulse, he helped disarm it.

Flannery O'Connor's short story "A Temple of the Holy Ghost" tells of a precocious twelve-year-old girl and two country boys who have come to court her visiting cousins. The girl overhears her teenage cousins mock a nun, Sister Perpetua, who has suggested a formula to use in fending off fresh young men in the back seats of cars. "Stop sir! I am a Temple of the Holy Ghost!" the nun taught the girls to say. The cousins think such advice hilarious. The twelve-year-old girl, however, is moved. The news that she is the dwelling place of God makes her feel as if somebody has given her a present. She takes it seriously.

The nun's formula comes from a passage, 1 Corinthians 6, that is among Paul's strongest and most strange. In trying to shock the Corinthians out of their wild behaviour, Paul uses this astonishing argument: "Do you not know that your bodies are members of Christ himself? Shall I then take the members of Christ and unite them with a prostitute? Never! Do you not know that he who unites himself with a prostitute is one with her in body? For it is said, 'The two will become one flesh.'"

Whether or not such an argument might deter an adolescent's groping hands in the back seat—much less the Corinthians' worldly escapades—Paul does reveal something of the multilayered nature of desire. The biology of sex has a seamless integration with the deeply personal (Paul quotes God's original formula for marriage in Genesis) and also the spiritual. We cannot simply compartmentalize sexual desire.

"Lust is a serious burden," said Martin Luther, discounting neither its power nor the actual suffering involved in living with unfulfilled desires. Joseph resisted temptation and ended up serving time in prison. "By faith Moses ... chose to be mistreated along with the people of God rather than to enjoy the pleasures of sin for a short time," says Hebrews.

"He regarded disgrace for the sake of Christ as of greater value than the treasures of Egypt, because he was looking ahead to his reward." Joseph and Moses both made a calculated choice, not against pleasure, but against one particular kind of pleasure in determined pursuit of another. As with all temptation, lust entices us to believe a seductive lie rather than the hard truth.

Purity. In a remarkably candid book, Jean Vanier, founder of the worldwide l'Arche communities where the author and priest Henri Nouwen spent his last years, discusses what he learned in many years of working with the profoundly retarded. *Man and Woman He Made Them* describes individuals so disturbed or mentally challenged as to be incapable of a normal relationship with another human. Some cannot speak. Some are blind. Some cannot control their spastic movements. Some seem unable to process any sensory data from the outer world.

Still, most of the damaged people Vanier works with experience sexual desires. One young man masturbates almost constantly. Others "fall in love" with other residents, though they lack the social ability to express that love, and want to get married. Others have no comprehension of marriage and simply want to have sex.

Meanwhile Vanier, a lay theologian, tries to live out his life of celibacy. He confesses the difficulty of that struggle, a struggle to which others succumb. He tells of the loneliness on the road, away from the supportive community that he serves, when he feels most vulnerable to seduction.

Vanier concludes that every choice we make about sex will involve a kind of suffering. The young man who masturbates every day does so out of inability to connect to others, his compulsive act more an expression of suffering than of pleasure. Marriage introduces suffering of a different sort: often expectations are not met, and sexual incompatibility creates even more conflict. "The human being is constantly straining towards this infinity," concludes Vanier: "a thirst to be filled, to be recognized in one's uniqueness, a thirst to be free, to be loving, to be a source of life for others.... Our thirst is infinite but it is carried in fragile vessels."

Vanier admits that his life of chosen celibacy includes very real suffering. Yet he prefers his own suffering to the suffering of those who exercise genital sexuality without responsibility or commitment. In his work, he has heard many of their stories in confession. Often they end up disappointed, and more isolated than ever. Relationships based primarily on sex do not wear well, for when the physical attraction fades, so does the love.

For Vanier, a commitment to purity is a sign of hope, an effort to bring personal order into a disordered world. Purity can be sought as a celibate single person or as a married person. Either state involves loneliness and sometimes anguish as well as hope. "Blessed are the pure in heart, for they will see God," Jesus promised. Note the extent of the promise: not that they will find complete sexual fulfilment and solve all loneliness, but that they will see God.

"We all have to choose between two ways of being crazy," says Vanier: "the foolishness of the Gospel and the non-sense of the values of our world." Both Jean Vanier and Henri Nouwen (who looked upon him as a mentor) cast their lot with the foolishness of the Gospel, leaving prestigious careers and living in community with some of the saddest, most neglected human beings on earth. To those who have known these two men, however, the choice looks like wisdom and not foolishness. A life of resisting temptation and pursuing purity involves a loss, yes, but also a gain, the very gain promised by Jesus in the Beatitudes.

At times I have given in to lust. I cannot deny that nude women, whether in art museums or magazines or over the Internet, exert on me a power like gravitational force. Our culture has mastered the disconnected "technique" of sex, and I have fallen victim. I must also say, though, that when I resist the temptation and pour sexual energy into my marriage—a much more complicated and less selfish transaction, to be sure—the obsessive power of sexuality fades away. The air clears. Marriage becomes more of a haven. My life with God yields unexpected rewards.

"Adherence to Jesus allows no free rein to desire unless it be accompanied by love," wrote Dietrich Bonhoeffer, engaged to be married, from a Nazi concentration camp:

Instead of trusting to the unseen, we prefer the tangible fruits of desire.... Lust is impure because it is unbelief, and therefore it is to be shunned. No sacrifice is too great if it enables us to conquer a lust which cuts us off from Jesus.... When you have made your eye the instrument of impurity, you cannot see God with it.

Bonhoeffer never got to experience the tangible fruits of desire; he died, still trusting to the unseen, at the hands of SS guards.

Romance. "We use a most unfortunate idiom when we say, of a lustful man prowling the streets, that he 'wants a woman,'" wrote C. S. Lewis. "Strictly speaking, a woman is just what he does not want. He wants a pleasure for which a woman happens to be the necessary piece of apparatus. How much he cares about the woman as such may be gauged by his attitude to her five minutes after fruition (one does not keep the carton after one has smoked the cigarettes)."

Lewis went on to say that true love makes a man want, not a woman, but one particular woman—the beloved herself, not the pleasure she can give. He wrote those words in 1960, not long after he, a confirmed British bachelor, had fallen joyously in love with the American Joy Davidman. For much of his life Lewis the scholar had treated romantic love as a purely literary phenomenon. "I know better now," he had to admit. "It's funny having at 59 the sort of happiness most men have in their twenties ... 'Thou hast kept the good wine till now.'"

Lyrics from the love songs broadcast on pop radio stations tap into romantic yearnings but promise more than any person can deliver. "You are my everything." "I can't live without you." Sexual desires and romantic longings are a kind of debased sacrament. If humanity serves as your religion, then sex becomes an act of worship. On the other hand, if God is the object of your religion, then romantic love becomes an unmistakable pointer, a rumour of transcendence as loud as any we hear on earth.

I credit three things—classical music, the beauties of nature, and romantic love—as responsible for my own conversion. The first two convinced me of the goodness of this world, and prodded me to search for the One who had made it. The third convinced me of the possibility of change in myself. I met a woman who saw worth in me where I had seen little. The hard, cynical shell I had carefully cultivated as a form of protection split apart like a carapace, and to my surprise I discovered that vulnerability need not mean danger.

Romance gives intriguing hints of transcendence. I am "possessed" by the one I love. I think of her day and night, languish when she leaves me, perform brave deeds to impress her, revel in her attention, live for her, even die for her. I want to be both heroic and meek at the same time. For a time, and only for a time, I can live on that edge of exaltation. Then reality sets in, or boredom, betrayal, old age, or death. I cannot sustain a state of complete absorption forever. At least, though, I can see in it a glimpse of God's infinite capacity for such attention. Could this be how God views us—views *me?*

Charles Williams, a colleague and close friend of C. S. Lewis, attempted a kind of natural theology based on romantic love. Others had traced the fingerprints of God in nature; he sought to do so in romance. He never fully completed the project, but the result, *Outlines of Romantic Theology,* follows Dante's path in exploring the sacred shadow of romantic love.

Williams suggests that romantic love gives us a new vision of one other human being, an *in*sight into his or her "eternal identity." To the rest of the world, such a vision may seem a delusion. "She's moonstruck," we say of someone in love, or "Love is blind." Parents look at a pimply introvert and wonder why on earth their daughter wants to spend all evening talking to him on the telephone. "They have changed eyes," says Shakespeare.

For a brief time, at least, romance gives us the ability to see the best in one other person, to ignore or forgive flaws, to bask in endless fascination. That state, says Williams, gives a foretaste of how we will one day view every resurrected person and how God now views us.

Romantic love does not distort vision but corrects it, in a very narrow range. The Bible uses explicit romantic images to describe God's love for us: what we feel in passing for one person, God feels eternally for the many. If we receive romantic love not as an end in itself but as God's gift, a shining grace, it can become like a shaft of light beckoning us toward what we will someday experience more fully as resurrected beings.

I cannot love every person in my neighbourhood, let alone every person on the planet, in the way I love my wife. I have neither the capacity nor the desire. Some day, perhaps, I will. C. S. Lewis again:

> The event of falling in love is of such a nature that we are right to reject as intolerable the idea that it should be transitory. In one high bound it has overleaped the massive wall of our selfhood; it has made appetite itself altruistic, tossed personal happiness aside as a triviality and planted the interest of another in the centre of our being. Spontaneously and without effort we have fulfilled the law (towards one person) by loving our neighbour as ourselves. It is an image, a foretaste, of what we must become to all if Love Himself rules in us without a rival. It is even (well used) a preparation for that.

Sex. Dostoyevsky's *Notes from the Underground* contains a chilling scene in which the underground man, a disturbed egoist, visits a prostitute. He pays his money, she performs, and then the two of them lie there in silence. Suddenly he looks to the side and sees two wide-open eyes staring at him. "The look in those eyes was coldly indifferent and sullen, as though it were utterly detached, and it made me feel terribly depressed." Then it occurs to him that for two hours he has not said a word to the naked creature beside him and has not even thought it necessary.

> Now, however, I suddenly saw clearly how absurd and hideous like a spider was the idea of vice which, without love, grossly and shamelessly begins where true love finds its consummation. We went on looking at each other like that for a long time, but she did not drop her

eyes before mine, nor did she change her expression, so that in the
end it made me for some reason feel creepy.

An extraordinary conversation takes place. The underground man
asks the prostitute's name. "Liza." He inquires about her nationality and
her parents. He speaks of a funeral he observed that morning. He asks
about her profession, and they discuss love, sex, and married life.

Gradually the two, who have wordlessly completed the most intimate act of physical union, become human to one another. A relationship,
guarded and manipulative but a relationship nonetheless, stirs to life. In
the remainder of the book, a plot plays out in which Liza cuts through the
underground man's armour of cruel egoism by responding to him with
tenderness and selfless love. "Something was not dead within me," he
finally realizes; the prostitute Liza, a person even more pitiable than himself, has coaxed it out.

We instinctively recognize the lie when sex becomes a mere transaction. I know of some societies that legally tolerate prostitution, but none that
honour the profession. Even high school students mock the "easy" girl who
offers her body cheaply. No amount of apparent pleasure can silence the nag-
ging sense that intimacy should involve more than a joining of body parts.
Dostoyevsky's despicable underground man intuits the error in "grossly and
shamelessly" beginning where true love finds its consummation.

A few mysterious passages in the Bible hint that, besides being a
token of human intimacy, sex has layers of further meaning. Weddings
often include the passage from Ephesians in which Paul declares, "After
all, no one ever hated his own body, but he feeds and cares for it, just as
Christ does the church—for we are members of his body. 'For this reason
a man will leave his father and mother and be united to his wife, and the
two will become one flesh.' This is a profound mystery—but I am talking
about Christ and the church."

You could look at such passages as God borrowing one of the most
thrilling human experiences, sexual intimacy, and using it as a verbal
appetizer to quicken our desire for eternity. Or you could travel in the
other direction, as Paul seems to do in Ephesians, and consider sexual

intimacy as a sacred pointer to something even greater, something truly out of this world.

In one sense, we are never more Godlike than in the act of sex. We make ourselves vulnerable. We risk. We give and receive in a simultaneous act. We feel a primordial delight, entering into *the other* in communion. Quite literally we make one flesh out of two different persons, experiencing for a brief time a unity like no other. Two independent beings open their inmost selves and experience not a loss but a gain. In some way—"a profound mystery" not even Paul dared explore—this most human act reveals something of the nature of reality, God's reality, in his relations with creation and perhaps within the Trinity itself.

I will go no further because to do so seems a kind of sacrilege, an ignorant probing of what we cannot possibly comprehend, an attempt to reduce an irreducible mystery. Simply recognizing the sacramental nature of sex does, however, shed light on some of the sexual taboos of the Bible. I now see them not as capricious rules to spoil our sexual adventures but rather as guidelines protecting something of great value that can only be realized in an exclusive, covenant relationship.

Confining sex to marriage does not guarantee that we will realize anything beyond physical gratification in our sex lives. It may, however, create an environment of safety, intimacy, and trust where the true meaning of sex, the sacramental meaning, may at times break through. Marriage provides the security we need to experience sex without restraint, apart from guilt, danger, or deceit. Teenagers worry that they will miss out on something if they heed the Bible's warnings against premarital sex. Actually, the warnings are there to *keep* them from missing out on something. Fidelity sets a boundary in which sex can run free.

When California adopted a sex education programme, the American Civil Liberties Union responded with an official memorandum: "The ACLU regrets to inform you of our opposition to SB 2394 concerning sex education in public schools. It is our position that teaching that monogamous, heterosexual intercourse within marriage is a traditional American value is an unconstitutional establishment of religious doctrine in public schools. . . . We believe SB 2394 violates the First Amendment." Many Christians felt outrage. The more I think about it, the more I understand the ACLU's position. Sex within a monogamous marriage *is* a religious doctrine, one that would be difficult to defend apart from such belief.

Marriage. I once heard an actor being interviewed on late-night television. "Tell me," said David Letterman. "You're a sex symbol who plays all sorts of exciting roles with gorgeous women. How does that compare to your real life, off-screen?"

The actor reminded Letterman that he had been happily married for twenty years. Then he said, "Here's the difference in a nutshell. In the movies, life is mostly about sex and occasionally about children. Married life is mostly about children and occasionally about sex."

Sex is such a powerful force that a young person may have trouble understanding how anything else could ever eclipse it. Most married people, like the actor, will tell you that sex within marriage is neither as easy nor as important as they had imagined before marriage. It expresses intimacy, yes, and provides pleasure. But much of marriage consists in making day-to-day decisions, managing the complexities of careers and schedules, rearing children, negotiating differences, juggling finances, and all the other effort involved in keeping a home running.

Marriage strips away the illusions about sex pounded into us daily by the media. Few of us live with oversexed supermodels. We live instead with ordinary people, men and women who get bad breath, body odours, and unruly hair; who menstruate and experience occasional impotence; who have bad moods and embarrass us in public; who pay more attention to our children's needs than our own. We live with people who require compassion, tolerance, understanding, and an endless supply of forgiveness. So do our partners. Such is the ironical power of sex: It lures us into a relationship that offers to teach us what we need far more, sacrificial love.

Every married person I know wonders at times if he or she has married the wrong person. For that reason we need something more than a

93

relationship built on emotions of the moment. We need something big enough to envelop circumstances rather than be enveloped by them. The old wedding vow sets out the commitment required of marriage: "for better for worse, for richer for poorer, in sickness and in health, to love and to cherish, till death us do part, according to God's holy ordinance . . ."

Puritans called marriage "the little church within the Church," a place to test and also develop spiritual character. Every day marriage calls both partners to love and forgive and stay faithful—hard work that only makes sense if we are convinced somehow that we are participating in a kind of alternate history, one set in eternity. I persevere in the difficult times in my marriage for the same reason I persevere in the difficult times in my faith: because I believe that both touch something of eternal significance.

For most of us, it takes years, perhaps a lifetime, to realize what unity with another person means. We learn each other's strengths and weaknesses, and work out power-sharing. We learn when to probe and when to back off, when to soothe and when to challenge. Gradually, as two independent people share a common reality, a kind of transfiguration takes place. A "second love" emerges.

After thirty-three years of marriage, I have difficulty separating my point of view from my wife's. She has taught me so much about human nature that when I encounter people, I encounter them as much through her eyes as my own. I cannot imagine travelling overseas without factoring in her taste in food, her observations of a foreign culture, her perceptions of beauty.

Over a long time, after much prayer and considerable effort, something new has come into being: a unity sealed by God, which enables us to face economic pressures, relocation, illness, and the loss of family and friends, as well as the delights that attracted us to each other in the first place. What affects her affects me; what affects me affects her. I went into marriage thinking love would hold us together. I learned instead that it required marriage to teach me what love means.

Jesus pointed to the original source for that unity: God designed and intended it, from the moment of creation. (In the same passage in

Matthew 19, significantly, Jesus also upholds singleness as a high calling, not for everyone, but a "vocation" in the kingdom of heaven with rewards unattainable in any other way. Jesus himself showed the way, living a fulfilled life despite his commitment to celibacy.) By declaring marriage a sacrament, the church did nothing but acknowledge formally a reality that already existed. It is a vocation, a calling, to spend a life together in self-giving partnership.

Increasingly, marriage as a sacrament is a quaint concept that few couples take seriously and fewer still could explain. The notion, though, is rooted in creation itself, a calling to be living witnesses, to establish settlements or "signs" of God's kingdom within an uncomprehending wider culture. The sociologists who authored *Habits of the Heart* found that few individuals in their survey except committed Christians could explain why they stayed married to their spouses. Marriage as a social construct is arbitrary, flexible, and open to redefinition. Marriage as a sacrament established by God is another matter entirely.

Because marriage is a sacrament, every test of fidelity poses a spiritual test as well as a moral one. God intended marriage to be a sign of the kind of love relationship he wants with us. Jacques Ellul said, "When I witness the end of a marriage because one of the spouses is gripped by a passion for someone else, I am as sad as at the death of a child." No wonder. A planted flag of the kingdom from another world has fallen to the ground.

It is precisely because of the eternity outside time that everything in time becomes valuable and important and meaningful. Therefore, Christianity . . . makes it of urgent importance that everything we do here should be rightly related to what we eternally are. "Eternal life" is the sole sanction for the values of this life.

DOROTHY L. SAYERS

PART TWO

signs of disorder

It is not we alone, it is not the house,
It is not the city that is soiled,
But the world that is wholly foul.

T. S. ELIOT

out of order

> Imaginary evil is romantic and varied; real evil is gloomy, monotonous, barren, boring. Imaginary good is boring; real good is always new, marvellous, intoxicating.
>
> SIMONE WEIL

A question has been looming in the background—a series of questions really, colliding and agitating each other like thunderheads in a summer sky. If this is God's world, why is it such a mess? And why do so few people experience good things, like sex, in the way God supposedly intended? And why must we pay attention and actively search for God? Why only rumours and not proofs of another world?

In short, if there is another world out there, shouldn't this one give more evidence of it? Obviously, a great rift has opened up between the ideal world Christians describe as God's creation and the world we actually inhabit. We stand at the edge of a precipice and peer into a fog for guidance. Some enthusiasts wave their arms and point, convinced of a reality beyond eyeshot, but the rest see only the milky white of clouds.

Christians explain the rift with a three-letter word, "one little, flat, deadly word that covers a lifetime," as novelist Evelyn Waugh put it.

Something in me recoils against that word *sin,* for reasons I will explain. Yet who can doubt that the world has undergone a kind of breakdown, the cosmic counterpart to a psychological breakdown in an individual. As a species we have lost a sense of self and of meaning, and we struggle to put life together in a coherent whole. A sly, chronic disease prevents us from relating to creation and each other, let alone God, as we should.

———

We have a deep intuition about how the world should operate and how it should not. Where did we get that sense?

Investigators of an airplane wreck assemble every fragment, poring over the blackened shards of metal in search of how the machine failed to fulfil its original design. Something went badly wrong, bringing instant chaos to a well-ordered system. In a similar way, the introduction of evil disordered the world's original design.

In a few brush strokes, the book of Genesis paints a scene of few rules, no shame, bountiful joy, and an unlimited range of pleasure and creative work. Despair, drought, sickness, death, conflict—all that has cursed human history—did not exist in Eden. John Milton bravely tried to render scenes from paradise, of a naked Eve serving Adam ambrosia and cups of pleasant liquors (". . . in those hearts Love unlibidinous reigned, nor jealousy was understood"), though most critics judge him more successful at depicting the fallen state all too familiar to us his readers.

The Hebrew prophets predict a return to Paradise, a time when the elderly can sit safely in the streets watching children play, when vineyards gush wine and deserts gush water, when carnivores and herbivores lie side by side and human races too live in peace—in other words, exactly the opposite of what transpires in the land of the prophets today. Modern Jews still greet each other with the gentle word used by the prophets to describe such a time, *shalom,* the salutation nowadays an aching reminder of how faraway is that state.

When I hike through a field of wildflowers toward a snowfield on a brilliant Colorado summer day, when I sit for hours with an old friend revealing parts of myself that no one else knows, when I add the final satisfying touches to a project that has taken me months or even years—at such times a memory stirs, a vestige of the world God intended.

And when I hear the relentless, dreary news of more human cruelty and global conflict, or come face to face with my own stubborn selfishness, I recoil because of that same memory. Something is wrong. As Lewis Smedes put it, "Christians must forever pick their way between delight in creation's gifts and sorrow for sin's distortions."

Genesis records that in Paradise a great severing took place. Adam and Eve reached too far, trusting themselves rather than God to set the rules. They tasted of the tree of the knowledge of good and evil, and ever since, human beings have known evil as a daily reality and good as a daily longing. Christians believe that sin, arguably the most "natural" human act, is from God's viewpoint distinctly *un*natural, the very opposite of God's intent for the planet.

I found a website, *www.notproud.com,* in which visitors anonymously post confessions of their sins. Listen to these voices of sadness and remorse, reproduced with their original spelling and grammar:

- If I could smack every co-worker and take their responsibilities and salaries, I'd do it. If I could take all competitors incomes and services, I'd do it. If I could hit your face and steal your wallet without looking you in the eye, I would do it.
- Sloth: I should be working now, but I am doing this instead.
- When my father was in a pschatric hospital after a suicide attempt, I wouldn't visit him in order to get back at him.
- i go to college. i used the money i should have spent on housing to buy dope, alcohol, entertainment, and food. i am bad, i know it, but stopping is soooo hard.
- I wish I was rich. I want to buy things I don't need with money I can afford to waste.
- I want one laptop, one cool flip phone, one Mercedes, two beers everyday for the rest of my life, and one million bucks in my bank account, thats it all I want.

• i lie about things i have done to hide the fact that my life has been
a meaningless timeline of uninteresting events, characters and
experiences. i lie to make up for the fact that i have no soul ...

Sin tempts us to choose the artificial over the real, the fleeting plea-sure over the lasting good. We follow our longings, only to find them dis-ordered and unquenchable. Thomas Merton wrote about his own disquiet, "The sense of exile bleeds inside me like a hemorrhage—it is always the same wound, whether it is a sense of sin, or of loneliness, or of one's own insufficiency, or of spiritual dryness: they are all really the same, in the way we experience them."

———

Morton Hunt's book on the human mind, *The Universe Within,* explores the limits of artificial intelligence. Cognitive scientists, he explains, rec-ognize a restlessness in the human mind, a need to do something with our thoughts and to pursue goals. Being human means grasping for some-thing more, just as Adam and Eve did. "The computer, in contrast, is a passive system: its goals and the strength of its drive to reach them are those given it by the designer. Left to itself, it will sit inert, awaiting fur-ther orders. We will not; we look for new goals, and, to reach them, are forced to solve problems we did not have before; we do not let well enough alone."

Artificial intelligence researchers doubt whether they can build a similar restlessness or curiosity into a computer. They can program a com-puter to seek new avenues and investigate new problems, but it does so because of its program, not because it wants to. Computers don't "want." Hunt concludes, "Maybe the biggest difference between artificial and human intelligence is just that simple: we care about the things we choose to do. Solving a new problem, discovering some new fact, visiting a new place, reading a new book, all make us feel good; that's why we do them. But how would one make a computer feel good?" Perhaps, he speculates, that mystery suggests why computer compositions of music and poetry so far fail to impress: the computer is neither pleased nor displeased by its own creation, unlike every human artist.

The challenge facing computer programmers may shed light on the choices God faced in creating human beings. Presumably, God could have designed a human brain more like a computer CPU, leaving out any neurological restlessness. Animals seem content living out the singular goal of survival, without the need to reflect on themselves or grasp for more. Yet when God created a being in God's own image, he built in restlessness, along with curiosity and desire, in full awareness they could lead the human to choose the wrong path.

That freedom, a reflection of God's image and our greatest "advantage" as human beings, can turn into a terrible disadvantage. Like Adam and Eve, we too can overturn the order of creation. "I am not an ordinary man, and the laws of morals and of custom were never made for me," said Napoleon. At times, who doesn't think something similar on smaller scale?

I have read critiques of God's decision to grant such freedom. Couldn't God have set tighter boundaries around our freedom so that people like Adolf Hitler would self-destruct if they exceeded those boundaries? More to the point, couldn't God have created human beings who would always choose good rather than evil, in a world that combines perfect freedom and perfect goodness?*

Maybe not. Most of the science fiction films I have seen circle around the same basic plot. Human beings, weak, error-prone, fools of passion, dangerously "free," encounter aliens who at first glance seem superior: the unflappable *Star Trek* Vulcans, the miracle-working Starman, the all-wise Yoda, the bureaucratic Agents of *Matrix*. Yet somehow by the end of the movie it is the humans, not the extraterrestrials, who save the universe.

---

*Using the complex language of symbolic logic, in the essay "God, Evil and the Metaphysics of Freedom" Christian philosopher Alvin Plantinga offers compelling reasons why it is logically impossible for God to control the amount of evil in a world that also includes free will.

In many of these films, the "superior" beings begin to feel a strange attraction for our humanoid qualities. Even Superman falls in love. As the movie plots suggest, despite our complaints we deeply cherish our humanity, notable for its freedom. (And to Christians, whose faith centres in Jesus, the God who became a man, it seems clear that God cherishes humanity as well.)

In a satire titled "The Wireless Wizard of Wonder," Karen Mains described a new electronic gadget that attaches to a person's arm. It works something like a lie detector, though with much greater sensitivity. Whenever any evil thought crosses the wearer's mind, the machine sets off a warning buzz. Unfortunately, the magazine article carried nothing labelling it as satire, and soon the publisher received a letter from a high school teacher wondering where she could purchase the Wizard Wonder for her students. The teacher missed the point of the article entirely: God, a respecter of our freedom, does not use such overt behaviour-modification techniques.

Apparently God did, in earlier times. Intriguing stories from the Old Testament tell of the prophet Elijah who called down fire from heaven on each company of soldiers that came to arrest him (2 Kings 1); both a king and a servant who contracted leprosy when they defied God (2 Kings 5; 2 Chronicles 26); and another king, Jeroboam, whose hand promptly shrivelled when he outstretched it to do wrong (1 Kings 13). These rebels experienced immediate punishment for their mistakes.

I grew up hearing the Old Testament stories, and they helped form my early image of God. As I read them now, however, what stands out is the contrast between their pattern of instant punishment and Jesus' style. He refused to call down fire from heaven on a town that rejected him. He healed, rather than afflicted, people with leprosy. When opponents took up arms against him, he did not fight back, and even restored a servant's ear severed by an overprotective disciple. I can only conclude that God mercifully changed his style of relating to cantankerous human beings. Although we may deserve instant punishment for rebellion, God has chosen a gentler, freedom-enhancing way.

Once, while celebrating with notorious sinners, Jesus fielded criticism from religious people scandalized by his dinner companions. In response he said, "It is not the healthy who need a doctor, but the sick. I have not come to call the righteous, but sinners [to repentance]." I heard the fiery stories from the Old Testament as active warnings: if I disobeyed, God might strike me down with leprosy. Somehow I missed the change introduced by the Great Physician, a change from judgement to grace.

Jesus' famous parable of the prodigal son paints the picture clearly. By any standard of good and bad behaviour, the prodigal son failed, squandering his inheritance and cavorting with prostitutes. He deserved punishment, not celebration. But the father, representing God, had eyes only for healing and restoration: "This son of mine was dead and is alive again; he was lost and is found." God's method with evil is cure, not prevention.

———

In Chinese opera, heroes wear a certain colour of face paint with a few simple strokes, while villains wear a different palette in complex patterns. In real life, unlike Chinese opera, we cannot tell the heroes and villains by the colour of paint on their faces. Medieval saints spoke of the Fiend with his stench; more often evil appears as a friend with a smell like perfume.

We can identify some villains, to be sure: suicide bombers who target civilians, priests who abuse children, drug lords in Latin America. The problem is, evil rarely announces itself so brazenly. Like citizens of an industrial city who no longer notice the pollution, we cannot detect more subtle evils in our cultural atmosphere. Consider the seven deadly sins, a moral checklist that emerged from centuries of reflection. We live in a modern world so disordered from the original design that the entire notion of what is good for us has turned upside down.

In the modern United States, at least, the seven deadly sins might be renamed the seven seductive virtues:

Pride: In music, sports, and business, we reserve our applause for winners, and those who flaunt it with an attitude tend to garner the most publicity. We strut our medals at the Olympic Games, lavish rewards on winners, and read management books patterned after Machiavelli and Attila the Hun.

Envy: Our entire advertising industry is built on inciting envy of colleagues and neighbours, so that whatever new electronic marvel or body shape my neighbour has, I want too.

Anger: We must get in touch with and express our anger, counsellors tell us. Encounter groups, television trash-talk shows, town meetings, and political debates offer ample opportunity to do so.

Greed: The economic engine of our nation, and indeed the world, depends on a constant sense of discontent that motivates each consumer to desire ever more.

Sloth: Find an island with a beach, retire early, relax, slow down, feel good—it's all part of the American dream.

Gluttony: Every year the "big gulp" drinks and supersize French fries get bigger, as do the waistlines. Currently 64 percent of Americans are overweight, with half of that percentage qualifying as obese.

Lust: From Lycra-clad professional cheerleaders to dancing babes on MTV videos, lust is ubiquitous in modern America, the single most profitable industry on the Internet.

In the modern world, sin approaches in camouflage. Too late do we realize that it blocks the path to *shalom,* to wholeness and health. We miss the hidden dangers that prompted the ancients to regard these sins as deadly. I have learned that these sins diminish me and bring disorder to my life. Pride is a kind of addiction, a yearning for ego strokes that will never be satisfied. Greed tempts me to move my focus from people to things. Lust keeps me from connecting in the most meaningful way, diverting that desire in a direction that ultimately does not satisfy. God wants to set me free; evil attempts to enslave.

A Jewish friend once told me he found the list of seven deadly sins unsatisfactory. They seemed so inward-looking, he said—a list compiled by people who spent their lives cloistered in monasteries. In contrast Jews emphasize outward sins, like mistreatment of the poor, injustice, and racism.

At first I agreed with him that the seven deadly sins do not seem nearly as lethal as some others omitted from the list. I grew up among proponents of the Victorious Christian Life who worked hard at personal piety while ignoring the Jim Crow racism of the South and paying little attention to poverty. (Our ancestors didn't let slavery disturb their spiritual equilibrium either.) I know Christians who took more offence at Richard Nixon's profanity captured on the Watergate tapes than at the criminal acts themselves.

On reflection, though, I saw the wisdom of the monks who located the root problem of disorder in the human heart, from where it spreads outwards like a stain. Greed leads corporate executives to reward themselves with bonuses while their company lurches toward bankruptcy, and politicians to grant tax breaks to the rich while doing nothing to help the poor. Pride creates a feeling of superiority that devalues another race, or class, of human beings, as the caste system in India, apartheid in South Africa, and racism in the U.S. have demonstrated only too well. Anger, allied with power, can motivate a dictator like Saddam Hussein to gas his own citizens, or inspire a terrorist to blow up a building. Lust leads to the child sex-slaves of Southeast Asia.

Sinful people create sinful structures, which may then take on a life of their own. Human rebellion has spread across the planet so that every human institution—government, family, church—has been soiled. In some ways a structure or group of people is *more* inclined to evil than an individual and less inclined to love.

Heinrich Himmler, head of the SS during the Nazi reign in Germany, gives one example:

> What happens to the Russians, what happens to the Czechs, is a matter of utter indifference to me.... Whether the other nationalities live

in comfort or perish of hunger interests me only insofar as we need them as slaves for our society; apart from that, it does not interest me. Whether or not 10,000 Russian women collapse from exhaustion while digging a tank ditch interests me only insofar as it affects the completion of the tank ditch for Germany.

———

I have called desire a good thing, a rumour of another world that points back to the Giver. Yet at least four of the seven deadly sins (greed, envy, lust, and gluttony) suggest what may happen when desire becomes disordered. Of these, Jesus spoke most often against the commonplace sin of greed.

"Watch out! Be on your guard against all kinds of greed; a man's life does not consist in the abundance of his possessions," Jesus pronounced with a tone of alarm. He went on to tell of a rich man who built bigger and bigger barns to hold his grain, only to die with little to show for his life but a succession of large barns. Jesus' concern over the seductive power of greed shows in the fact that one-sixth of his sayings in the Gospels centre on money and its dangers. As the rich man demonstrated, wealth offers a glittering short-term satisfaction that obscures the real purpose of living.

Greed led Saddam Hussein to spend billions of dollars on massive, luxurious palaces while thousands of children in his country were dying from malnutrition (and a perverse inversion of greed prompted him to burn up Kuwait's oil fields when he lost control of them). Greed led Enron executives to pillage their company's assets by awarding themselves $745 million in bonuses while proposing a maximum of $13,500 in compensation for each laid-off employee.

"Greed is good," said Michael Douglas in the movie *Wall Street.* "Greed is right. Greed works." Indeed, in consumer economies such as the United States and Europe, greed drives the economy. We want more and more, and advertisers play on our fears that we never have enough. ("There are two ways to get enough," said G. K. Chesterton; "one is to continue to accumulate more and more. The other is to desire less.")

Greed exerts its power on those who have little as well as those who have much. The memoir *Shantung Compound* includes Langdon Gilkey's account of sharing a prison camp with other foreigners during Japan's occupation of China in World War II. Food supplies shrank so that eventually each prisoner received only 1,200 calories per day: six slices of bread, boiled water, and a bowl of stew. All the prisoners were losing weight and feeling malnourished. They dreamed of little else than food.

One day a shipment of two hundred parcels arrived from the American Red Cross, one for each American prisoner. The Americans felt they had struck gold. Each fifty-pound parcel contained a pound of powdered milk, four tins of butter, three of Spam, one pound each of cheese, chocolate, and sugar, as well as cans of powdered coffee, jams, salmon, and a package of dried prunes or raisins.

Gilkey recalls, "After a diet made up largely of bread, low on meats and oils, and lacking in sweets of all sorts—in fact, without real taste— fifty pounds of this sort of rich, fat-laden, and tasteful food was manna from heaven." In addition to the food, the parcels supplied much-needed clothing, far more than the Americans could use. They generously distributed the extra food and clothes to the more numerous prisoners of other nationalities.

Six months later, all the food was gone and conditions had deteriorated. Winter had set in, and morale in the camp hit an all-time low. A few days after Christmas, a donkey train suddenly appeared at the gates like a mirage, bearing more Red Cross parcels, this time too numerous for the prisoners to count. The Japanese commandant catalogued 1,550 parcels in all, and calculated that he could distribute one parcel to each of the 1,450 prisoners, and an extra half-parcel to the two hundred Americans. Joy and excitement gripped the camp: "It was as though everyone were living through every Christmas Eve of his lifetime all rolled into one."

The next morning, to their dismay, the prisoners read a notice that no parcels would be distributed. A small group of Americans had protested the arrangement, insisting that only they were entitled to the gifts from the *American* Red Cross. In other words, they demanded seven-and-a-half parcels for each American, with none for the other prisoners. Disgusted, the commandant appealed to Tokyo for a decision, and for ten days Gilkey and the other Americans had to face the resentment and hostility of prisoners from other nations.

Gilkey reports,

> It was the same story all over. A community where everyone had long forgotten whether a man was American or British, white, Negro, Jew, Parsee, or Indian, had suddenly disintegrated into a brawling, bitterly divided collection of hostile national groups. Ironically, our wondrous Christmas gift had brought in its wake the exact opposite of peace on earth. The massive mounds of life-giving parcels lay inert in the centre of the camp, while gusts of human conflict and ill will swirled turbulently around them.
>
> For the first time, I felt fundamentally humiliated at being an American.

The Japanese authorities, not known for their sense of justice, in this case showed more of it than the prisoners. Tokyo ordered that each prisoner receive one parcel, with the extra hundred parcels to be distributed instead to other camps.

From that experience and others, Gilkey learned a painful lesson. He had entered the camp with a liberal-optimist view of human nature. After spending two-and-a-half years in a prison camp, among missionaries, priests, educators, and business people, he emerged with a much darker view and a new understanding of selfish humanity. He saw firsthand the enormous consequences of a simple sin like greed.

Greed, like all sin, has its root in disorder. Human freedom allows us

an ambiguous privilege not granted to the rest of creation: we can throw the balances of nature out of joint. We can accumulate in such a way as to deprive others, and through wars to destroy them as well. The entire planet shudders at the results of our attempts to make ourselves and not God the centre of existence.

And to try to be happy by being admired by men, or loved by women, or warm with liquor, or full of lust, or getting possessions and treasures: that turns you away, soon, from the love of God; then men, women, and drink and lust and greed take precedence over God; and they darken His light.... And then we are unhappy and afraid and angry and fierce, and impatient, and cannot pray, and cannot sit still. That is the bitter yoke of sin: and for this we leave the mild and easy yoke of Christ.

THOMAS MERTON

a word unsaid

Bad is so bad, that we cannot but think good an accident; good is so good, that we feel certain that evil could be explained.

G. K. CHESTERTON

For thirty years Lancelot Andrewes Lamar, the main character in Walker Percy's novel *Lancelot*, has been drifting through life in a dreamlike state, following a rut so predictably that his neighbours can set their watches by his daily routine. Everything abruptly changes when he learns his daughter is a product of his wife's infidelity, not his biological child.

Lancelot wonders if proofs of the existence of God based on the order and beauty of the universe have been off track:

> But what if you could show me a *sin?* a purely evil deed, an intolerable deed for which there is no explanation? Now there's a mystery. People would sit up and take notice. I would be impressed. You could almost make a believer out of me.

In times when nobody is interested in God, what would happen
if you could prove the existence of sin, pure and simple? Wouldn't that
be a windfall for you? A new proof of God's existence! If there is such
a thing as sin, evil, a living malignant force, there must be a God!

In view of all the injustice and violence in the world, perhaps
Lancelot has it right: belief in evil offers a backhand proof of God's existence. Indeed, the very outrage we feel against evil acts—hijackers steering jetliners into buildings full of civilians, concentration camp guards
torturing their prisoners, kidnappers abusing and killing young children—
points to a built-in sense that some things are desperately wrong, blame-
worthy, damnable.

———

I have mentioned my resistance to the word *sin*. It has a slithery, reptil-
ian sound to it, and for me the word summons up memories from my
past, when heavy-breathing Southern revivalists would drawl the word in
a two-syllable fury. "See-yun," they would shout and raise their fists
against the devil's agent that crouched inside us.

As a child, I trembled when I heard about sin. My concept of God was
forming as I listened to the angry preachers. I did not think of God as
Father, for my own father had died just after my first birthday and I had
no experience to draw on. God more resembled a policeman, or a scowl-
ing teacher eager to catch me in some wrongdoing. The great Enforcer
would bring down swift and terrible punishment on all who misbehaved.
Church members cruelly fanned those fears when they told me that my
earthly father, now in heaven, was looking down day and night to spy out
my hidden sins.

Later, in teenage years, I got downright cynical about the fixation
with sin. I remember one summer camp meeting when the visiting
speaker, a fervent young student from Bob Jones University, strove to get
every person present to come forward in an altar call. We sang four verses
of "Just As I Am" while he coaxed the unrepentant to receive Christ. He

then gradually expanded the invitation to encompass other needs. Soon, fully two-thirds of the audience had come forward to kneel at the front. I glanced wistfully at the corrugated tin roof overhead, because sometimes a summer thunderstorm would blow through, unleashing a downpour that rattled the roof so loudly the meeting had to adjourn. Not tonight.

"If you just feel a need for someone to pray with you, we have counsellors standing by," the speaker entreated. Another trickle made their way forward. Finally, the clincher. "I have one last invitation. Now listen carefully. Any of you with unconfessed sin in your life—any sin whatsoever—God is calling you to come forward and confess it." Campers streamed down the aisles as he went through a list of suggestions: "A careless word, perhaps ... a flash of anger ... a lukewarmness in your spiritual life. Have you looked on anyone with lust this week? Have you thought ill of anyone?" The stream became a flood as the pianist gallantly pounded away on yet another refrain.

This was my sixth straight week at camp and every other week I had gone forward at the final service. Tonight, my soul was callous. Eventually, only two of us remained standing in the large auditorium.

I edged closer to my friend Rodney for moral support as the pianist began yet another round of verses. Fellow campers kneeling down front glared back at us in irritation; we were, after all, delaying the evening's round of refreshments and games. "I don't know, Rodney," I whispered, "I can't think of any sins tonight, can you?"

"No unconfessed ones," he replied with a tight grin. The two of us held out until at last the revivalist gave up, said a closing prayer, and called it a night.

As I now look back on that scene, I realize that I completely missed the point of the Christian concept of sin. I envisioned God as a frowning Enforcer rather than a loving Creator who desires the best for us in life, with sin as the main obstacle preventing it. I missed any sense of sin as a negative marker pointing toward life as it is meant to be—it, too, a telling rumour of another world.

A misconception of sin has turned people away from faith. Nathaniel Hawthorne reacted against the stern judgement of New England Puritans by writing stories that exposed their hypocrisy. John Muir fled the harshness of his Scottish Presbyterian father, who scorned his son's interest in nature as frivolous and ungodly, and "made every duty dismal." George Orwell lost his faith at an English boarding school where the staff beat him and condemned him as a sinner every time he wet the bed. Instead of helping people understand the world, the notion of sin alienated them.

Coming from a sin-saturated upbringing myself, I read such accounts with great sympathy. At various times, the church has hammered away at "original sin" while ignoring the presence of an original grace in which God provided the cure for sin even before it occurred. That risky act of rescue—"the Lamb that was slain from the creation of the world"—lies at the heart of Christian belief. "God is love," proclaims the Bible in absolute terms, which seems a very long way from my childhood image of God as stern Enforcer.

———

Something strange has occurred in more recent times, however. Although almost every sermon in my childhood church centred on sin, the word has vanished in the years since then. I seldom come across the word these days in Christian books or magazines, rarely hear it railed against from the pulpit, never hear it mentioned on network television. Politicians, who often speak in the language of morality, hardly ever invoke the word *sin*. Fear of sin, the dominant force of my childhood, has nearly disappeared.

In retrospect, my early encounters with the word *sin* seem to belong to another planet. Psychiatrist Karl Menninger wrote a book titled *Whatever Became of Sin?* and the answer today is more elusive than ever. Menninger's question poses a challenge to modern culture. Christians did not invent the concept of sin, after all. Anthropologists find something similar, acts of wrongdoing that cause a sense of guilt, in every culture. How did this most basic insight into human nature simply vanish from the radar screen of modern thought? And what are we missing if we delete the word from our vocabulary?

Today, although we hear about a health crisis associated with promiscuous sex and drug abuse, or the problem of illegitimate births, or the social injustice of poverty and homelessness, we do not often hear the word sin. Try dropping *sin* into a conversation on these topics, and you will see what I mean.*

Caught red-handed in criminal activity, President Richard Nixon grudgingly admitted, "Mistakes were made," and insisted he had acted in the best interests of the nation and was resigning as a "personal sacrifice." Under oath, President Bill Clinton responded to direct questions with such deflections as "That depends on what the definition of the word *is* is." When Clinton finally did use the word *sin,* confessing his guilt before a breakfast gathering of religious leaders, journalists treated it as something freakish; you could almost see them winking to each other and smirking out of camera range.

Modern society is caught in a dilemma. We can afford to be optimistic about human nature, those of us who live in prosperous nations with strong economies and ever-rising life expectancies. We certainly don't want to come across as moralistic and judgemental, and yet we keep encountering contradictory signs of disturbance. The alcoholic down the street beats his wife and wrecks the car. A woman confides that sexual abuse by her father has made her suspicious and angry toward all men. A security camera at a shopping mall records a man abandoning his three-year-old son. Gang members in New York "brand" their women with heated coat hangers. Much as we would wish otherwise, we have a deep, inescapable sense that something is wrong with the world, with our neighbours, and even with ourselves.

---

*A literature professor at Wheaton College told me he gave a test question about the effect of the Fall on Adam and Eve in Milton's *Paradise Lost*. Two different students who were not sitting together wrote the same first sentence, which naturally caught the professor's eye. Their answer nearly jolted him out of his chair: "The main effect of the Fall on Adam and Eve was the need for them to change their lifestyle." If students at theologically conservative Wheaton College view sin so benignly, what must the rest of society think?

At its core, sin assumes a relationship between a Creator who sets the rules and free human beings who break them. A reductionistic world has little place for a Creator, and little place for individual souls who are morally accountable. We like to negotiate our own rules and set our own punishments, and for most people the fusty category of sin does not apply. Instead we substitute euphemisms such as "addicted," "inappropriate behaviour," "emotionally impaired," or "suffering from an affective disorder."

We use these euphemisms confidently and comfortably—until monstrous evil, sin's radical cousin, intrudes. In *Humanity: A Moral History of the Twentieth Century,* Jonathan Glover wrote what turned out to be a history of modern evil. As societies increased in knowledge and technological skill, they descended to depths of depravity and mass violence never before imagined in history. Nations such as Turkey, the Soviet Union, Germany, Cambodia, Yugoslavia, and Rwanda perfected the strategy of mass murder and genocide. The first few years of a new century, plagued by suicide bombers, nuclear threats, and a clash of civilizations, give little reason for optimism that humanity will outgrow evil on its own.

I have visited the concentration camps at Dachau and Bergen-Belsen and watched the grainy films of Allied soldiers removing the emaciated bodies, stacked like cordwood, which they found there. Near Anne Frank's home in Amsterdam I listened to an elderly Dutchman recount for me the days when Nazis forbade the Jews to use trolleys and ride bicycles and shop in stores, and then one by one arrested them and shipped them off in cattle cars to be worked to death or gassed. I have visited Russia and listened to chastened communists wonder at how an ideology they believed in with all their hearts could have led to the state-sponsored murder of sixty million citizens. Old-fashioned words like *evil* inevitably creep into those conversations.

The American commentator Walter Lippmann, writing during World War II, reluctantly admitted we must come to terms with the fact that human nature includes what he called *ice-cold evil:* "The modern sceptical world has been taught for some 200 years a conception of human nature in which the reality of evil, so well known to the ages of faith, has been discounted.... We shall have to recover this forgotten but essential truth—along with so many others that we lost when, thinking we were enlightened and advanced, we were merely shallow and blind."

In 1995 the *New York Times Magazine* published a long, reflective article, "Staring into the Heart of Darkness," which examined recent atrocities that had both outraged and mystified the public. A young woman named Susan Smith strapped her three-year-old and fourteen-month-old sons into her Mazda and drove them into a lake and watched them drown. In Liverpool two ten-year-old boys lured a two-year-old away from his mother, beat him to death, and discarded his body on some railroad tracks. (The trial judge characterized the two boys not as misguided, abused, or troubled, but as wicked and evil.) Lyle and Erik Menendez emptied a shotgun into their mother and father, then left the house to retrieve more ammunition and returned to fire again at the mother's twitching body. Jeffrey Dahmer not only killed his victims, he cut them up, cooked and ate them, and stored the leftover body parts in his refrigerator.

"What does it mean to call someone evil?" the *Times* author asked. On his search for answers, he interviewed Susan Smith's pastor and survivors of the Oklahoma City bomb blast, and sought ethical wisdom from such sources as former governor of New York Mario Cuomo and Christian philosopher Alvin Plantinga. To his surprise, two scholars of Hitler, one a historian and the other a psychoanalyst, could not bring themselves to pronounce Hitler evil. The German leader was "convinced of his own rectitude," said one, and delusively believed that he was doing good. He "was a prisoner of his pathological unconscious drives," said the other.

The *New York Times* had a close-up encounter with evil on September 11, 2001, when hijackers steered airplanes into the two tallest buildings in the city, causing the deaths of people from eighty different countries. Over the next few months the newspaper devoted an entire daily section to the event and its aftermath, including an obituary on each person who had died. Secretaries, janitors, bond traders, waiters, gardeners, husbands, wives, mothers, fathers, grandparents—all had commuted to Lower Manhattan that day, like any other day, never to return, most of them incinerated so that no body parts survived as a physical residue of their lives.

We have seen the face of evil, said the news reporters, and then they showed us nineteen faces of ordinary Middle Eastern men such as you might meet on the streets of any major city.

For a society unsure whether evil even exists, and embarrassed by the word *sin*, it takes an atrocity of historic dimensions to raise the question once again. Moral ambiguity tends to recede as the nightly news portrays the stark contrast between death and life, between murder and rescue, between those who joke in Afghan caves about their unexpected success and those who dig for bodies in the pile of twisted steel.

———

As a rule, people find it easier to recognize the existence of evil—some dark force present in criminals and mass murderers—than the possibility of more subtle, personal sins lurking inside themselves.

We live in an age of rationalization: "I was following my heart ... He started it—what else could I do? ... I have an addiction ... I come from a dysfunctional family ... That's the way business works, you know...." A character in a John Cheever story captures perfectly the tone of scapegoating: "My left eye had begun to twitch again, and the inability of one part of my consciousness to stand up under the reproach that was being heaped into it by another part made me cast around desperately for someone else who could be blamed."

We also live in an age of victimization. When the mayor of Washington, D.C., was videotaped smoking crack cocaine, he blamed it on a racist plot. A murderer blamed the Twinkies he ate for altering his brain chemistry. And when sixteen women accused Senator Robert Packwood of gross sexual harassment, he at first denied the charges, then attacked his accusers' credibility, then promised to seek professional help to determine if his behaviour was related to the use of alcohol. Each of these knee-jerk responses helps the offender feel better temporarily, by transferring the blame somewhere else.

Yet if moral guilt is indeed a rumour of another world, a God-given sense that something is wrong, no amount of victimization or rationalization will make it go away. Graham Greene's novel *The Quiet American* ends with the main character lamenting his life of misery and moral failure: "How I wished there existed someone to whom I could say I was sorry."*

Ironically, the most successful modern treatment of human failures—twelve-step groups for those who admit to alcoholism or other addictions—takes a rather old-fashioned approach. Psychiatrists, pharmacologists, and scientific reducers cannot improve on a spiritual programme devised by a couple of Christian alcoholics sixty years ago. Professionals may use the phrase "addictive behaviour" as a euphemism for sin, but not the addicts themselves. They combat denial by insisting on naked honesty about transgressions.

The alcoholic must first recognize his or her own helplessness and then fall back in the arms of an unseen Higher Power. "First of all we had to quit playing God," concluded the founders of Alcoholics Anonymous (AA); and next, allow God himself to work in their lives. Every time addicts repeat the twelve steps, they reject a reductionist view of life. Addiction tempts the addict to reduce life down to the longing for alcohol or narcotics that seems more real and more urgent than everything else combined. With the support of fellow alcoholics, the addict learns to face the lie.

---

*Contemporary literature remains one of the few refuges for sin. Novelists and short-story writers present human characters in all their complexity and realism, which unavoidably includes sin. Try to imagine a novel by Dostoyevsky, William Faulkner, Graham Greene, or John Updike—not to mention the entire genres of murder mysteries and legal thrillers—without a richly nuanced depiction of sin. Sin provides the hook, the pull that keeps a reader turning pages. Apart from sin and its consequences, fiction would read like a flat, deterministic tale of animal behaviour.

Using the AA model, addicts must weave together the torn fabric of life, making restitution to people they have harmed. They admit themselves incapable of seeing the whole picture and living accordingly. They must accept at face value their own incompetence, and humbly seek to rebuild relationships with others and with God.

Bill Wilson, the cofounder of Alcoholics Anonymous, reached the unshakeable conviction, now a canon of twelve-step groups, that an alcoholic must "hit bottom" in order to climb upward. Wilson wrote his fellow strugglers, "How privileged we are to understand so well the divine paradox that strength rises from weakness, that humiliation goes before resurrection, that pain is not only the price but the very touchstone of spiritual rebirth." The apostle Paul could not have phrased it better.

A broken relationship with God, accepting moral responsibility, admitting the need for outside help, a commitment to make restitution to all who have been harmed—the formula for twelve-step groups comes straight from the pages of the Bible. As an alcoholic once told me, "I have to publicly declare 'I am an alcoholic' whenever I introduce myself at group. It is a statement of failure, of helplessness, and surrender. Take a room of a dozen or so people, all of whom admit helplessness and failure, and it's pretty easy to see how God then presents himself in that group."

The same alcoholic said that he has heard this comment repeatedly in AA meetings and has made it himself: "I know I have another drunk left in me. I have a real doozy of another drunk left in me. The problem is that I am afraid I don't have another 'sobering up' left in me."

William James, the Harvard philosopher and psychologist, subjected to scientific scrutiny the spiritual claims of converted alcoholics, saints, and ordinary believers, publishing his findings in a book that became a classic: *The Varieties of Religious Experience.* James came up with two overall classifications of belief: "healthy-minded" and "morbid-minded."

Healthy-minded faith was booming in James's day, an era of unprecedented peace and prosperity. "What we call evil and immorality must disappear. It is certain that man must become perfect," predicted his contemporary Herbert Spencer. "Every day in every way the world is getting better and better" became a slogan for the times. James contrasted these optimists with morbid-minded Christians who declared the only hope to be a "twice-born" experience that offered a new start.

After surveying the two groups, James came away surprisingly impressed with the morbid-minded. He fully understood the appeal of the optimists: they discounted or denied evil, sickness, and death. But their faith did not account for all the facts, he concluded. At least the evangelicals described a world that actually existed, one riddled with sin and suffering.

William James died in 1910, and before long many of the healthy-minded faiths around him passed away too. As James had prophesied, they did not account for all the facts. They were crushed by the terrible weight of World War I, which exposed the flaws in their vision of the world. Like it or not, our understanding of the world must somehow take into account this most basic disorder which Christians diagnose as sin.

I encounter sin as a point of view as much as a series of choices—a point of view that avoids the truth about God's world. At the moment of sin, I declare it my world, not God's. Like an alcoholic choosing whether or not to drink, I begin with a bias, a "selfish gene," if you like.

Malcolm Muggeridge expressed the subtle danger of sin this way:

Christianity ... does not say that, in spite of appearances, we are all murderers or burglars or crooks or sexual perverts at heart; it does not say that we are totally depraved, in the sense that we are incapable of feeling or responding to any good impulses whatever. The truth is much deeper and more subtle than that. It is precisely when you consider the best in man that you see there is in each of us a hard core of pride or self-centredness which corrupts our best achievements and blights our best experiences. It comes out in all sorts of ways—in the jealousy which spoils our friendships, in the vanity we feel when we have done something pretty good, in the easy conversion of love into lust, in the meanness which makes us depreciate the efforts of other people, in the distortion of our own judgement by our own self-interest, in our fondness for flattery and our resentment of blame, in our self-assertive profession of fine ideals which we never begin to practise.

On a trip to Russia just after the collapse of communism in 1991, I had a conversation with a Marxist scholar who was devastated by revelations about the horrors just then coming to light in his country. "I had no idea things like this were taking place," he said. "I became a communist with the best of ideals, to fight racism and poverty, to bring about a just society. Now I learn that we created a monster. We saw the evil in others—the capitalists, the rich, the exploiters—but not in ourselves. I have learned to distrust any utopian philosophy, especially one that sets 'us' against 'them.' The danger of evil is inside all of us, rich or poor, socialist or capitalist."*

The disillusioned Marxist had just accepted a fundamental Christian belief about sin, that it affects everyone ever born. Christians have a most realistic view of humanity, believing that human beings have failed, are failing, and will always fail.

As I review my own pilgrimage of faith, I find it has mirrored the schizophrenia of the larger culture. Sometimes I am dominated by sin-consciousness, sometimes I rebel vigorously against it, often I avoid thinking about it altogether. I do recall, though, that amid all the unhealthiness of my childhood church one unmistakable message seared itself deep inside me: What I do *matters*. More, what I do matters to God, who created this world and set the rules we disregard at our peril. Somehow, I must keep that conviction in the foreground of my life.

---

*Lenin himself admitted "I made a mistake. Without doubt, an oppressed multitude had to be liberated. But our method only provoked further oppression and atrocious massacres. My living nightmare is to find myself lost in an ocean of red with the blood of innumerable victims. It is too late now to alter the past, but what was needed to save Russia were ten Francis of Assisis."

"Character is how you behave when no one is looking," a child psychiatrist once told me. He went on to say that psychopaths, crooks, and thieves do what they do because in their heads "no one is looking." I have often thought of his remark, not in the way he meant it but in the way Jesus must have meant when he prayed that God's will be done on earth as it is in heaven. God, after all, is always looking. I now envision God not so much as a policeman upstairs watching my every move but rather as a Spirit within, coaxing me to realize fully what I was created to be in the first place.

> Man is ruining the pleasant earth & man.
> What at last, my Lord, will you allow?
>
> JOHN BERRYMAN

the good life

> God may reduce you
> on Judgement Day
> To tears of shame,
> reciting by heart
> The poems you would
> have written, had
> Your life been good.
>
> W. H. AUDEN

A few years ago I had a scary encounter with a masked man wielding a knife. I remember him with gratitude, though, since he was an orthopaedic surgeon to whom I paid thousands of dollars to correct some problems with my left foot. The horizontal recovery period gave me a chance to ponder pain that we choose voluntarily, sometimes for our own good and sometimes to our peril.

While rehabilitating, I persisted in exercises that hurt me because I knew that working through the soreness would allow my foot to regain its usefulness. On the other hand, for three months the surgeon forbade bicycling, hiking, running, and other activities that might endanger the healing process. Basically, anything that sounded fun he vetoed.

On one visit I tried to talk him into permitting a premature golf match. "Some close friends get together only once a year, and this one's important to me. I've been practising my swing, and if I use only my upper body, and keep my legs and hips very still, could I join them? I think I could keep most of my weight on my right foot."

Without a flicker of hesitation, my doctor replied, "It would make me very unhappy if you played golf within the next two months."

"I thought you were a golfer," I said, seeking sympathy.

"I am. That's how I know you can't swing without rolling that foot inward and putting weight on the bones that are trying to heal."

Later, I told my wife about his strange way of expressing disapproval. "Why should I care if my doctor is unhappy?" I joked. "I'm not his psychiatrist."

Of course, my doctor had nothing against my playing golf; a fellow golfer, he understood my frustration. Yet he also had my best interests at heart. It would truly make him unhappy if a patient were to indulge in some short-term pleasure that might jeopardize a full recovery. He wanted me to play golf the next year, and the next, and the rest of my life, and for that reason he could not sanction a match so soon after my surgery.

I began to appreciate my doctor's odd choice of words. If he had issued an edict, "Absolutely no golf!" I might have obstinately rebelled. He left me the free choice, while presenting the consequences in a most personal way. My ignoring his orders would sadden him because, as guardian of my health, he cared whether I damaged myself further.

For a time I resisted thinking of God as an authority figure; harsh images from childhood had scarred too deep. Like many people, I saw religion mainly as a set of rules, a moral code handed down from an invisible world that we on this planet were somehow obligated to obey. Why it might matter to God whether puny creatures on a tiny planet kept his rules, I had no clue. I only heard the dire warnings that if I broke the rules, I would pay.

More recently, however, I have come to recognize that sometimes I submit gladly to authority. When my computer software acts up, I call technical support and scrupulously follow the technician's orders. When I want to master a difficult sport, such as golf, I pay for lessons. And when I get hurt or sick, I see a doctor.

A doctor is probably the most helpful image for me to keep in mind while thinking about God and sin. Why should I seek out God's view on how to live my life? For the same reason I seek my doctor's opinion. I defer to my doctor, trusting that we share the same goal, my physical health, but that he brings to the process greater wisdom and expertise. And I am learning to view sins as spiritual dangers—much like carcinogens, bacteria, viruses, and injuries—that must be avoided at all costs, for my own sake. I am learning to trust that God wants the *best* life for me in this world, not some diminished, repressed life.

At the Body Worlds exhibit in London, I bought a catalogue of the human organs I had seen on display. In the section on respiration, facing pages show photographs of two different sets of lungs. The lungs on the left are white like the meat of a turkey breast, so shiny and smoothly textured they could have been taken from a newborn. In dramatic contrast, the lungs on the right look as if they have been used to clean a chimney. Black sediment coats and fills them, clogging the delicate membranes designed to capture oxygen molecules. The photo caption explains that the lungs on the right came from a chain-smoker.

I cannot comprehend how any doctor who has seen such lungs, side by side, could ever smoke again. If I feel a temptation toward tobacco, I turn to page 66 of the catalogue. So many of the displays in Body Worlds show how human behaviour brings disorder to the body, subjecting its organs to stresses they were not designed to bear. I remind myself of the two sets of lungs when I think about sin: it too retards growth, ravages health, and chokes off the supply of new life.

———

Every society judges certain actions wrong—murder, theft, incest, rape— and imposes sanctions against them. "Vicious actions are not hurtful because they are forbidden, but forbidden because they are hurtful," said Benjamin Franklin, ever the pragmatist.

In recent years, and especially since the 1960s, the democratic societies of the West have been enlarging the boundaries of acceptable behaviour, in effect redefining sin. The sexual revolution of my youth dismantled barriers against premarital sex and encouraged open marriages. Not just rock stars but Harvard professors such as Timothy Leary advocated the use of LSD and other hallucinogenic drugs. A single decision by the U.S. Supreme Court reversed a centuries-old ban on abortion. Pornography came out of the closet and grew into a multibillion-dollar industry. Binge-drinking swept across college campuses.

Christians who opposed these new trends all too often came across as finger-wagging spoilsports. I think back to the moral environment in which I grew up, when good Christians did not smoke, drink, use drugs, divorce, or fool around sexually. Into that stale environment, the sixties revolution swept like a gust of fresh air, promising freedom and liberation. Many of my friends cheerfully discarded what seemed to them the straitjacket of religious subculture.

As it turned out, however, the subculture was right about many of those issues, at least in terms of their effect on physical health. The sexual revolution fostered the spread of venereal diseases, the plague of AIDS, and numerous other health problems (for example, a man who has many sex partners increases his wife's risk of cervical cancer by eleven times). Now secular activists and public health officials are warning of the health dangers associated with unprotected sex, smoking, binge-drinking, and drug use.

I have had to learn, against my instincts, that what seems attractive and alluring may in fact prove destructive. I need outside help in determining what is truly good for me.

The surgeon Paul Brand, with whom I have written three books, told me about a conference he attended in the 1980s with representatives from each government agency involved in health matters, including the Public Health Service, the Centres for Disease Control, the National Institutes of Health, and the Food and Drug Administration. Once a year experts from these agencies get together to pool their knowledge about the major health crises facing Americans.

As the conference progressed, Dr Brand began jotting down the urgent health concerns being discussed. It struck him that the primary health issues were lifestyle-related: heart disease and hypertension related to stress, cancers associated with a toxic environment, AIDS contracted through drug use and sexual activity, sexually transmitted diseases, emphysema and lung cancer caused by cigarette smoking, foetal damage resulting from maternal alcohol and drug abuse, diabetes and other diet-related disorders, violent crime, automobile accidents involving alcohol.

These were the endemic, even pandemic concerns for health experts in the United States in the 1980s, and nothing has altered the trend since then. Studies at the Jimmy Carter Centre in Atlanta show that two-thirds of deaths prior to age sixty-five can be traced to the very same list of behavioural choices.

Having spent much of his working life in India, Dr Brand had attended comparable medical conferences there. "In India," he told me, "our top ten health concerns would consist of infectious diseases: malaria, polio, dysentery, tuberculosis, typhoid fever, leprosy. If you promised Indian health experts the eradication of their top ten diseases, they could hardly imagine such a paradise. Yet look what has happened here. After conquering most of those infectious diseases, the U.S. has now substituted new health problems for old, the majority of them stemming from lifestyle choices."

Dr Brand recalled that the U.S. meeting was held in Arizona. That state's neighbour to the west, Nevada, ranks as the very worst on most mortality tables, while its northern neighbour Utah ranks as the best. Both states have a relatively wealthy and well-educated population, and they share a similar climate. The difference in health is best explained by lifestyle factors. Utah is the seat of Mormonism, which frowns on alcohol, tobacco, and caffeine. Nevada has twice the incidence of divorce and a far higher rate of alcohol and tobacco use, not to mention the unique stress associated with gambling.

Another physician I have interviewed, David Larson, made a career out of researching how religion affects health, focusing not so much on the harmful effects of behaviour but rather on the positive benefits of a spiritual life. What he discovered shocked him. For example, people who describe themselves as religious have a markedly lower incidence of heart attack, arteriosclerosis, and hypertension. Churchgoers average a blood pressure reading 5 mm. lower than nonchurchgoers. Religious people are also less likely to abuse alcohol and far less likely to use illicit drugs. People who attend church regularly, pray, and read their Bibles are hospitalized less often, recover from surgery faster, have stronger immune systems, and normally live longer.

Dr Larson told me that statistics on marriage impressed him most. Married people seem to handle illness better, earn larger incomes, and adopt healthier lifestyles. Indeed, divorce represents one of the greatest health hazards facing modern Americans, dramatically increasing the likelihood of early death from stroke, heart disease, hypertension, respiratory cancer, and intestinal cancer. Suicide rates double for divorced people. Astonishingly, a divorced non-smoker faces roughly the same health risks as a married person who smokes a pack or more a day.

Many other studies document the potentially devastating toll of divorce on children. As vice president, Dan Quayle attracted scorn for his *Murphy Brown* speech in which he questioned the wisdom of glamourizing births out of wedlock. A year later, a well-documented cover story in the *Atlantic Monthly* concluded "Dan Quayle Was Right" about the potentially harmful effects of single-parent families. By any measure—intelligence, earnings potential, suicide attempts, violence, crime, emotional stability, substance abuse, physical health, mental illness—children from one-parent homes face additional challenges. No responsible politician or sociologist would now argue otherwise.

132

Dr Larson concluded, "In essence the studies empirically verify the wisdom of the book of Proverbs. Those who follow biblical values live longer, enjoy life more, and are less diseased."

I used to think, as does much of the world, "If it feels good, it must be sinful." Such a sentiment stems from a tragic misconception of God. The state God desires for us, *shalom,* results in a person fully alive, functioning optimally to the Designer's specifications. For the best life in this world, it helps to listen to wisdom transmitted from another world.

———

In my childhood, thinking about sin terrified me. In adolescence it repulsed me. But as I learn to envision God more accurately, as a physician or a loving parent, my defences crumble. I once had a caricature of God as a cranky old codger who concocted an arbitrary list of rules for the express purpose of making sure no one had a good time. I now see those rules as given not for God's sake but for ours.

Every parent knows the difference between rules designed primarily for the benefit of the parent ("Don't talk while I'm on the telephone! Clean up your room—your grandmother's coming!") and those designed for the benefit of the child ("Wear mittens and a hat—it's below freezing outside. But don't skate on the pond yet!"). God's rules primarily fall into the latter category.* As creator of the human race, God knew how human society would work best.

I began to look at the Ten Commandments in this light, as rules designed primarily for the benefit of the people themselves. Jesus underscored this principle when he said, "The Sabbath was made for man, not man for the Sabbath." The Bible is a most realistic book, and it assumes human beings will at times be tempted to lust after a neighbour or covet someone else's property, to work too hard, to strike out in anger at those who wrong them. In short, it assumes humanity will bring disorder to whatever we touch.

---

*Some of the cultural rules applied exclusively to Israel, the nation selected to be "a kingdom of priests and a holy nation," and the New Testament eventually dismantled many of these laws for non-Jewish believers. Even many of the cultural and diet regulations, however, included a clear benefit for the people who followed them. The regulation to dig latrines and cover them up helped prevent the spread of infectious diseases, as did the strict quarantine of sick people. A prohibition against eating fat would help guard against coronary disease; abstaining from pork protected against trichinosis. Rules against marrying close relatives eliminated many genetic disorders, and strict laws against promiscuity helped control sexually transmitted diseases.

Each of the Ten Commandments offers a shield of protection against that disorder, stated negatively. Unlike the animals, we have the freedom to say no to our base instincts. By doing so, we avoid certain harm.

If I give my loyalty to a lesser god, I am the one who suffers, as any alcoholic or sex addict can attest. If I work seven days a week, my own body pays the price. Murder harms another person, of course, but it also exacts a cost on the murderer, searing his conscience and embittering his soul (Dostoyevsky's *Crime and Punishment* describes this process in clinical detail). Adultery and lying destroy trust and relationship. Coveting harms no one but the coveter; the neighbour who inspires such feelings may remain blissfully unaware.

Taken together, the Ten Commandments weave life on this planet into some kind of meaningful whole, the purpose of which is to allow us to live as a peaceful, healthy community under God. Three hundred years ago the commentator Matthew Henry observed, "God has been pleased therein to twist interests with us, so that in seeking his glory we really and effectually seek our own true interests."

Of course, no one can legislate goodness. William J. Stuntz, a professor of law at the University of Virginia, makes a fascinating observation about laws. He reckons that the highest incidence of lawbreaking by ordinary citizens involves cheating on income taxes, even though the tax code specifies the law's intent in a most detailed way. No matter how many thousands of pages it takes to spell out the IRS code, taxpayers ardently seek ways to get around the rules. Says Stuntz, "It is a little like the behaviour of a child who, when told to stop throwing his ball in the house, starts to throw a hockey puck instead. (And, as every parent knows, when caught, the child immediately says, 'But you said no throwing *balls* in the house.')"

On the other hand, Stuntz notes that the family, the setting perhaps least subject to legal regulation, tends to inspire the opposite kind of behaviour: genuine altruism, sacrificial love, unselfishness. A parent of a two-year-old with the flu knows well the meaning of self-sacrifice. "Law teaches many things," concludes Stuntz, "but the most important thing it teaches is its limits, what it cannot do." Where law falters, love steps in.

Reading Stuntz's musings, I could not help thinking of the contrast between the Old Testament's hundreds of detailed regulations and the New Testament's emphasis on love. Echoing Jesus, the apostle Paul said, "The entire law is summed up in a single command: 'Love your neighbour as yourself.'" He added, "We serve in the new way of the Spirit, and not in the old way of the written code."

Rules serve an important function: like training wheels on a bicycle, they point the beginner in the right direction and protect against injury. The ultimate goal, though, is to ride safely on your own, without props. "Love God, and do as you please," said Augustine, in a famously misconstrued word of counsel. If our actions truly are motivated by love for God, we will act in ways that not only please God but please ourselves as well.

In many ways, sin is the punishment for sin. The more I choose against God's design and give in to my baser impulses, the more I suffer— even if I never get caught, even if no one else knows. And as I study the accounts of how Jesus, the Great Physician, dealt with cheats, prostitutes, and other notorious sinners, I see that he came not merely to save us from the punishment for sin but to save us from the sin itself. He came, in short, to liberate us, promising "So if the Son sets you free, you will be free indeed."

———

I remember the first time I met a murderer. I was working for *Campus Life* magazine, a cub reporter in my early twenties on my first visit to California. I rented a car in Los Angeles, drove north on the spectacular, winding highway along the Pacific coast, and cut over toward Lompoc, descending the coastal hills to a stunning patchwork scene of red, yellow, and blue flowers planted in orderly rows as far as the eye could see. Lompoc sits in the heart of the nation's flower-growing region, and my trip happened to coincide with blossom time.

On my visit to a maximum-security prison the next day, I left behind all remnants of the natural world and entered a wholly artificial one of concrete walls, barbed wire, sliding steel gates, and inch-thick glass. After passing through a metal detector and enduring a pat-down search, I entered a booth where I could talk to Frank over a telephone. Even though Frank sat six feet away, separated from me only by the glass, the telephone line was thick with static. "Don't forget, this is not a private line," Frank began, motioning with his eyes toward a booth where guards monitored all calls.

I found it surprisingly easy to talk to Frank, who was my age and seemed glad for the company. Serving a twelve-year sentence, he spent his time either working out with weights (the results apparent in his bulging biceps) or completing correspondence courses. He answered every question I asked him without hesitation. He told me of his hellish upbringing, of being shipped from one abusive foster home to another. In one of them, the father would beat him with a two-by-four when he disobeyed. He dropped out of high school and joined with a friend to steal enough money to buy cigarettes and beer. One robbery went awry when the attendant followed the pair outside and Frank's partner blasted the man with a shotgun, killing him.

In my stereotype at the time, murderers comprised an entirely different category of human being. I expected a hardened personification of evil, a leering Charles Manson–like figure. Instead, Frank reminded me a lot of my friends. Unlike other prisoners I had met, he did not try to deny his involvement in the crime for which he was sentenced. He spoke with regret, even remorse, yet quickly pointed out that he had not pulled the trigger and that he had come from an abusive background. He did not exactly rationalize, but he explained, put his actions in context, made them understandable.

I could not help thinking of my own sins as I drove away from that prison and as I kept up a correspondence with Frank over the next few years. I had avoided overt crimes against the state, the kind that could put me behind bars. My sins were more internal, befitting a writer who spends life staring inward.

In time, I made a list of those sins—not just a stray sin here or there, but patterns that keep breaking out. Here are a few from my list:

Deceit. I am ashamed to admit it, but I struggle against a pattern of deceit. Years ago, justifying my deceit as a creative way to oppose "the system" that was constantly ripping me off, I would get even by mailing in bill payments without postage stamps, making the utility and other companies pay postage (until the Postal Service wised up and stopped delivering such mail). I subscribed to music clubs, recorded the albums, then sent them back for a refund. If Napster had been around in those days, I'm sure I would have been a regular user. My conscience stricken, I eventually cut out such practices, but I still recognize within me a temptation to rely on deceit as a survival tactic. When a credit card company or airline mileage programme makes a mistake in my favour, I think I deserve it; when it goes against me, I fight it tooth and nail.

Permanent Discontent. You may not find this one on any biblical list of sins—although the medieval term *acedia,* or spiritual melancholy, comes close—but the root attitude affects me in many sinful ways. Years of working as an editor honed in me an editor's personality that is never satisfied. I spend my days looking for mistakes, striking out words, re-arranging sentences, crumpling up first drafts. Such a dyspeptic outlook serves a worthwhile purpose in editing, but not in the rest of life. I yearn for what I cannot have and cannot be. Looking back, I tend to remember all the people who have hurt me. I find myself editing my wife's behaviour, and my friends'. I react to new people with initial suspicion. People can win me over, but it is exactly that, a winning-over process.

Hypocrisy. All Christians fight this sin to some degree (there I go again, rationalizing), but writers perhaps more than most. A columnist writes a stirring call to civil disobedience. A Nebraska citizen reads it, defies the law in defence of some moral principle and lands in jail. How does the columnist feel? I write about leprosy patients in India and about the extraordinary humility and sacrifice of missionaries I have visited there, yet I write from the comfort of an office in the mountains, with the strains of classical music filling the room. How do I live with that? How should I?

Greed. Writing about the Christian faith is the only form of "ministry" I know of that has a one-to-one correspondence to income. Each person who buys my books means more money in my pocket. Need I detail the mixed motives that may result? Greed changes the questions I ask from *Is this thought true? Does it have value?* to *Will it sell?*

Pride. Again, a most embarrassing admission I would much prefer to leave off my list of sins. As an author, I begin with the rather audacious assumption that I have a viewpoint worth your interrupting your life to consider. If I did not believe that, I would not go through the laborious process of writing. The danger of pride rides on every thought, every sentence, every word.

My list of sins excludes many overt ones I heard about from Frank in prison: child abuse, drunkenness, theft, disorderly conduct. I feel no temptation toward those sins, and that fact offers a clue into the nature of evil: it strikes at the point of greatest vulnerability. I spend my days secluded in an office, susceptible to an introvert's self-absorption. Discontent, pride, and greed are internal sins that grow like mould in dark, moist corners of the psyche, nourished by slight rejections, mild paranoia, and loneliness—the precise occupational hazards of the writing profession.

Frank, who grew up under a reign of abuse, succumbed to the temptation to strike back violently at a world that had mistreated him. A charismatic public figure will face a different set of temptations. And those who depend for a living on the appeal of their bodies will likely fall at different points; adultery tempts them, as Hollywood divorce rates easily prove.

We who battle internal sins may think our sins more dignified than blatant sins such as adultery and drunkenness. When I begin to entertain such thoughts, I simply turn to the Sermon on the Mount, in which Jesus paints with one brush lust and adultery, hatred and murder.

I now see that each of the sins I allow to grow, or even cultivate, is a form of selfish reductionism. It blocks relationship with other people and with God, and keeps me from experiencing *shalom*. It disorders my own small world and keeps me from attending to rumours from another world. When I choose myself rather than others, rather than God, in a cruel irony I end up with a sick and disconnected self. In the process, I miss out on life as God intended it to be.

The more I see my sins in this light, the more I see beyond the harshness of God's warnings. Instead, I find myself gazing into the grieving eyes of a parent whose children are destroying themselves. Augustine, something of an expert on the topic, said it best: "The soul lives by avoiding what it dies by desiring."

———————

> Evil is unspectacular and always human,
> And shares our bed and eats at our own table.
>
> W. H. AUDEN

the gift of guilt

> When other people commit them [sins], you are startled, but when you commit them yourself, they seem absolutely natural.
>
> ELSPETH HUXLEY

Three straight hours one morning I sat in front of a television and listened to a U.S. president confess his sins: Bill Clinton was giving testimony before a grand jury. For months the press had leaked juicy details about his dalliance with a twenty-one-year-old intern named Monica. Both the president and his wife had initially denied the reports, only to be forced to amend their statements as evidence—taped phone conversations, letters, gifts, a soiled dress—piled up. Now the president of the United States sat before a camera and subjected himself to legal scrutiny.

For Americans who lived through the Watergate scandals, the drama had a painfully familiar plot: wrongdoing, denials, a web of deception, solemn declarations that turned out to be lies. Europeans rolled their eyes at the naiveté of Americans who judge public leaders by their private acts. Republican politicians gravely insisted the central issue was perjury, not sexual immorality. Like an avalanche gathering force as it slides down the mountain, the scandal swept aside other current events. The most private of Bill Clinton's acts became the most public, resulting in the second impeachment in American history.

Eventually, of course, Clinton weathered the storm and served out his term. Some people remember him as the Comeback Kid, able to rebound from every crisis. Some remember him as Slick Willie, the politician who prevaricated about marijuana, Arkansas land deals, presidential pardons, and the definition of the word *sex*. I remember a single image: the most powerful man in the world, pale, flinching at some of the questions, staring at the video camera like a wild animal frozen in headlights.

"I am so sorry," he said, fully conscious of the trauma he had caused his family and nation, and of the stain on his own historical reputation. The leader of the world seemed its least free citizen, a slave of passions, a man humbled by his inability to control basic urges.

———

What is it, what nameless, inscrutable, unearthly thing is it; what cozzening, hidden lord and master, and cruel, remorseless emperor commands me; that against all natural lovings and longings, I so keep pushing, and crowding, and jamming myself on all the time; recklessly making me ready to do what in my own proper, natural heart, I durst not so much as dare?

Captain Ahab is speaking, the obsessed hunter of Moby Dick, the great white whale. Ahab ignores dreadful warnings against his fateful mission; his crew's pleas to abandon the chase fall on deaf ears; he even coldly refuses to search for another captain's lost son in order to continue his quest. He cannot control himself. The whale, "all a magnet," has Ahab in its mighty field of force. First mate Starbuck sees to the heart of the matter, crying out to Ahab, "Desist. See! Moby Dick seeks thee not. It is thou, thou, that madly seekest him!"

Here lies the inscrutable power of evil. I can calmly identify my own sins and affirm how much better my life would be if rid of them. Yet knowing that I should choose the good, even willing that I should, does not make me choose the good. Like Captain Ahab and, yes, like Bill Clinton, sometimes I feel caught in a force field I can neither explain nor resist.

"There remains in [us] a smouldering cinder of evil, from which desires continually leap forth to allure and spur to commit sin," said John Calvin. If only evil did resemble a smouldering cinder that we could locate and stomp out. Instead, we more resemble tiny magnets, with one end attracted to and the other end repelled by the same force. Cut a magnet in half and you get a smaller magnet with the same polarity. Cut it again, and again, into sixteen pieces, and you have sixteen pieces attracted on one end and repelled on the other. In just that way the tendency to yield to evil and also to resist it infuses every part of my body, as a kind of inbuilt cellular tension.

When Raskolnikov commits murder in *Crime and Punishment,* he describes it "as though someone had taken his hand and pulled him along irresistibly, blindly, with supernatural strength." At the same time, he confesses that he has freely chosen the foul deed. Somehow, he can neither excuse nor avoid the crime.

I see the power of sin at work most clearly in addictions. As a social worker in Chicago, my wife watched helplessly as an elderly Polish man, cultured and well educated, handed over his welfare cheque to a prostitute each week. He lost his subsidized housing, landed in an abominable nursing home, attempted suicide, and sank into a profound depression. Even so, when the prostitute tracked him down in his new quarters, he signed his cheque over to her once again.

A high-society friend of mine in San Francisco, a patron of the opera and connoisseur of the arts, experimented with drugs, recreationally at first, then compulsively. He lost his beautiful Victorian home and ended up frequenting rescue missions and homeless shelters. Another friend in Mississsippi hoped to earn enough money as a night watchman to live somewhere other than a cheap motel. When a family member died and left him a $25,000 inheritance, he lost it all in one weekend, gambling on a riverboat near New Orleans.

Søren Kierkegaard likened the human condition to a person who has a three-storey house and yet insists on dwelling in the dank cellar. I feel no attraction to prostitutes, drugs, or gambling, yet in a way these obvious addictions merely exaggerate my own tendencies. Mine may seem less earthy, but in them too I detect the musty scent of a cellar dripping water and crawling with silverfish. A law of entropy governs the moral universe as well as the physical, tending toward disorder. Something tugs us downward and prevents us from realizing the good life, the *shalom*, that God intended for us.

The Bible informs about sin mainly through stories, and its most complete story of sin involves a national leader whose crimes easily overshadow those of Richard Nixon and Bill Clinton. The sin in question began as a spark of everyday lust by King David, perhaps the greatest leader in Israel's history, who spied a married woman bathing on a nearby rooftop. It ended in adultery and murder, as well as a needless battle that cost the lives of many soldiers.

Interestingly, the account of this notorious sin has one central theme: a broken relationship with God. "Against you, you only, have I sinned," prayed King David after he got caught, a remarkable response considering he had just committed adultery and murder. Bathsheba, her husband, and the others who died as a result of his wrongdoing faded in the background as David dealt with the most important aftereffect of his misdeeds.

That theme reminded Israel that even the king reported to a higher authority. And the rest of the Bible underscores this insight into the most serious consequence of sin: it blocks contact between the natural and spiritual worlds. Sin introduces a kind of static interference in communication with God and as a result shuts us off from the very resources we need to combat it.

David's story, told in all its seamy detail, provides a case study of communication with the spiritual world blocked and then restored. There is no magic secret to restoring contact with God. In fact, it follows the same basic path required to restore any broken relationship, whether family, spouse, or friend. The path begins with guilt and ends with restoration.

Guilt. Guilt is the early warning sign of danger, the first rumour of something wrong. "Man is the only animal that blushes. Or needs to," observed Mark Twain. Uniquely in creation, humans have a complex method of registering moral failure. The guilty conscience presents itself as an inner voice, a most personal form of communication, and can proceed to have a powerful effect on both body and psyche.

While not an exact science, the polygraph machine, or "lie detector," shows that guilt can influence heart rate, respiratory functions, and galvanic skin resistance. Sometimes local police departments will administer the test to reporters or other volunteers. Even though they have committed no crimes and are taking the test as an experiment, without stress, the needle on the paper strip will usually catch them in any intentional lie.

Some therapists mention guilt as one of the chief problems of their disturbed clients and blame religion for its role in inducing guilt. They suggest we would all be better off if we could learn to overcome our feelings of guilt.

My own perspective on guilt changed during my work with Dr Paul Brand, the first person I met who championed physical pain. As an orthopaedic surgeon working among leprosy patients in India, Dr Brand had made the startling discovery that all the manifestations of that feared disease came about as a result of painlessness. A tiny pain cell that makes most people blink every few seconds falls silent, and the leprosy patient soon goes blind for lack of the lubrication provided by blinking. Patients lose toes by wearing too-tight shoes, and fingers by common injuries that go undetected. Diabetics face a similar danger: losing sensation in their feet, they become prone to injuries and infections that often lead to amputation.

Dr Brand and I wrote a book together called *The Gift of Pain,* and after spending time among leprosy patients, I became solidly convinced of the need for pain in a normal life. I began to view pain not as my enemy but as the language the body uses to alert me when something needs attention. The very unpleasantness of that language makes it effective: pain-sensitive people almost never duplicate the injuries of leprosy patients.

The direct parallel between physical pain and guilt became obvious. Both force me to pay attention to parts of my life I would prefer to ignore or cover up.

Psychologists use the term "cognitive dissonance" as a sort of euphemism for guilt, a symptom of the inner battle raging inside a person who believes one way and acts another. For example, a priest will feel intense cognitive dissonance if he secretly carries on an affair with a parishioner. Even if his church suspects nothing he will feel a lack of peace and harmony, and the mind will seek to resolve the contradictions. The priest may lose his train of thought while delivering a homily or blurt out his lover's name at an inappropriate time.

At times I experience cognitive dissonance in my marriage. When I am trying to keep something from my wife, quite unconsciously I let out clues. Even if I have the best of intentions—for instance in planning a surprise birthday party—I find it difficult to deceive her. And if I have done something wrong and want to hide it from her, the cognitive dissonance loudens into guilt. When I try to repress it, my behaviour gives me away and she knows something is amiss. Ultimately, the guilt so disturbs me that I must take the difficult step of confessing to her what I have been hiding.

I believe such guilt is essential to a mature relationship. "Love means never having to say you're sorry," proclaimed *Love Story*, a sappy romance novel from the 1970s. No, just the opposite: love means precisely having to say you're sorry. Guilt deserves my gratitude, for only such a powerful force can nudge me toward reconciliation with those I have wronged.

Guilt reminds us of our place, as moral beings accountable to God. In his response to guilt, King David saw beyond the damage to human relationships and confronted the rupture with God. As his poetry makes clear, David regularly monitored his conscience for signs of danger in his life with God. How we behave, how we treat others in this world matters far more than we can see.

Like everything in our disordered world, guilt is subject to misuse. Instead of serving as a prod for us to deal with a problem, it becomes the problem. Therapists often work with clients who have a harmful obsession with guilt and who confuse false guilt with true guilt. False guilt occurs when a person punishes himself or herself for not measuring up to somebody else's standards—perhaps a parent's or the church's or society's. True guilt occurs when a person does not measure up to God's standards.

A fourteenth-century mystic, Dorothy of Montau, once wept for hours after realizing she had committed the "sin" of wanting to eat a piece of spiced fish. Martin Luther, in his early days as a monk, would wear out his confessors with hours of introspection about minuscule sins and unhealthy thoughts. "My son, God is not angry with you: it is you who are angry with God," said one of his exasperated advisers. Eventually, Luther came to agree that his fear of sinning actually showed a lack of faith. "To diagnose smallpox you do not have to probe each pustule, nor do you heal each separately," he concluded.

Just as my physical body speaks loudly through pain so that I will attend to the injury site, my conscience speaks in the language of guilt so that I will take the steps necessary for healing. The goal in both is to restore health, not to feel bad. When I feel a twinge of conscience, I should first ask whether I've done something deserving true guilt. In other words, have I really sinned? If the answer is yes—as it was in King David's case— then I dare not avoid or repress that guilt. Like pain, it warns of something that endangers my health.

Guilt is not a state to cultivate or a mood you slip into for a few days. It should have directional movement, first pointing backward to the sin and then pointing forward to change. A person who feels no guilt can never find healing. Yet neither can a person who wallows in guilt. The sense of guilt only serves its designed purpose as a symptom if it presses us toward cure.

I once thought Christians went through life burdened by guilt, in contrast to carefree unbelievers. I now realize that Christians are the very people who can go through life free of that burden. Benedict Groeschel puts it this way: "A saint is just a sinner who is more repentant than most of us."

Repentance. Sometime after his sin, King David wrote a poem to express his thoughts and emotions during the act of repentance. Ever since, many Jews and Christians have made Psalm 51 their own prayer in response to true guilt. A psalm prayed in public by the people of Israel, it confesses a horrible private sin committed by their king.

Recall again the U.S. parallels in Watergate and Monica-gate. In lengthy television interviews with David Frost, Richard Nixon never admitted guilt. He used words like "errors of judgement" and "mistakes," but never bluntly confessed, "I was wrong. I'm sorry." President Clinton proved more forthcoming only after the evidence mounted against him. In front of television cameras, the two U.S. presidents responded precisely as most of us do when caught: we rationalize, explain away, justify ourselves, grudgingly admit error.

Nixon's and Clinton's squirming denials revealed under bright lights that national leaders are just like everyone else, which is what makes David's approach so extraordinary. He, the king, turned his humiliation into a public document, one that became enshrined as a national song. To David, restoring a right relationship with God counted far more than maintaining his reputation as a ruler.

Something in us resists repentance at all costs. We would rather deny, lie, blame, rationalize—anything but repent. Yet the first words of Jesus, in the earliest Gospel, include the straightforward command "Repent!" Repentance emerges as his consistent theme, repeated to a variety of audiences that include rich and poor, powerful and weak, religious and irreligious alike.

Whenever I find such dissonance between a requirement set forth by Jesus and my own natural resistance, I try to explore why. What keeps me from following Jesus' clear command? I can identify two main forces that tug mightily against a call to repentance.

First, when I mess up I like to work my way out of it. Most religions have elaborate techniques for penitents to demonstrate their remorse. If you sit in a sweat lodge, embark on a pilgrimage, crawl on your knees, or sacrifice an animal, you can walk away with a feeling of self-satisfaction. You did something that somehow balances out the sin. You paid for it.

Christianity has at its core a most unnatural concept called *grace,* which means that we can do nothing to counterbalance our sins. God has already paid the penalty, and we need merely accept it, by trusting him for the remedy.* Grace is God's free gift, with repentance the way to access it.

The second barrier to repentance is that I like to look good in front of other people. I want to appear respectable and in control, a veneer that repentance slices through. It requires me openly to acknowledge failure and weaknesses that I normally seek to keep hidden.

Author Keith Miller notes that, paradoxically, honest confession before others is the only way to silence the "shaming voices" within, the secrets about ourselves that we try diligently to hide. Our secrets control us, as any therapist can attest. Their power comes from the threat of revealing the shameful acts of our past. When we voluntarily share these secrets in a spiritual community, says Miller, we break the power of the shaming voices.

Twelve-step programmes insist on the painful fifth step, in which the addicted person has to make a no-holds-barred confession to another person. The programme insists, "You are as sick as your sickest secret and you will remain sick as long as it remains a secret." One AA pamphlet estimates that sobriety is 10 percent about alcohol and 90 percent about honesty. When a person stubbornly denies having a serious problem,

---

*After writing a book titled *What's So Amazing About Grace?* I received a letter from a reader who made an error in typing. She complimented me on my book *What's So Annoying About Grace?* Subconsciously, she expressed what a lot of people feel: we would rather do something to earn forgiveness than subject ourselves to repentance, the path to grace.

treatment centres may stage an intervention, in which they bring in relatives, bartenders, and colleagues who force the alcoholic to confront the truth in its most searing and despicable form.

I once heard Keith Miller describe his own experience with this difficult fifth step. Miller, a Protestant, called a Catholic priest who lived five hundred miles away and asked, "Would you hear my confession?" He made a long list of his character flaws and defects and the many people he had wronged. Then he travelled to the priest's home city, sat before him, and read aloud the entire list without looking up.

At the end, Miller held his head in his hands, waiting for a response. Silence. Miller kept expecting the blow to fall. Nothing. When he forced himself to raise his head, he saw that the priest was crying. "My God, Keith," he said, "that's my list too." A path opened toward healing.

After experiencing the power of repentance, Miller developed a ritual of confession, a mini-inventory he goes through each night in a review of the day. He looks for signs of self-pity, self-justification, dishonesty, resentment, selfishness, and fear. As he identifies each instance, he confesses it to God and jots a note to make amends to the people he wronged, if appropriate. Then, having cleared himself of the day's toxins, he lists the good things that happened, breathes a prayer of gratitude, and goes to sleep.

My own attitude toward repentance has changed dramatically as my view of God has changed. In adolescent years I thought of repentance as something like courtroom interrogation. I, the accused, was sitting on the witness stand while a prosecuting attorney constructed a case against me. Anything I said might incriminate me. If I admitted a failure or defect, the attorney (or God, in this case) would seize on it as proof of my guilt.

The New Testament uses that courtroom analogy, though with an important twist: "And if any man sin, we have an advocate with the Father, Jesus Christ the righteous." God restores us through his Son, now the advocate of our innocence—our defence attorney, as it were.

Again I turn to the image of the Great Physician. Recently I visited a specialist about an infection that had been spreading inside my mouth.

If I had denied all symptoms, dismissed the pain, and kept my mouth shut as he tried to examine me, I would have received no help. Instead, because I trusted him, I opened my mouth wide, moved my tongue back and forth at his command, let him take tissue samples, and went away with a prescription for treatment. I have come to see repentance as something like that visit to a specialist. The goal is not to cause me pain, though treatment may require that. The goal is to restore my health, which can only take place if I fully cooperate in the process.

C. S. Lewis said about repentance, "It is not something God demands of you before He will take you back and which He could let you off if He chose; it is simply a description of what going back is like." By humbly accepting my place as a flawed creature in God's world, I get a tiny glimpse of God's point of view. I see at a glance how my sins stunt growth and threaten health. In the same act, I acknowledge the disease and ask for the cure.

Consequences. Many people think of sins as accumulating like parking tickets. In Chicago, where I used to live, one parking ticket matters little. You can ignore it and never get into trouble. Once you get ten, however, you start receiving threatening letters and your name goes into a computer database. If you get stopped for a traffic violation, the police officer will know about your unpaid tickets. And if you collect twenty-five tickets, you become a "scofflaw." One day you'll walk outside and find your car immobilized, with an ugly steel contraption called a Denver Boot clamped onto your front wheel. To get the boot removed, you must appear in court and pay all your fines.

Similarly, some view individual sins as nuisances that cause problems only if you accumulate too many. A few niggling little sins may not matter, but eventually you will reach a crisis point and have to face the consequences. The Bible has a different perspective, of sins operating more like cancer cells. One or two loose in the bloodstream do make a difference—often the difference between life and death. Unchecked, cancer cells multiply and metastasize, undermining the health of the entire body.

King David's story follows the pattern of a moral cancer: a ruler's lust for a beautiful woman leads to adultery and then a bungled cover-up and then a conspiracy to murder. The same pattern, on a different scale, played out in Watergate and Monica-gate. And the same pattern can appear in my life. A seemingly harmless white lie or act of lust can lead to lasting consequences.

Sometimes the Bible lays out the consequences of sin as a stern deterrent—for instance, in the dire warnings of the prophets—but often it simply chronicles the aftermath in the sinner's own life. God lets punishment work itself out in the natural course of this life.

In King David's case, punishment played out within the royal household. Having forfeited his moral authority, David seemed to lose his grip on his family. One son raped his half-sister. Another son, Absalom, seethed against that crime for two years and then committed a murder of revenge. Eventually Absalom launched an armed revolt against David and nearly brought down the kingdom. The later troubles of the kingdom, including a bloody civil war, all trace back to the early "petty" sins of King David.

Fear of consequences can be a powerful deterrent against wrongdoing. A clinic for cocaine abusers operated by the University of Colorado School of Medicine has shown impressive success in helping people kick a cocaine habit through a technique of self-blackmail. The drug abusers themselves devise the penalty for failure. An addicted nurse wrote a letter to the state board of nursing confessing her habit and surrendering her licence. The letter would remain in the clinic vault as long as she passed the drug tests; if she failed, the letter would be mailed. An addict who happened to be a diehard Republican made a pact that if he failed a drug test he would donate $1,000 to Democratic Senator Edward Kennedy—the worst punishment he could think of. Doctors and lawyers have written self-blackmail letters that would end their careers. In each case, the abusers make the consequence of misbehaviour so harsh that it deters them from resuming their habit.

Usually, the consequence of sin flows naturally from the act. Smoke two packs a day and your lungs pay the price; abuse alcohol and your liver will suffer the penalty. Inject drugs or live promiscuously, and you may end up with AIDS or a sexually transmitted disease. Tell lies, and you'll find yourself isolated—as George Bernard Shaw said, the liar's punishment is not being able to believe anyone else. A careless fit of anger by a parent can inflict wounds that take years to overcome; a society's racism or economic injustice may have an effect over many generations.

Oscar Wilde's novel *The Picture of Dorian Gray* depicts personal consequences through an allegory. Having sat for a portrait of himself, the dashing young Dorian Gray regrets that he will age and change while the picture stays the same. If only their roles could be reversed, he sighs. Gray gets his wish. He remains a handsome young socialite while the portrait, hidden away in his attic, begins to age.

Soon the portrait starts to bear the consequences of the real Gray's behaviour. He makes a cruel comment, and the mouth on the portrait twists into a cruel grin. As he nurses hatred toward a rival, the eyes on the portrait narrow in rage. Finally, when he murders a man, the hands on the portrait drip with blood. At the end of the book, Gray despises the portrait so much that he slashes it with a knife. When a servant ascends to the attic to check on his master, he finds that the portrait has vanished and Dorian Gray is lying on the floor with a knife through his heart. The painting had visibly represented his true self, and when he finally faced it, he killed himself.

Restoration. I have a tendency to bury issues of contention with people. They rarely go away, I find. Instead, they gather force even as I try to repress them. While working out in a health club or driving, I find myself buttressing arguments in my defence, building my case, justifying myself. When I finally do screw up the courage to confront, however, many of these arguments simply dissolve. Determining who is at fault seems far less important than restoring the relationship.

After his sin, King David followed the path of guilt, repentance, consequences, and forgiveness in textbook fashion. Psalm 51 expresses the sorrow and remorse he felt, and God answered his plea for a new start. David got a clean heart and renewed joy. David's reconciliation with God became a centrepiece in the Old Testament, an indelible picture of God's amazing grace. Despite his history of adultery and murder, David gained the reputation of "a man after [God's] own heart."

"I ain't got to, but I can't help it," said one of William Faulkner's characters about sin. None of us can help it. Born sinners, we never completely slough off our flaws and imperfections. But we were also born thirsting for forgiveness. We yearn for the clean, fresh feeling of restoration, of *shalom*, of being washed and made new.

When we do fail, we face options of how to respond. We can yield to the attraction, ignore the consequences, and sin for all we're worth. We can wallow in remorse and live under a constant cloud of guilt. Or we can call out for help.

Living in Colorado, I climb mountains. Colorado has fifty-four mountains rising above 14,000 feet, and every summer I climb some of them. On a summer weekend in the mountains, I see casual hikers who have no idea what they are doing. In sandals, shorts, and T-shirts, carrying a single container of water, they start up a trail at mid-morning. They have no map, no compass, and no rain gear. They also have no apparent knowledge of the lightning storms that roll in many summer afternoons, making it imperative to summit before noon and head for the safety of the timberline.

My neighbour, who volunteers for Alpine Rescue, has told me hair-raising stories of tourists who must be rescued from certain death after wandering off a trail, falling, or simply being exposed to a sudden hailstorm or thirty-degree drop in temperature. Nevertheless, regardless of the circumstances, Alpine Rescue always responds to a call for help. Not once have they lectured a hapless tourist, "Well, since you obviously ignored the most basic rules of the wilderness, you'll just have to sit here and bear the consequences. We won't assist you."

Their mission is rescue, and so they pursue every needy hiker in the wilderness, no matter how undeserving. A whistle, a cry, a flashing mirror, a bonfire, an "SOS" spelled out in pine branches, a message of distress from a cellphone—any of these signals will cause Alpine Rescue to mobilize teams of medically trained searchers.

I have come to see the central message of the Bible, too, as one of rescue. In the book of Romans, Paul takes pains to point out that none of us "deserve" God's mercy and none of us can save ourselves. Like a stranded hiker, all we can do is call for help.

A hardened park ranger could look at the efforts of Alpine Rescue as indulging the bad habits of irresponsible tourists. Shouldn't they spend their energy instead handing out rewards to hikers who follow the rules? ("God, I thank you that I am not like other men—robbers, evildoers, adulterers," prayed the Pharisee.) When I posed such a question to my neighbour, she looked at me uncomprehending. "But our business is rescue!" she said. "Do you expect us to leave any hiker stranded in the wilderness? I don't care who they are—they need help." ("In the same way," said Jesus, "I tell you, there is rejoicing in the presence of the angels of God over one sinner who repents.")

I ask myself why I so seldom call for spiritual rescue. In the wilderness, I would have no problem signalling for help. I carry whistles, mirrors, and other signalling devices for just that purpose. Yet often after I have sinned I shun the path of repentance that leads to restoration. What diverts me?

Sometimes I simply find ways to avoid facing my sin, whether out of pride, denial, or stubbornness. At other times, I shrink from the steps required for restoration for just the opposite reason. I think of myself as unacceptable, incurable, beyond the range of God's grace. Whenever I sense that, I realize I have a distorted vision of God that needs correcting. "God is love," says the apostle John. God cannot help extending grace. Forgiveness, reconciliation, rescue define God's nature.

When I resist calling for help, I tend to focus on the cost: my wounded pride, an admission of failure, the changes I need to make. But as Jesus' story of the prodigal son makes clear, the object of repentance is what we turn *toward,* not what we turn away from. Sitting in a pigsty, beset with hunger pains, the prodigal remembered a home with lanterns burning and food aplenty, and a father who longed to embrace him. Did he even remember the pain after the banquet, tucked in his own bed, welcomed back into a loving family?

———

Early in my marriage I would haltingly reveal secrets about myself to my wife, secrets I had never told anyone. "Do you still love me?" I would ask. Yes, she would assure me, even when the secrets may have caused her pain. I learned from her a truth I would later understand about God: only if you are fully known can you be fully loved.

My spiritual growth has meant bringing a succession of secrets, in fear and trembling, to God, only to find that God of course knew the secret all along, and loved me anyhow. I have learned that God is hardly surprised by my failure. Knowing me better than I know myself, God expects failure from me. I am more sinful than I ever imagined—and also more loved by God.

"Adam, where are you?" God called out in the garden. It was Adam, not God, who hid. God takes the initiative to come searching; we are the ones who hide. And Jesus, the Great Physician, sees our sins not as disqualifiers but as the reason for his journey from another world to ours. Rescue is God's business.

A pastor friend told me that when he sits in his office and hears tearful confessions from people who have failed, he realizes at that moment they are closer to God than he is, the religious professional. King David knew well what God most desires from us: "You do not delight in sacrifice, or I would bring it; you do not take pleasure in burnt offerings. The sacrifices of God are a broken spirit; a broken and contrite heart, O God, you will not despise."

In childhood I thought of each of my sins as a brick filling in a space that walled me off from God. My guilt feelings blinded me to the truth that I was busily constructing a wall God had already destroyed. I now believe that God accompanies me at each stage of my struggle, present with me even as I flee from him. At the moment I am most aware of my own inadequacy, at that moment I am probably closest to God. As C. S. Lewis wrote to an American correspondent, "It is when we notice the dirt that God is most present in us; it is the very sign of His presence."

Once a week or so my church schedules a "Mom's Night Out," with free babysitting for single mothers who need a night off or mothers who simply want to spend an evening with their husbands. Our pastor's wife once happily took advantage of this programme to go out to dinner with her husband. Later, when Peter, my pastor, went to pick up his three-year-old son, the babysitter told him about one of the games they had played. She had asked each of the preschoolers what was Mummy's favourite thing to do with them. "You know what your son answered? He said that Mummy's favourite thing was to 'clean me up.'"

"In truth," said Peter the next Sunday, "that isn't Susan's favourite thing to do with her son. Cleaning him up is an excuse to hold him. Absorbing the mess is just part of the process of getting close. And it's the same with God."

One deep and serious groan is more acceptable
to God than the creation of a world.

THOMAS TRAHERNE

PART THREE

two worlds

In the history of humanity there are no civilizations or cultures which fail to manifest, in one or a thousand ways, this need for an absolute that is called heaven, freedom, a miracle, a lost paradise to be regained, peace, the going beyond History.... There is no religion in which everyday life is not considered a prison; there is no philosophy or ideology that does not think that we live in alienation.... Humanity has always had a nostalgia for the freedom that is only beauty, that is only real life, plenitude, light.

EUGENE IONESCO

why believe?

Who were the two artists of ancient times who competed to see who could paint the visible world most faithfully? "Now I shall prove to you that I am the best," said the first, showing the other a curtain which he had painted. "Well, draw back the curtain," said the adversary, "and let us see the picture." "The curtain is the picture," replied the first with a laugh.

NIKOS KAZANTZAKIS

In his whimsical autobiography, the cartoonist James Thurber tells of flunking a college course in botany. Other students peered through their microscopes and drew the cellular structure of plants. Meanwhile Thurber, who suffered from an eye disorder, would protest, "I can't see anything." Each time this happened, the professor would begin patiently, making fine adjustments to the microscope, and then end in a fury when Thurber still could not see. A year later, attempting the class again, Thurber finally detected something worth drawing. He excitedly sketched the series of specks, dots, and patterns he saw in the eyepiece. The professor approached him with a broad smile, only to squint into the microscope and lose his temper once again. "That's your eye!" he shouted. "You've fixed the lens so that it reflects! You've drawn your eye!"

Are we missing something, we moderns who bestride history and peer at the world around us with scientifically trained eyes? For the

Christian, the greatest disorder of the planet is that it disguises the true nature of things. The natural world, so evident to our senses, draws a curtain across spiritual reality. Those who believe in another world keep pointing, perhaps until we are red in the face like Thurber's professor, and still sceptics cannot see past the surface. The writer William Irwin Thompson likens such people to flies that crawl across the ceiling of the Sistine Chapel, blissfully unaware of the magnificent shapes and forms that lie beneath—or above—the threshold of perception.

"Where are you?" God called to Adam after the fateful choice in the garden. Once, God and human beings had walked and talked together as friends. Suddenly, a rupture opened between the visible world of Eden and the invisible world of God and spiritual reality. Adam and Eve were lost and alone on a strangely tilted planet.

Despite the rupture, rumours of another world proved so convincing that for most of history people accepted without question the reality of two worlds, one visible and one invisible. They lived their everyday lives in the visible world of trees, rocks, and soil, while always acknowledging an unseen world as more powerful and significant. What they could not explain—sunrise, thunder, volcanoes—they credited to God or the gods. Indeed, the unseen world undergirded the world they could see and gave it purpose.

Only in the last few centuries, as science advanced and the ideas of the Enlightenment spread, have people lived with no belief in an unseen world. In 1900 the historian Henry Adams wrote a famous essay, "The Dynamo and the Virgin," which claimed that in the new industrial age the electric motor had displaced the Virgin Mary as the power that drives history. A century later, we might substitute the computer chip or atom for his dynamo, but for many educated people the formula still holds. Whoever masters the material world determines future's fate. What other world is there?

"If you could select any one person across all of history to interview, who would it be?" someone asked Larry King, turning the tables on the television interviewer. "Jesus Christ," he responded. And what would

King, a sceptical Jew, ask him? "I would like to ask him if he was indeed virgin-born. The answer to that question would define history for me."

Both Henry Adams and Larry King settled on the Virgin as the hinge of history because Christians hold up Jesus' birth as an example of the unseen world impinging on the visible, God's own Son entering the world of matter with full humanity but no earthly father. King is right: such an "invasion" would redefine history. No longer could we see ourselves as cosmic orphans, inhabiting a speck of a planet in an insignificant galaxy. We would become central characters in a drama involving not merely now but time beyond, not this world only but worlds beyond imagining.

Henry Adams' contemporary, William James, made a lifelong study of religious people, reading the accounts of hundreds of mystics and conducting many personal interviews. In a series of Gifford Lectures (which became *The Varieties of Religious Experience*), he concluded that all religions have in common a belief in an unseen, spiritual world from which the visible world draws its significance. Furthermore, all share a sense of living in a disordered world and propose as the cure a means of contacting the unseen world, which is our true end.

An agnostic, James could not accept the mystics' accounts of such experience at face value, yet as a scientist neither could he deny them. He noted that contact with the unseen world had produced actual, transforming effects on individual personalities in this world. "God is real since he produces real effects," he summed up.

I have a physicist friend who doubts the evidence. "The worst physics is better than the best metaphysics," he insists. Matter, you can count on. You can measure and quantify it and break it down into particles. Metaphysics deals with the unseen, that slippery world of first principles and invisible forces and regenerated souls. Yet the books he gives me on modern physics seem to me more metaphysical than anything I read in William James. I learn that consciousness plays a key role in physical reality, that quantum events depend on an outside observer, that measuring the spin of one particle may affect the spin of another billions of miles away, that string theory proposes as many as ten dimensions (or eleven, or maybe twenty-six) to explain how the forces of the universe work together, that parallel universes may exist which influence us in ways we cannot detect.

In psychology, theology, and physics, the line separating the two worlds, physical and spiritual, is uncertain at best.

———

To fully appreciate the modern outlook, we would have to go back in time. A peasant in medieval Europe oriented life around two worlds.* Although the world around him contained much hardship—poverty, disease, crime, near-constant warfare—he took solace in the images of another world portrayed in his place of worship. The scenes painted in the Sistine Chapel, or on the walls of his village church, he accepted as literal truth. He understood life on this physical planet as one small slice of eternity and sought to make connection with the spiritual world he could not see. He believed that God has revealed how we ought to live, and will one day hold us accountable.

In contrast, the average citizen of modern Europe perceives only one world, the here and now. She assumes that rational people make society's rules based on a common good, not on any revealed or "natural" law. She also believes that at the moment of physical death, existence ends, and there is no God to hold us accountable. Without question, her material well-being in the physical world shows impressive improvements over the peasant's. She sleeps in a more comfortable house with regulated temperatures, eats better food, and lives a healthier and longer life.

Which view of the world, the medieval's or the modern's, more closely resembles that articulated by Jesus? "What good is it for a man to gain the whole world, yet forfeit his soul?"—if Jesus was in fact visiting this planet from another dimension, he could not have asked a more penetrating question. Apparently to him, a connection with the spiritual

*In his journals, Thoreau remarked that the ancients, with their gorgons, unicorns, and sphinxes, imagined more than existed, whereas moderns cannot even imagine so much as exists.

world had more value than all material goods put together. With such pronouncements, Jesus bluntly rejected a one-world outlook on life. The apostle Paul echoed the theme: "So we fix our eyes not on what is seen, but on what is unseen. For what is seen is temporary, but what is unseen is eternal."

Throughout its pages, the Bible presents a wholistic view of reality that encompasses both the familiar visible world and an invisible world that coexists as a kind of parallel universe. In every instant of human time, eternity is present. An act of love, justice, compassion—or hate and cruelty—has consequences in this world and in the unseen world as well. Indeed, as Paul grandly proclaims in Romans 8, what happens on earth has enormous consequences for the entire cosmos: "The creation waits in eager expectation for the sons of God to be revealed."

Such notions seem quaint and almost primitive to many moderns. As I reread them in the Bible, however, my mind goes back to scenes from a trip to Russia that took place as I was writing this book. Building a society on a myopic view of reality, one that does not take into account a spiritual world, to which we are accountable, can lead to catastrophe.

The trip began in Sweden, where I spent time with churchgoing Christians, a distinct minority in Sweden these days. I mentioned to them that even though many Swedes had turned away from church, their admirable society continued to live off the moral capital accumulated during centuries of Christian faith. Honesty, peacefulness, generosity, cleanliness, charity, compassion—the Vikings were not noted for such qualities before their conversion.

"What would Sweden look like if we used up our moral capital and those qualities disappeared?" one woman asked me. I replied that she could answer that question by visiting her near neighbour, Russia.

There, brilliant men and women with a doctrinaire outlook—"dialectical materialism," they called it—set into motion an experiment on a huge scale to establish a society based on a one-world view of life. Quite properly, they saw religious faith as an obstacle to their experiment and thus shuttered 98 percent of the churches, killing 42,000 priests in the process.

Some large cathedrals they turned into museums of atheism; village churches they converted into apartments or barns. They banned religious instruction to children and published a national newspaper called *The Godless*.

Soviet communists mocked any belief in "pie in the sky when you die." In the days of Stalin, kindergarten teachers would tell children in their classes to close their eyes and pray to God for a bag of candy. None appeared. "Now, pray to Stalin," they would urge. As the children prayed, the teachers would place bags of candy on each desk. Prayer never gets anything, the teachers would announce. The lesson is to trust our Leader for your needs.

Over the next seventy-five years in the Soviet Union, a terrible irony played itself out. A society committed exclusively to justice in the visible world, here and now, achieved just the opposite. "With the best of intentions, we ended up creating the greatest monstrosity the world has ever seen," a shaken editor of *Pravda* told me. Dostoyevsky's prophecy, "Without God, everything is permitted," proved tragically true in his nation's history.

Archives that were recently released detail the deaths of sixty million people at the hands of their own government. *The Moscow Times* estimates that one-half of all Russian males who died in the twentieth century died of unnatural causes, from war, famine, execution, or imprisonment. A massive economy collapsed of its own incompetence, and by many social standards—life expectancy, nutrition, disease, poverty rate— mighty Russia found itself among the world's developing countries.*

---

*Estimates of the death toll from communism have varied wildly. At the height of Stalin's purges, 3,800 people—more than the number killed in the World Trade Centre attacks—were executed every other day. Alexander Yakovlev *(A Century of Violence in Soviet Russia)* has established the figure of 60 million fatalities through execution, forced starvation, or prison through documents brought to light while he was heading a committee to seek restitution for the victims. Under Mikhail Gorbachev, Yakovlev served on both the Politburo and Central Committee.

Because of disease, alcoholism, and a collapsing economy, Russian men now have a life expectancy of fifty-nine. The birth rate has fallen so precipitously that Russia's population may well sink back to the level of 1917. Seventy percent of Russian marriages end in divorce, and the average woman has had four abortions.

At the same time, communism succeeded in suppressing much of the Russian "soul." Visitors today comment on the scarcity of smiles, rudeness on the subways, the fear of crime, the quantity of alcohol consumed. Even Russian politicians complain about the lack of honesty and charity and, in response, have commissioned foreign organizations to teach the Ten Commandments in the schools. Giant statues of Lenin, Stalin, and other Soviet idols lie toppled in a Moscow sculpture park, mute testimony to the failed substitute gods. Lenin's own body still lies embalmed in Red Square, but few bother to visit it anymore.

Of all the statistics coming out of Russia, the most astonishing to me is the finding of a recent poll in which 61 percent of Russians identified themselves as Christians—this despite the most determined attempt in history to obliterate faith.

"Aim at heaven and you will get earth thrown in. Aim at earth and you get neither," wrote C. S. Lewis. The Soviet experiment of the twentieth century vividly illustrates the second part of his formula. As if a symbol of repentance, a sparkling new Cathedral of Christ the Saviour now overlooks the Kremlin, replacing one that Stalin destroyed to make way for a swimming pool.

———

If communism had succeeded spectacularly, bringing prosperity and happiness to the Soviet Union, I doubt anyone would be building new cathedrals there today. Across the globe, faith is flourishing mainly in places where the physical world is not working out so well, where poverty and hardship press people to look for hope and meaning somewhere else.

Meanwhile affluent societies such as Sweden and the U.S. face a different challenge. With the luxury of indulging in the delights of the physical world, their citizens may ignore the spiritual world altogether. A typical guide to digital cable television in the U.S. lists page after page of adult movies and only a few columns of religious programming. The Siren calls of the visible world—something we can gaze upon, fondle, smell, taste—drown out whispers from the unseen world.

Can faith withstand the seductive powers of the visible world? J. F. Powers' novel *Wheat That Springeth Green* poses the intriguing question "How can we make sanctity as attractive as sex?" The novel tells of a sexually adventurous track star who enters the priesthood and discovers that a hunger for truth, no matter how urgent, is no match for the pleasure principle.

I think of my friends who have, against their own consciences, succumbed to extramarital affairs. "I know it is wrong," said one. "But she makes me feel loved and even heroic. I have lost a lot—my reputation, my family, maybe my career. What have I gained? A love that satisfies my body as well as my soul. A cellular love. That's something I never get with God."

An addiction to anything in the physical world, not just sexual desire, may drown out God's thin, quenchable voice. "Substance abuse," the professionals' term for an addiction to narcotics or alcohol, is perhaps more freighted with meaning than intended. I marvel at the humility of a God who entrusts us with pleasures that would, as God must have known, dampen or displace whatever spiritual desire we might feel.

After returning from Russia, I went to the local supermarket and looked over the magazines as I stood in line at the checkout stand. The progression of magazine titles over the past few decades tells a story of narrowing interests: from *Look* and *Life* to *People* to *Us* to *Self*, from *Ladies' Home Journal* and *Good Housekeeping* to *Shape* and *Cosmopolitan*. Every magazine on the rack featured a beautiful woman showing off her curves in workout gear, a bikini, or other revealing clothes. Does America have no men?

I looked around at the women standing in line. This being the U.S., a majority were overweight. They wore glasses, had moles and imperfect skin, dressed sloppily, slumped at the shoulders—qualities absent from the magazine cover girls. We all know the lie being sold by the magazines, yet still we buy the promise that straight teeth, an ideal shape, and glossy hair will satisfy forever.

Not long afterward I visited the nursing home where my wife works as a chaplain. People who live in nursing homes have, by and large, given up on perfect bodies. They wear sweatsuits and loose clothes with Velcro fasteners, apparel chosen for ease and convenience, not sexiness. Some drag portable oxygen tanks behind them. Some wear adult diapers. All have wrinkles. Body parts sag and do not work as they once did. J. F. Powers' question, "How can we make sanctity as attractive as sex?" loses much of its provocative force in a nursing home.

In that nursing home, one of the city's leading athletes in the 1970s—yellowed clippings from the newspaper's sports pages decorate the walls of his room—lies in a ward for dementia patients, unable to recognize family members or respond to his own name. An old Italian proverb comes to mind: "When the chess game is over, the pawns, rooks, kings, and queens all go back into the same box."

I once visited a church in the town of Waterford, Ireland, to see its renowned tomb carving. Considered one of the finest monuments in Ireland, the stone carving portrays the devout Mayor Rice's decomposing body being gnawed and devoured by toads, vermin, and insects. The mayor died at a time when the shadow of the Black Death shrouded all of Europe. "Whoever you are that pass by, stand, read, weep," says the mayor's inscription. "I am what you will be and I was what you are." The physical world, no matter how attractive, has its limits.

———

Jacques Ellul begins one of his books with the frank admission "I try to do here the same thing I do in all my books: face, alone, this world I live in, try to understand it, and confront it with another reality I live in, but which is utterly unverifiable." Every explorer of the spiritual world faces a similar challenge.

In his memoir *The Seven Storey Mountain,* Thomas Merton tells of encountering the poetry of William Blake and being convicted of the "dead, selfish rationalism which had been freezing my mind and will." Merton became convinced that "the only way to live was to live in a world that was charged with the presence and reality of God."* His search led him to a monastery, the Abbey of Gethsemani, where he was overwhelmed by the power of a place strictly dedicated to prayer: "I had wondered what was holding the country together, what has been keeping the universe from cracking in pieces and falling apart."

Early in his pilgrimage, Merton wrote, "Very soon we get to the point where we simply say, 'I believe' or 'I refuse to believe.'" Faith swings like a pendulum, in individuals as well as societies.

It did not surprise Jesus in the least that some would disbelieve him, regardless of evidence. He had predicted as much: "They will not be convinced even if someone rises from the dead." It does not surprise me either that some disbelieve the reality of an unseen world, especially in an age that excels at mastering the visible world, an age dominated by images. For many, God cannot possibly exist unless he makes himself visible— and God does not perform on our terms.

Why do I believe? I ask myself. Why do I struggle, like Ellul, in all my books to confront my certain world of mountains, trees, computers, and telephones with another reality that is utterly unverifiable? Why do I, like Merton, continue to make that defiant leap of faith?

I could point to a conversion experience during college days, a transforming moment that bisected my life into two parts, an age of unbelief and an age of belief. Yet I know that a sceptic, hearing that story, could propose alternate explanations.

I could point to shafts of light that have (rarely, I must admit) pierced the veil between the visible and invisible worlds. These, too, the sceptic would dismiss, forcing me to fall back on what William James called "the convincingness of unreasoned experience."

---

*Blake offered a good model, for he saw more in a cloud, or in a wildflower, than any scientist. He sought "To see a world in a grain of sand / And a Heaven in a wild flower, / Hold infinity in the palm of your hand / And Eternity in an hour." When Blake read *Essays,* by the rationalist Francis Bacon, he scribbled his judgement on the title page: "Good advice for Satan's Kingdom."

In my own days of scepticism, I wanted a dramatic interruption from above. I wanted proof of an unseen reality, one that could somehow be verified. In my days of faith, such supernatural irruptions seem far less important, in part because I find the materialistic explanations of life inadequate to explain reality. I have learned to attend to fainter contacts between the seen and unseen worlds. I sense in romantic love something insufficiently explained by mere biochemical attraction. I sense in beauty and in nature marks of a genius creator for which the natural response is worship. Like Jacob, I have at times awoken from a dream to realize, "Surely the Lord is in this place, and I was not aware of it."

I sense in desire, including sexual desire, marks of a holy yearning for connection. I sense in pain and suffering a terrible disruption that omnipotent love surely cannot abide forever. I sense in compassion, generosity, justice, and forgiveness a quality of grace that speaks to me of another world, especially when I visit places, like Russia, marred by their absence. I sense in Jesus a person who lived those qualities so consistently that the world could not tolerate him and had to silence and dispose of him. In short, I believe not so much because the invisible world impinges on this one but because the visible world hints, in the ways that move me most, at a lack of completion.

I once heard a woman give a remarkable account of achievement. An early feminist, she gained renown in the male-dominated field of endocrinology. She brushes shoulders with Nobel laureates and world leaders, and has lived as full and rich a life as any I have known. At the end of her story she said simply, "As I look back, this is what matters. I have loved and been loved, and all the rest is just background music."

Love, too, is why I believe. At the end of life, what else matters? "Love never fails," Paul wrote. "It always protects, always trusts, always hopes, always perseveres." He could only be describing God's love, for no human love meets that standard of perfection. What I have tasted of love on this earth convinces me that a perfect love will not be satisfied with the sad tale of this planet, will not rest until evil is conquered and good reigns, will not allow its object to pass from existence. Perfect love perseveres until it perfects.

Jesus' disciple John brought the two worlds together, a unity forged through love: "For God so loved the world that he gave his one and only Son.... For God did not send his Son into the world to condemn the world, but to save the world through him." Love deems this world worth rescuing.

———

From Bill Broyles, former editor of *Texas Monthly* magazine, I heard a story of two worlds coexisting, a story that became for me a kind of parable. During the Vietnam war, Broyles served the U.S. military near Danang, one of the finest air bases in the world and the pride of the American Air Force. No matter how well the Americans protected it with guards and barbed wire, however, the enemy still managed to infiltrate and destroy valuable airplanes. Broyles could never understand how they did it.

Years later he returned to Vietnam as the guest of a Vietnamese officer, once an enemy, now a friendly host. He got a different view of Danang as the officer escorted him through tunnels no more than three feet high that wound in a labyrinthine network around and under the air base. Broyles reflected on the ironic contrast. Beneath the airmen at Danang, North Vietnamese soldiers were living in muddy tunnels, which they shared with rats, snakes, and slimy creatures of the night. They slept in pools of water and crawled from place to place along dimly lit passageways. They had pitifully inadequate supplies of food, ammunition, and medicines.

Meanwhile, above them, American GIs lounged in air-conditioned rooms, watching the latest movies available through the USO. The GIs kept away boredom by playing cards, smoking dope, and fathering a new race of Amerasians. Many American soldiers got shipped home early for disciplinary reasons; many still suffer from Vietnam syndrome.

The underground army endured temporary sacrifices because they fervently believed they would one day retake the world above ground. They staked their hopes on a future victory, and when that victory arrived the Vietnamese emerged into the daylight and claimed their territory.

Another story with poignant parallels comes from World War II. The classic movie *The Bridge on the River Kwai* starring Alec Guinness, gave some of the background, but not until recently did the book and movie *To End All Wars* fill in details on the extraordinary life of Ernest Gordon, a British Army officer captured at sea by the Japanese at the age of twenty-four.

Gordon was sent to work on the Burma-Siam railway line that the Japanese were constructing through the dense Thai jungle for possible use in an invasion of India. For labour, they conscripted prisoners of war they had captured from occupied countries in Asia and from the British Army itself. Against international law, the Japanese forced even officers to work at manual labour, and each day Gordon would join a work detail of thousands of prisoners who hacked their way through the jungle and built up a track bed through low-lying swampland.

The scene was straight out of Dante. Naked except for loin cloths, the men worked under a broiling sun in 120-degree heat, their bodies stung by insects, their bare feet cut and bruised by sharp stones. Death was commonplace. If a prisoner appeared to be lagging, a Japanese guard would beat him to death, bayonet him, or decapitate him in full view of the other prisoners. Many more men simply dropped dead from exhaustion, malnutrition, and disease. Under these severe conditions, with such inadequate care for prisoners, 80,000 men ultimately died building the railway, 393 fatalities for every mile of track.

Ernest Gordon could feel himself gradually wasting away from a combination of beriberi, worms, malaria, dysentery, and typhoid. Then a virulent case of diphtheria ravaged his throat and palate so severely that when he tried to drink or eat, the rice or water would come gushing out through his nose. As a side effect of the disease, his legs lost all sensation.

Paralysed and unable to eat, Gordon asked to be laid in the Death House, where prisoners on the verge of death were laid out in rows until they stopped breathing. The stench was unbearable. He had no energy even to fight off the bedbugs, lice, and swarming flies. He propped himself up on one elbow long enough to write a final letter to his parents and then lay back to await the inevitable.

Gordon's friends, though, had other plans. They built a new bamboo addition onto their hut on high ground, away from the swamp. They carried his shrivelled body on a stretcher from the contaminated earth floor of the Death House to a new bed of split bamboo, installing him in clean quarters for the first time in months.

Something was astir in the prison camp, something that Gordon would call "Miracle on the River Kwai." For most of the war, the prison camp had been a laboratory of survival of the fittest, every man for himself. In the food line, prisoners fought over the few scraps of vegetables or grains of rice floating in the greasy broth. Officers refused to share any of their special rations. Theft was common in the barracks. Men lived like animals, and hate was the main motivation to stay alive.

Recently, though, a change had come. One event in particular shook the prisoners. Japanese guards carefully counted tools at the end of a day's work, and one day the guard shouted that a shovel was missing. He walked up and down the ranks demanding to know who had stolen it. When no one confessed, he screamed "All die! All die!" and raised his rifle to fire at the first man in the line. At that instant an enlisted man stepped forward, stood at attention, and said, "I did it."

The guard fell on him in a fury, kicking and beating the prisoner, who despite the blows still managed to stand at attention. Enraged, the guard lifted his weapon high in the air and brought the rifle butt down on the soldier's skull. The man sank in a heap to the ground, but the guard continued kicking his motionless body. When the assault finally stopped, the other prisoners picked up their comrade's corpse and marched back to the camp. That evening, when tools were inventoried again, the work crew discovered a mistake had been made: no shovel was missing.

One of the prisoners remembered the verse "Greater love hath no man than this, that a man lay down his life for his friends." Attitudes in the camp began to shift. Prisoners started treating the dying with respect, organizing proper funerals and burials, marking each man's grave with a cross. With no prompting, prisoners began looking out for each other rather than themselves. Thefts grew increasingly rare.

Gordon sensed the change in a very personal way as two fellow Scots volunteered to come each day and care for him. One faithfully dressed the ulcers on his legs and massaged the useless, atrophied muscles. Another brought him food and cleaned his latrine. Yet another prisoner exchanged his own watch for some medicine that might help the infection and fever. After weeks of such tender care, Gordon put on a little weight and, to his amazement, regained partial use of his legs.

The new spirit continued to spread through the camp:

> Death was still with us—no doubt about that. But we were slowly being freed from its destructive grip. We were seeing for ourselves the sharp contrast between the forces that made for life and those that made for death. Selfishness, hatred, envy, jealousy, greed, self-indulgence, laziness and pride were all anti-life. Love, heroism, self-sacrifice, sympathy, mercy, integrity and creative faith, on the other hand, were the essence of life, turning mere existence into living in its truest sense. These were the gifts of God to men. . . .
>
> True, there was hatred. But there was also love. There was death. But there was also life. God had not left us. He was with us, calling us to live the divine life in fellowship.

As Gordon continued to recover, some of the men, knowing he had studied philosophy, asked him to lead a discussion group on ethics. The conversations kept circling around the issue of how to prepare for death, the most urgent question of the camp. Seeking answers, Gordon returned to fragments of faith recalled from his childhood. He had thought little about God for years, but as he would later put it, "Faith thrives when there is no hope but God." By default, Gordon became the unofficial camp chaplain. The prisoners built a tiny church, and each evening they gathered to say prayers for those with greatest needs.

The informal discussion group proved so popular that a "jungle university" began to form. Whoever had expertise in a certain field would teach a course to other students. The university soon offered courses in history, philosophy, economics, mathematics, natural sciences, and at least nine languages, including Latin, Greek, Russian, and Sanskrit. Professors wrote their own textbooks as they went along, on whatever scraps of paper they could find.

Prisoners with artistic talent salvaged bits of charcoal from cooking fires, pounded rocks to make their own paints, and managed to produce enough artwork to mount an exhibition. Two botanists oversaw a garden, specializing in medicinal plants. A few prisoners had smuggled in string instruments, other musicians carved woodwinds out of bamboo, and before long an orchestra formed. One man blessed with a photographic memory could write out the complete scores of symphonies from composers like Beethoven and Schubert, and soon the camp was staging orchestra concerts, ballets, and musical theatre performances.

Gordon's book tells of the transformation of individual men in the camp, a transformation so complete that when liberation finally came the prisoners treated their sadistic guards with kindness and not revenge. Gordon's own life took an unexpected turn. In an about-face from all his previous plans, he enrolled in seminary and became a Presbyterian minister, ending up as Dean of the Chapel at Princeton University, where he died in early 2002, just before the movie about his life was completed.

Two worlds lived side by side in the jungles of Thailand in the early 1940s. The miracle on the River Kwai was no less than the creation of an alternate community, a tiny settlement of the kingdom of God taking root in the least likely soil, a spiritual fellowship that somehow proved more substantial and more real than the world of death and despair all around.

To a man, the prisoners clung to the desperate hope that their lives would not end in a jungle prison in Thailand but would resume, after liberation, back in the hills of Scotland or on the streets of London or wherever they called home. Yet even if it did not, they would endeavour to build a community of faith, beauty, and compassion, nourishing souls even in a place that destroyed bodies.

Perhaps something like this was what Jesus had in mind as he turned again and again to his favourite topic: the kingdom of God. In the soil of this violent, disordered world, an alternate community may take root. It lives in hope of a day of liberation. In the meantime, it aligns itself with another world, not just spreading rumours but planting settlements-in-advance of that coming reign.

———————

To believe in the supernatural is not simply to believe that after living a successful, material, and fairly virtuous life here one will continue to exist in the best-possible substitute for this world, or that after living a starved and stunted life here one will be compensated with all the good things one has gone without: it is to believe that the supernatural is the greatest reality here and now.

T. S. ELIOT

earth matters

> We see either the dust on the window
> or the view beyond the window,
> but never the window itself.
>
> SIMONE WEIL

When the owner of the bed and breakfast suggested we arrive half an hour early for the evening performance of Shakespeare's *Measure for Measure,* we had no clue what awaited us. My wife and I and another couple had driven from Chicago to Stratford, Ontario, for a culturally enriching weekend of classical theatre—or so we thought.

We headed to the theatre early, as suggested, only to find our seats occupied by two characters who seemed quite out of place in a pleasant Canadian village. A young woman with spiky red hair and body-piercing jewelry, wearing a black leather bikini, was nonchalantly playing with chains and a whip. Next to her—actually, handcuffed to her—sat a gorgeous transvestite in full regalia.

The props onstage portrayed not sixteenth-century Vienna, Shakespeare's setting for the play, but rather a modern night club with a stripper's cage suspended from the ceiling. A sleazy master of ceremonies grabbed a microphone and began instructing the audience on how to handle arrests and drug charges, as well as encouraging patrons to remove whatever clothing they wished. As the play began, police officers walked the aisles shining flashlights in our faces. Strobe lighting and the wail of sirens lent realism to the simulated police raid.

Shakespeare's plot, wrenched by director Michael Bogdanov into a modern setting at Stratford, features a vigorous young ruler, Angelo, who decides to strengthen his appeal among the law-and-order crowd in decadent Vienna. Curiously, in a wide-open city that tolerates bribery, corruption, and bordellos, he chooses as his showcase victim a man named Claudio, who has made the single mistake of getting his fiancée pregnant. In order to demonstrate the new order, Angelo decides to enforce a long-neglected law making sexual immorality a capital crime.

Angelo's hypocrisy comes to light when Claudio's sister, Isabella, a beautiful young woman pledged to enter a convent, pleads with him for her brother's life. Smitten, Angelo offers her a cynical deal: if she becomes his secret lover, then he'll commute Claudio's death sentence. Otherwise, Claudio dies.

Torn between her scruples and love for her brother, Isabella agonizes while scenes of decadence play out in the background. Despite the high stakes, Isabella does not waver in her resolve. Reluctantly, she'll let her brother die rather than compromise herself with Angelo.

The play centres on one theme: In an evil time, will anyone stand against the tide? Isabella will, no matter the cost. Shakespeare ultimately resolves Isabella's dilemma through a series of plot twists, but only after she has proved her steadfastness. The play's title comes from the Sermon on the Mount ("For in the same way you judge others, you will be judged, and with the measure you use, it will be measured to you"), and in the end Angelo receives his due measure.

Bogdanov's Stratford production closed with a single spotlight illuminating Isabella, who stood underneath the cage now filled with the motley assortment of strippers, transvestites, and hoodlums from the bar. At last the beasts were confined. In a world of corruption, commercialized sex, and deteriorating values, the director seemed to imply, any remedy must start with one person taking an immovable stand.

I left the theatre that night with a vivid image of the contrast between seductions of the visible world and the spiritual strength required to resist them.

———

Before attending the production in Stratford, I had just read a book titled *Pagans and Christians,* a study of early Christians and the Roman empire. Upper-class Romans of that day practised a morality much like that portrayed in Shakespeare's play: an appearance of virtue on the outside, but decadence behind closed doors. Rome prided itself on tolerance of all points of view. Surely such a broad-minded society could find room for yet another religion spilling over from Palestine.

One emperor made an offer to install Chrestus (Christ) in the Pantheon among the other gods, but the Christians refused, having no interest in becoming one more item in the smorgasbord of Rome's tamed religions. They spurned meat that had been offered to idols, denounced the pagan gods, and boldly denied the emperor's claims to divinity. Instead, they pledged loyalty to an invisible kingdom that took precedence over any visible kingdom ruled by a Caesar.

Like Isabella in Shakespeare's play, early Christians believed they walked a precarious line between good and evil, with every choice tilting dangerously in one direction or the other. How they responded mattered greatly, to God and to God's kingdom they were working to establish on earth. During the persecutions, some sympathetic Roman officials begged the Christians merely to go through the motions of a loyalty oath, but most refused and chose a martyr's death instead.

Thanks to the theatre director's modern appropriation of Shakespeare, I thought too of parallels with our own day. The modern West also encourages tolerance of behaviour and beliefs, and views with alarm any claims to absolute truth. Likewise, we give a nod to civil religion as long as it does not require too much of us. Like the Roman empire and sixteenth-century Vienna, modern society has little place for the notion of an invisible kingdom that demands our loyalty at all costs.

By contrast, at the heart of the Christian view of reality is the stark belief that two worlds coexist on planet Earth, constantly interacting and sometimes colliding, with human beings playing a central role in that drama. Somehow I must come to terms with that point of view and allow it to shape my everyday life. Faith is being "certain of what we do not see," says the book of Hebrews, bringing the two worlds together.

Morton Kelsey, the Episcopalian author and speaker, once showed me a copy of the New Testament in which he had used scissors to cut out every verse dealing with the invisible world. The pages barely held together since Kelsey had excised one-third of its seven thousand verses. He used the tattered Bible to demonstrate how far we moderns have strayed from the emphasis of the New Testament. The apostle Paul yearned so strongly for the invisible world that he told the Philippians he could hardly think of a reason to stay around in this world. "We fix our eyes ... on what is unseen," he wrote elsewhere, as if unaware of the oxymoron.

Reading Paul's letters, I sense that to him the invisible world had a reality more substantial and more trustworthy than the visible world he lived in. I read such passages and hang my head, for many days I must pray for the faith just to believe in the reality of the unseen world. Often for me faith feels mostly like an act of will. I *choose* to believe, and rarely with anything resembling the certainty described by the apostle.

Frankly, the reality of evil is what has strengthened my faith in the invisible world. Shakespeare got it right. Evil reigns in the visible world, presenting itself brazenly and "in your face." God is more subtle, and must be sought. A scene comes to mind of Isabella kneeling onstage, eyes closed, as Angelo beckons her, surrounded by half-naked dancers.

Paul sets out the Christian's challenge in unmistakable terms: "For our struggle is not against flesh and blood, but against the rulers, against the authorities, against the powers of this dark world and against the spiritual forces of evil in the heavenly realms." Such passages used to embarrass me. I had no idea what to make of them. As a child of the modern age, I explained away any talk about supernatural "powers," unable to swallow the notion of a world ruled by invisible spirits. I have changed, however, for the simple reason that my reductionist instincts failed to account for the evil around me.

I had a conversation with Bob Seiple, then president of the relief agency World Vision, after he returned from Rwanda at the time of the massacres there. Standing on a bridge, he had watched thousands of bodies float beneath him on a river scarlet with their blood. Hutu tribesmen had hacked to death with machetes almost a million Tutsis—their neighbours, their fellow parishioners, their school classmates—for reasons no one could begin to explain. Seiple seemed badly shaken. "It was a crisis of faith for me," he said. "There are no categories to express such horror. Someone used the word bestiality—no, that dishonours the beasts. Animals kill for food, not for pleasure. They kill one or two prey at a time, not a million of their own species for no reason at all."

As I listened to Seiple, I too could think of no force in nature to explain what was happening in Rwanda, only a malevolent force from supernature—the same kind of inexplicable force that caused Hitler to divert badly needed resources during wartime in order to carry out genocide against the Jews.

We in the U.S. have recently seen another spiritual power at work, the force of greed, which impelled the directors of companies to siphon off millions of dollars in profits while allowing the companies to go bankrupt, wiping out the retirement savings of thousands of hardworking employees. When Jesus encountered a similar power, which drove people to build beautiful palaces and vast barns while some in Palestine lived as slaves—in other words, when Jesus encountered the first-century equivalent of greedy CEOs—he recognized it as a spiritual power and gave it the name of the god Mammon.

The Bible's language about spiritual powers speaks to actual realities that cannot be adequately described in the terms of evolution and politics. Try to explain on rational grounds the mass insanity that seized

Germany in Hitler's day. Explain the logic behind the Cold War arms race, in which the two strongest nations pursued the precisely named policy of MAD (Mutual Assured Destruction). Explain the rationale behind the overnight collapse of economies in Asia and Latin America, or a sniper who starts picking off suburbanites at shopping malls and gas stations. What keeps a wealthy nation like the United States from finding shelter for its homeless population? What keeps the world from feeding the thousands who die malnourished each day? The experts have no answer but "forces beyond our control." New Testament writers agree and do not hesitate to identify those forces.*

I have not changed my belief in spiritual powers because I learned anything new about this world. I simply learned to recast what I already knew in the language of the Bible. I came to accept the apostle Paul's assertion that our real struggle is waged against forces we cannot see. Much more is happening on this planet than is visible to the human eye. Isabella in Vienna, Ernest Gordon in the Thai jungle, and early Christians in Rome all recognized the struggle and gave their allegiance to an invisible kingdom arrayed against the spiritual powers of this dark world.

As I search the Bible for clues about the invisible world, I find that it consistently pulls the two worlds together, connecting them in a wholistic way. It presents history in parallel scenes, with the invisible world operating out of sight, like the stage machinery that remains hidden from a theatre audience. Occasionally the curtain lifts for a brief glimpse of God at work behind the scenes, but mainly the Bible keeps the focus on the visible world. God works through matter, through people.

The Bible insists the spiritual world is primary, the original source for matter: "By faith we understand that the universe was formed at God's

*The contemporary theologian Walter Wink has done more than any other writer to clarify the biblical concept of powers. His trilogy, *Naming the Powers*, *Unmasking the Powers*, and *Engaging the Powers* gives the full explanation; the one-volume *The Powers That Be* summarizes his thought.

command, so that what is seen was not made out of what was visible."
All of matter—the mountains outside my home, tropical fish darting about
in coral reefs, supernovas releasing more energy than a billion suns—
sprang into existence at the command of God. Its origin in the spiritual
world makes history more valuable, not less. It exists because God wants
it to exist; *we* exist for the same reason.

Much of the Bible, in fact, reads like a history book. Here is its "plot."
A single family of nomads migrates into Egypt, becomes a large tribe,
escapes from slavery, then travels to their original homeland, which they
must retake by force. They form a nation, which flourishes for a brief time
and then divides in two and succumbs to attacks by its larger neighbours.
After several centuries pass, the emerging empires of Greece and then
Rome conquer the territory, and in that puppet state a new prophet arises,
Jesus by name, whom some see as the promised Messiah. He is executed,
and a new religion forms around him, which opens up the Jewish heritage
to all other races.

That, at least, summarizes the outer level of history. The Prophets
give the inside view. God establishes a covenant with one family and later
rescues them from slavery in Egypt. God ushers these chosen people
through the harsh Sinai wilderness and leads them in a campaign to
retake a land that has been despoiled. They repeatedly break their
covenant with God, however, and each time punishment comes in the
form of foreign invasion. Finally, after sending many prophets to warn
them, God sends his own Son to earth. Jesus dies and is resurrected, and
as a result something permanently alters in the universe. For the first time,
all people have the opportunity for peace with God. Moreover, all of
human history points toward a culmination in which the Messiah will
return and restore the earth to its original design.

Note that both scenarios describe the same history. A secular historian would no doubt record the "natural" cycle of empires rising and
falling, while an Israelite prophet would emphasize instead the principle
that righteousness and justice exalt a nation. According to this inside
view, a nation built on the back of injustice—exploiting the poor,

oppressing slaves, forgetting God, raping the land—will inevitably pay the consequences.*

The Bible underscores the connection between the physical and spiritual worlds, not the division. Pierre Teilhard de Chardin tried to correct the modern bias by insisting, "We are not human beings having a spiritual experience, we are spiritual beings having a human experience." Even that fails to get it right. Rather, we are incomplete beings awaiting a complete experience, fragmented beings awaiting unity. Establishing contact with the unseen world while on this earth begins that process.

After death the two worlds will come together fully. Paul describes it as a kind of maturity or completion of what started on earth: "Now we see but a poor reflection as in a mirror; then we shall see face to face. Now I know in part; then I shall know fully, even as I am fully known." He gives few technical details, just a strong promise that life will be better: "The body that is sown is perishable, it is raised imperishable; it is sown in dishonour, it is raised in glory; it is sown in weakness, it is raised in power; it is sown a natural body, it is raised a spiritual body."

We have a model of the two worlds coming together in Jesus, the only human being who experienced completeness in this visible world. Sometimes he fasted, sometimes he banqueted. He pulled fish from a lake and transformed water into wine, apparently revelling in matter. While speaking of the invisible world he used these everyday objects and others—wheat, sheep, wildflowers, oxen—as signs of another world. The visible world was, for Jesus, a kind of medium: he lived in its environment while always aware of what lay beyond.

---

*One could apply the same model to modern states—fascist or Marxist governments that consolidate power by killing millions, rich nations that neglect the weak and aged and poor, multiracial states that keep one minority on the bottom—and predict a similar fate as befell ancient Israel (not to mention Babylon, Assyria, Persia, Greece, and Rome). In fact, modern prophets follow exactly this pattern. Martin Luther King Jr cast the war against racism as a spiritual movement, not just a political campaign. In city after city, Billy Graham has pointed to the spiritual roots of the problems in modern civilization. Aleksandr Solzhenitsyn summarizes the chaos of twentieth-century Russia as a fruit of a society that forgot God. In other words, prophets look beyond the outer signs to the inner powers at work.

To his followers, Jesus hinted at the effect they were having on the world beyond their vision. "I saw Satan fall like lightning from heaven," he told one group as they returned from a mission trip. They had been walking over hot sand, knocking on doors, asking to see the sick, announcing the coming of Jesus. All their actions took place in the visible world, which they could touch, smell, and see. Jesus, with supernatural insight, saw that those actions in the visible world were having a startling impact on the invisible world.

The world we live in is not an either/or world. What I do as a Christian—praying, worshipping, demonstrating God's love to the sick, needy, and imprisoned—is not exclusively supernatural or natural, but both working at the same time. Perhaps if Jesus stood in the flesh beside me, murmuring phrases like "I saw Satan fall" whenever I acted in his name, I would remember better the connections between the two worlds.

———

In the poem "Mans medley," George Herbert contrasts the lives of animals and angels, who inhabit different worlds. Only the human animal "makes them one, / With th' one hand touching heav'n, with th' other earth." We humans straddle visible and invisible realities.

I thought about my state of suspension between two worlds when I went out in a rubber Zodiac boat to watch sperm whales off the coast of New Zealand. The whale would rest on the surface for a while, then breathe deeply a few times, his exhalations creating a spectacular spout, before lifting his tail flukes high above the water and plunging a mile deep to feed on squid. Our guide would mark the spot, go hunt more whales, and return forty-five minutes later to let us watch the original sperm whale surface for a gigantic gulp of fresh air.

To the whale, most of my daily surroundings—mountains, cities, highways—exist in an "invisible" world, for its eyes can only take in sights level with the waterline. The whale has its own lively, congested habitat of marine plants and sea creatures. Yet unless it surfaces for oxygen once an hour or so, it dies. Though it knows little about the world above the sea, it needs vital contact with it simply to survive.

Spiritually, I sometimes feel like that whale, coming up for air at regular intervals to stay alive, then disappearing into a much more familiar environment in the cold and dark below. Even as I write that analogy, though, I realize its deceptive inadequacy, for it summons up the image of a universe with "upper" and "lower" stories that occasionally interact. Such an image has more in common with a pagan world view, of an angry Zeus aiming thunderbolts at the earth below.

The biblical view is at once more subtle and more connected. It presents reality as a seamless whole, with no neat division between sacred and profane or between natural and supernatural. There is only God's world, a sacred world, which has been profaned by human rebellion. Our mission is to bring the two together, to reconnect and hallow God's world, to build settlements of God's kingdom in the desecrated habitat of earth.

The same God who created the visible world actively sustains it. As Paul presents it, "For by him all things were created: things in heaven and on earth, visible and invisible, whether thrones or powers or rulers or authorities; all things were created by him and for him. He is before all things, and in him all things hold together." The picture more resembles the alternate universes described by theoretical physicists, in which two different worlds coexist, with every action in one having an immediate but hard-to-detect impact on the other.

Surely the Bible tells of miracles, when the invisible world seems for an instant to change the rules of the visible world. It is all too easy, however, to focus on the supernatural exceptions, to celebrate the miracles surrounding the Exodus from Egypt without noticing the four centuries of silence that preceded it or the four decades of wilderness misery that followed.

In fact, as I review the record, it almost seems that God prefers to work through means that to the human observer seem least supernatural. Consider Jesus' birth, the event that started the entire Christian faith. Miracles did occur—the Virgin Birth, some dreams, a bright star, frightened shepherds—though few observers knew of them. In many ways the first Christmas was a fairly normal process. A young girl went through nine months of pregnancy. Then came a tiresome journey on a donkey and the most humble birth imaginable, in an animal shelter. The Son of God came quietly.

Behind the scenes, however, God had been at work. Alexander the Great had conquered the region and taught it a common language. The Romans subsequently built a superb system of roads (which the disciples would use to spread the faith). A government census forced a difficult journey, changing Jesus' birthplace. Many factors that had no obvious supernatural significance came together at the precise point in history when Christianity was born.

As I have mentioned, the apostle Paul had an acute awareness of the unseen world. Yet as I read his story in Acts and in his letters, I see him commonly relying on "natural" means: using logic to debate the Athenians, accepting hospitality in order to establish churches, training and cajoling subordinates, insisting on his rights in Roman courts, fleeing from danger. He fills his letters with practical advice—settle lawsuits, feed the hungry, comfort the sick, forgive offences, love your spouse—presenting these as spiritual acts, offerings of service to God.

"Work out your salvation with fear and trembling," Paul tells the Philippians, and then adds an apparent contradiction, "for it is God who works in you to will and to act according to his good purpose." Paul saw no contradiction. The two worlds, visible and invisible, appear distinct only to those of us with limited vision.

———

All over the world today, millions of Christians prayed the Lord's Prayer, including the phrase "your will be done on earth as it is in heaven." We do not need to look far to see how much remains to be answered in that prayer. "As above, so below," Jesus prayed, in essence, and then left us to give flesh to that request.

For the planet, God's will done on earth as it is in heaven would mean food, water, and homes for all who lack, justice in politics and economics, peace between nations, harmony with nature, healing and comfort for the sick, souls reconnected to their spiritual source. For each of us, God's will means some small role in furthering the above.

Of course, every religion accepts some version of "As above, so below." Hesiod wrote of the Greek gods, "Zeus rules the world, and with resistless sway / Takes back tomorrow what he grants today." Even now taxi drivers in India mount their favourite idols on the dashboard so the gods will look favourably on them in the day's traffic. Jesus introduced a further, far more radical notion, a reversal of the formula: "As below, so above." This time, earth provokes heaven.

"I tell you the truth, whatever you bind on earth will be bound in heaven, and whatever you loose on earth will be loosed in heaven," Jesus told Peter. He said that our practical response to the sick and imprisoned, the hungry and needy, would contribute to our eternal destiny—would be the same, in fact, as if we had ministered to him in person.

As below, so above: Transposing two words changes everything. The most common, mundane tasks we do on earth—writing a prisoner, visiting a nursing home, comforting a neighbour, standing strong like Isabella against a decadent world—become charged with eternal significance. The ultimate destiny of the world, and of ourselves, is being played out right now. Everything matters, in ways we cannot yet see.

If we lived in a state where virtue was profitable, common sense would make us good, and greed would make us saintly. And we'd live as animals or angels in the happy land that needs no heroes. But since in fact we see that avarice, anger, envy, pride, sloth, lust, and stupidity commonly profit far beyond humility, chastity, fortitude, justice and thought, and have to choose to be human at all, why then perhaps we must stand fast a little, even at the risk of being heroes.

Sir Thomas More in Robert Bolt's *A Man for All Seasons*

CHAPTER TWELVE

eyes of faith

One man succeeds in everything, and so loses all. Another meets with
nothing but crosses and disappointments, and thereby gains more than all
the world is worth.

WILLIAM LAW

I first learned about the Elephant Man through the book about him by
anthropologist Ashley Montagu. Later I saw a play based on his life,
starring David Bowie, and also the David Lynch movie that made him
famous. The Elephant Man was an actual person named John Merrick
who lived in England in the nineteenth century, and who died in 1890 at
the age of twenty-seven. I know no better illustration of the clash in values between two worlds, still less the eternal mystery of a human being.
Montagu must have agreed, for this is how his book begins:

> What is a human life? A pulse in the heartbeat of eternity? A cry that
> begins with birth and ends with death? A brief and tempestuous
> sojourn on an inhospitable shore, where there is really neither joy, nor
> love, nor light, nor certitude, nor peace, nor help for pain? Or is it, is
> it, something more?
>
> In this book, I think, lies something of the answer to these questions.

Montagu seems genuinely puzzled by the Elephant Man. According to the principles of behaviourism, the kind of treatment John Merrick received in childhood should have produced an adult with the personality of a beaten dog. It did not.

Merrick was possibly the ugliest human being who has ever lived. A disorder known as *neurofibromatosis* worked progressively from the earliest years of childhood to turn him into a human freak. At the age of four he was abandoned by his mother and sent to a workhouse. At fourteen a carnival showman discovered him and decided to make money from his freakish appearance. Onlookers would pay a few pennies to step into a booth and gawk at a person so misshapen that, at a certain angle, he resembled an elephant with its protruding trunk and leathery folds of skin.

One day Frederick Treves, a surgeon at London Hospital, wandered across the street to the carnival after hours, noticed the crude rendition of a human elephant on the canvas flap of one booth, and paid the showman a shilling to let him inside. He saw a creature huddled next to a Bunsen burner for warmth, lit by the faint blue light of the gas jet. This hunched-over figure shrouded under a blanket seemed the embodiment of loneliness and despair.

As if giving orders to a dog, the showman yelled, "Stand up!" The creature arose and let the blanket fall to the ground, revealing to Treves "the most disgusting specimen of humanity that I have ever seen."

Treves goes on to describe the Elephant Man's deformities in clinical detail: a bony mass protruding from his brow; spongy skin, with a fissured surface resembling brown cauliflower hanging in folds from his back; a huge, misshapen head the circumference of a man's waist; the mouth a distorted, slobbering aperture; the nose a dangling lump of skin; a bag of flesh like the dewlap of a lizard suspended from the chest. His right arm was overgrown to twice its normal size, its fingers stubby and useless. Flaps of skin in the shape of a paddle descended from one armpit; deformed legs supported him only if he held onto a chair. A sickening stench emanated from the fungous skin growths.

His repulsion overcome by curiosity about the man's medical condition, Dr Treves arranged to have John Merrick, now twenty-one years of age, examined in his hospital. Because of the mouth deformities, Merrick spoke in unintelligible splutters, and Treves judged him an imbecile. After taking photographs and copious notes, he tried in vain to communicate further, gave Merrick his card, and returned him to the custody of the showman. The next day police raided the carnival, and Treves assumed he would never see the Elephant Man again.

For two more years John Merrick lived the life of an outcast, housed like a circus animal and led out to entertain curiosity-seekers, who invariably responded with shrieks of horror. When authorities in Belgium shut down the roving carnival for good, his keeper pocketed Merrick's share of the ticket proceeds and shipped him back to London.

During the journey other passengers tormented him, lifting the hem of his cloak to peek at his grotesque body. At the train station in London, policemen rescued him and took him to an unused waiting room, where he sank into a heap in a dark corner, muttering words they could not understand. He had only one ray of hope: the card of Dr Frederick Treves, which he had kept in a pocket for two years.

Treves answered the police summons, found Merrick huddled whimpering in a corner, and escorted him to the hospital's isolation ward. He had had nothing to eat or drink since leaving Belgium. Treves ordered a tray from the hospital cafeteria, but the nurse who delivered it, unprepared for such a sight, screamed, dropped the tray, and fled from the room. The patient, inured to such reactions, hardly noticed.

Over time, the hospital staff got accustomed to their unusual resident. Daily baths eliminated the stench. With practise, Treves learned to understand Merrick's speech, and much to his surprise he discovered that, far from being an imbecile, Merrick was literate and in fact a voracious reader. He had studied the Bible and the Book of Common Prayer, and knew Jane Austen and Shakespeare. Treves writes,

> His troubles had ennobled him. He showed himself to be a gentle,
> affectionate and lovable creature ... without a grievance and without

an unkind word for anyone. I have never heard him complain. I have never heard him deplore his ruined life or resent the treatment he had received at the hands of callous keepers. His journey through life had been indeed along a *via dolorosa,* the road had been uphill all the way, and now, when the night was blackest and the way most steep, he had found himself, as it were, in a friendly inn, bright with light and warm with welcome.

It mystified Treves that a person robbed of childhood, treated like a wild beast, exploited, with not a single memory of pleasure, a creature reviled and void of hope, could survive, let alone emerge with such an agreeable disposition. At first Merrick meekly inquired whether he might enter an asylum for the blind. He had read about such places and longed to live among people who could not stare at him. Gradually, though, Treves and the staff earned his trust, and a room in the hospital attic became the Elephant Man's home.

Treves determined to introduce Merrick to the pleasures he had never known. He owned no possessions other than a cane, a full-length black cloak that hid his deformities, an oversized hat with a veil, and a portrait of his beautiful mother. He spoke adoringly of women, even though every woman had treated him as an object of loathing. Treves persuaded a friend of his, a young and pretty widow, to enter Merrick's room with a smile, wish him good morning, and shake his hand—in short, to treat him as a human being.

"The effect upon poor Merrick was not quite what I had expected," Treves reports. "As he let go her hand he bent his head on his knees and sobbed until I thought he would never cease.... He told me afterwards that this was the first woman who had ever smiled at him, and the first woman, in the whole of his life, who had shaken hands with him. From this day the transformation of Merrick commenced and he began to change, little by little, from a hunted thing into a man."

The widow was not the last woman to shake his hand. As word of the Elephant Man spread, celebrities, actresses, and even the princess of

Wales, soon to be Queen Alexandra, stopped by the hospital for a visit. The hospital chaplain befriended him and served him communion. Dr Treves arranged to smuggle Merrick into the private boxes of London theatres, where he saw his first plays.

When Treves found a guest house available in the country, Merrick got an introduction to the world of nature, away from the prying eyes of humans. He listened to songbirds, flushed a rabbit, befriended a dog, watched trout darting in a stream. He picked wildflowers and brought samples back to Treves. To each new life experience he responded with childlike wonder. "I am happy every hour of the day," he kept repeating.

Using his left hand, the only one functional, Merrick began constructing models of buildings, gluing together carefully chosen bits of coloured paper and cardboard. He presented the finished models to the celebrities who visited him and to hospital staff. From his room, which overlooked the Church of St Philip on one corner, he could watch a new hospital church going up, and using the two churches as models he worked for many days to create an exquisite model of a cathedral, fitting in place a cardboard replica of each tiny stone and tile. He called the new church outside "an imitation of grace flying up and up from the mud," and his own model, "my imitation of an imitation."

After four years of happiness, the only happiness he had ever known, Merrick died in his sleep. His massive head had fallen back on his pillow, crushing the vertebrae in his neck and asphyxiating him. The hospital made plaster casts of his body as a record of his rare disorder. Some can still be seen in the London Hospital museum, along with the model cathedral, "an imitation of grace flying up and up from the mud." Like John Merrick's life.

———

I have retold the familiar story of the Elephant Man because I believe it poses a crucial test for Christians and materialists alike.

For those who regard the visible world as all there is, the question arises whether the Elephant Man should have been allowed to live.

Friedrich Nietzsche scorned Christianity for taking the side of all that is weak, base, and unfit. A religion based on pity, he said, went against evolution and its principles of fitness and competition. In Nietzsche's one-world philosophy, the Elephant Man had no right to existence, no intrinsic worth, no "soul" worth preserving. Why value an obvious freak of nature? Best to eliminate such a defect from the gene pool. The Nazi regime carried Nietzsche's sentiment to its logical conclusion, setting up extermination centres for the mentally handicapped and severely disabled.*

Nietzsche's cold logic reverberates in some places today. In early 2003 the *New York Times* magazine published an article by Harriet McBryde Johnson, a disability rights attorney who suffers from a muscle-wasting disease. She hunches over, makes uncoordinated movements, has difficulty feeding herself, and gets about in a power wheelchair. The article tells of her confrontation with Peter Singer, a professor of ethics at Princeton University, often called the most influential philosopher of our time.

Johnson debated Singer on behalf of an activist group called Not Dead Yet, for Singer proposes that parents should have the right to kill their disabled babies so they can replace them with nondisabled babies, who would have a greater chance at happiness. Before agreeing to the debate, Johnson reflected on the terrible plight of being "sucked into a civil discussion of whether I ought to exist." Singer, an atheist, sees the issue in terms of the laws of nature and utilitarian philosophy.

---

*Charles Darwin himself did not shrink from the logical conclusions of natural selection. As he wrote in *The Descent of Man,* "With savages, the weak in body or mind are soon eliminated; and those that survive commonly exhibit a vigorous state of health. We civilized men, on the other hand, do our utmost to check the process of elimination; we build asylums for the imbecile, the maimed, and the sick; we institute poor laws; and our medical men exert their utmost skill to save the life of everyone to the last moment. There is reason to believe that vaccination has preserved thousands who from a weak constitution would formerly have succumbed to smallpox. Thus the weak members of civilized society propagate their kind. No one who has attended to the breeding of domestic animals will doubt that this must be highly injurious to the race of man."

Darwin used the same logic in speaking of "higher" and "lower" races, predicting that "the civilized races of man will almost certainly exterminate, and replace, the savage races throughout the world."

Also an atheist, Johnson gropes for the best response and defends her right to live what Singer considers an "inferior" life. Johnson's article—more, her very life—offers a passionate, witty, and compelling defence of her right to existence, contra the principle of survival of the fittest. At one point she wonders, "Am I a person of faith after all?"

For Christians, people like Harriet Johnson and the Elephant Man pose a different sort of test. We assume their right to exist, as human beings made in God's image. Can we, though, see the weak and "unfit" as God sees them? "Give us weak eyes for things of no account," prayed the philosopher Søren Kierkegaard. Perhaps he should have prayed for strong ones, eyes of faith, for such are required in a world that so highly values appearance and competence.

In a way, Nietzsche was right: Christ's followers are called to defy the merciless scheme of evolutionary struggle. The Elephant Man stands as an extreme example of history's great divide between winners and losers. The beautiful have always enjoyed rewards beyond the reach of the ugly, the strong have always dominated the weak, a small number of rich have always lived at the expense of the poor. Against that reality, God's kingdom flies a flag of divine opposition.

As biological creatures, we share a planet with animals that flaunt their beauty to attract mates, fight off competitors for food, and abandon the sick and lame that might slow down the herd. Yet we humans are called to transcend instinct, to look past the surface appearance to the image of God inside, to cherish and not disdain the weak and unlovely.* God's own Son, after all, put himself on their side.

Jesus was the first world leader to inaugurate a kingdom with a heroic role for losers. He spoke to an audience raised on stories of wealthy patriarchs, strong kings, and victorious heroes. Much to their surprise, he honoured instead people who have little value in the visible world: the poor and meek, the persecuted and those who mourn, social rejects, the

---

*American theologian Jonathan Edwards based his concept of justice on his belief that no one is so worthless "but the Lord shows him to be one to whom he has deigned to give the beauty of his image."

hungry and thirsty. His stories consistently featured "the wrong people" as heroes: the prodigal, not the responsible son; the good Samaritan, not the good Jew; Lazarus, not the rich man; the tax collector, not the Pharisee. As Charles Spurgeon, the British preacher and John Merrick's contemporary, expressed it, "His glory was that He laid aside His glory, and the glory of the church is when she lays aside her respectability and her dignity, and counts it to be her glory to gather together the outcasts."

In the same vein, the apostle Paul gave this frank appraisal of those who comprise God's kingdom: "Not many of you were wise by human standards; not many were influential; not many were of noble birth." The wise, the influential, the nobly born find too many attractions in the visible world, a milieu in which they thrive. "But God chose the foolish things of the world to shame the wise; God chose the weak things of the world to shame the strong. He chose the lowly things of this world and the despised things—and the things that are not—to nullify the things that are, so that no one may boast before him."

The few scraps of writing John Merrick left behind show that he found a home in a faith that gathers together outcasts. God himself assured the prophet Samuel, "The Lord does not look at the things man looks at. Man looks at the outward appearance, but the Lord looks at the heart." Everyone who met the Elephant Man went away marvelling that such a pure and gentle soul—such a heart—could live inside that monstrous exterior.

———

Modern society excels at the visual image, the external. We get a steady barrage of eye-catching images on billboards, TV screens, the Internet, and even cellphone displays. (Visitors to the U.S. are often surprised to see so many overweight and ugly people walking the streets, for on television shows and billboards they have seen sexy bodies, chiselled faces, clean hair, and perfect teeth.) As a result, more than ever before we ascribe worth based on appearance. Disabled Americans tell of people responding to them with shame, indignation, revulsion, and even anger—a mild version of what the Elephant Man dealt with continually.

A book titled *The Body Project* points out the modern fixation on the body and external appearance by comparing the diaries of adolescent girls from a century ago to those of modern times. One typical girl of the 1890s wrote, "Resolved, to think before speaking. To work seriously. To be self-restrained in conversations and actions. Not to let my thoughts wander. To be dignified. Interest myself more in others." Her counterpart in the 1990s recorded these goals: "I will try to make myself better in any way I possibly can.... I will lose weight, get new lenses, already got new haircut, good make-up, new clothes and accessories."

Our culture values youthful appearance above all else, an understandable ideal for a people unsure about an afterlife. Youth represents the only sure stay against an uncertain future. As a result, whatever preserves the illusion of youth flourishes: vitamin supplements, diet programmes, exercise machines. Conversely, any sign of ageing brings to mind the end of life and so the health industry promotes cures for baldness and impotence, along with wrinkle creams, cosmetic surgery, and other elaborate means to mask the effects of ageing.

The average news-stand gives a straightforward display of these and other values of modern life. *Cosmopolitan, Shape, Swimsuit,* and soft porn titles like *FHM* and *Maxim* focus on physical appearance. *Fortune, Money, Travel and Leisure,* and their competitors trumpet the advantages of wealth and economic success. A magazine rack, designed to appeal to impulse buying, broadcasts cultural values: large breasts on women, firm muscles on men and women, an obsession with food and clothing, hot cars, stereo sound.

I admit it: I buy some of those magazines, the ones that cover my interests. I sample new foods, look for travel hints, and shop for advances in computer technology. I follow a few professional sports and exercise faithfully three times a week. I feel a constant tension between enjoying the good things abundant on this planet and not allowing them to blind me to the less fortunate. How can I celebrate the contributions of both the super-athlete Lance Armstrong and the Elephant Man?

The key, I have found, is to think of myself as an amphibian living in two different environments at once, physical and spiritual. In one, I breathe without thinking. In the other, I must set my mind to the task. It takes no effort to notice a gorgeous specimen of humanity or a neighbour's new sports car. It takes continuous effort to pay attention to a homeless person with a hand-lettered sign asking for food or a single mother with a disabled child who lives down the block.

Those who believe only in the visible world have a single proving ground of worth, and for this reason they celebrate beauty, success, wealth, talent—the values on prominent display at the magazine rack. The winners who excel get an ample reward in our celebrity culture.

On the other hand, if I believe in two worlds I will look on the same values differently. With gratitude I accept the grace of athletes, the beauty of supermodels, the talent of successful people as God's gifts. God is, after all, the creator and sustainer of all good things on this earth. At the same time, I ask that my eyes be opened to a different kind of beauty, one that lies beneath the surface, as manifest in the Elephant Man. Those who have no chance for success in the visible world may, after all, lead the way in God's kingdom.

All too often, the attractions of the visible world simply overwhelm those of the invisible. Three centuries after Jesus, when the church had already spread throughout the Roman Empire, John Chrysostom complained, "We admire wealth equally with them [non-Christians], and even more. We have the same horror of death, the same dread of poverty, the same impatience of disease; we are equally fond of glory and of rule.... How then can they believe?"

To keep some sort of balance, I must consciously call to mind the apostle Paul's advice, "Set your minds on things above, not on earthly things." He said that in full knowledge we would continue to fill our minds with earthly things. Earthlings have little choice, for the visible world is our home and we absorb its surrounding culture by osmosis.

Daily we breathe the air of an environment that exalts success and physical appearance.

There are exceptions to the trend, of course, lingering whispers of truth. As I stand before the magazines, I notice that the values on display have something in common. Net worth, body shape, muscle tone, beauty secrets, possessions: each of these is transitory. I have attended my share of funerals, and not once have friends and family members eulogized about the deceased's bank account or physical shape or surround-sound stereo system. Instead, they speak of qualities like kindness and generosity and love for family—sometimes even stretching the truth—as if conceding that in the end only these qualities endure.

Left alone, we humans too often make judgements based on the surface: appearance, race, income. Jesus entered our world—he "came down from heaven"—to establish a kingdom based on those more lasting values. What we emphasize too late, at a person's funeral, he set as a baseline. Jesus' vision of life does not "make sense" in the visible world. We are taught to look out for number one, to compete, to insist on fairness, to protect ourselves, to build a secure nest egg, to minimize risk—all reflexes that the Sermon on the Mount directly contradicts.

Rather, the kingdom of heaven recasts life on this planet from Jesus' own perspective, the perspective of two worlds. His words seem revolutionary to us only because we think like people who live an average of sixty or seventy years on a planet made of rocks and trees and soil. Jesus introduced a new way of thinking, raising sights to a life that extends into eternity and involves unseen worlds we have not the capacity to detect. He came to establish an alternate community centred on values from that invisible world, "on earth as it is in heaven."

Seen in that light, the kingdom of heaven prescribes a way of life that promotes what matters most and lasts longest.

———

From now on we regard no one from a worldly point of view," Paul wrote the Corinthians. He concluded by saying that God has now relegated to the followers of Jesus the message of reconciliation with God, adding this remarkable phrase: "as though God were making his appeal through us." I shudder at the sheer audacity of God entrusting such a task—*God making his appeal through us*—to a species known for making divisions between beautiful and ugly, rich and poor, dark-skinned and light, male and female, strong and weak.

Taking God's assignment seriously means that I must learn to look at the world upside down, as Jesus did. Instead of seeking out people who stroke my ego, I find those whose egos need stroking; instead of important people with resources who can do me favours, I find people with few resources; instead of the strong, I look for the weak; instead of the healthy, the sick. Is not this how God reconciles the world to himself? Did Jesus not insist that he came for the sinners and not the righteous, for the sick and not the healthy?

This, then, is the final step in resolving the tension between the values of two worlds. God's gifts are best used in the visible world when we give them away in serving those who have less. In the process we learn, as Henri Nouwen wrote of his experience in a South American slum, "to recognize the Lord's voice, his face, and his touch in every person we meet." As though God were making his appeal through *them* as well as through us.

Dr Frederick Treves found treasure hidden in the misshapen disguise of the Elephant Man. These are his final words about the patient who became his friend: "As a specimen of humanity, Merrick was ignoble and repulsive; but the spirit of Merrick, if it could be seen in the form of the living, would assume the figure of an upstanding and heroic man, smooth browed and clean of limb, with eyes that flashed undaunted courage."

The founder of the l'Arche homes for the mentally disabled, Jean Vanier, says that people often look upon him as mad. The brilliantly educated son of a Governor-General of Canada, he recruits skilled workers (Henri Nouwen was one) to serve and live among damaged people whose IQs register in the low double digits. Vanier shrugs off those who second-guess his choices by saying he would rather be crazy by following the foolishness of the Gospel than the non-sense of the values of our world. Furthermore, Vanier insists that those who serve the deformed and damaged benefit as much as the ones whom they are helping. Even the most disabled individuals respond instinctively to love, and in so doing they awaken what is most important in a human being: compassion, generosity, humility, love. Paradoxically, they replenish life in the very helpers who serve them.

In India I have worshipped among leprosy patients whose physical deformities provoke the same response from onlookers that John Merrick's did. Most of the medical advances in the treatment of leprosy came about as a result of missionary doctors, who alone were willing to live among patients and risk exposure to study the dreaded disease. As a result, Christian churches thrive in most major leprosy centres.

In Myanmar, the former Burma, I have visited homes for AIDS orphans, where Christian volunteers try to replace parental affection the disease has stolen away. In Jean Vanier's centre in Toronto, I have watched a scholarly priest lavish daily care on a middle-aged man so mentally handicapped that he could not speak a word. The most rousing church services I have attended took place in Chile and Peru, in the bowels of a federal prison. Among the lowly, the wretched, the downtrodden, the rejects, God's kingdom takes root.

Jesse Jackson tells the story of a visit to the University of Southern Mississippi. While touring the campus with the university president, he noticed a towering male student, six-feet, eight-inches tall, holding hands with a midget coed barely three-feet tall. His curiosity piqued, Jackson stopped to watch as the young man, dressed in a warm-up suit, tenderly picked up the midget, kissed her, and sent her off to class. The president explained that the student was a star basketball player. Both parents had died in his youth, and he made a vow to look after his sister. Many scholarship offers came his way, but only Southern Mississippi offered one to his sister too.

Jackson went over to the basketball star, introduced himself, and said he appreciated him looking out for his sister. The athlete shrugged and said, "Those of us who God makes six-eight have to look out for those he makes three-three."

———

I spent an afternoon with a man whose life trajectory has described an arc of success in both worlds, physical and spiritual. Jimmy Carter succeeded at everything he tried: as an officer in the U.S. Navy, as a nuclear engineer, as a gentleman farmer, as a governor of Georgia. He came out of nowhere to gain the most powerful position in the world, that of president of the United States.

Jimmy Carter has never made a secret of his Christian faith. Even while president, he taught a weekly Sunday School class at a Baptist church. He spoke openly to foreign leaders about his faith and continues to do so whenever asked. As well as any public figure in recent times, Carter understands the difference between the kingdom of heaven and the kingdom of this world.

After an artery-clogging Southern feast, I asked the former president to reflect on what he had learned while exercising his gifts in two different kingdoms. To my surprise, Carter spent much of his time discussing failure, not success. His descent from fame reversed his meteoric rise. After losing the 1980 election to Ronald Reagan, he returned to Plains, Georgia, a broken man, scorned even by fellow Democrats. His family business, held in a blind trust during his term, had accumulated a million-dollar debt.

From that shaky platform, Carter began to rebuild. After writing a book to pay off debts, he established a centre in Atlanta to foster programmes he believed in. Due mainly to his emphasis on human rights, many developing nations still looked to him as an important leader, and Carter responded with visionary programmes. A democracy project began monitoring elections all over the world. His support of Habitat for Humanity brought publicity and funding to that fledgling organization. His foundation targeted a handful of major diseases that plague poor nations, and as a result both guinea worm and river blindness have nearly been eliminated.

Every weekend he was in town, Carter also taught Sunday School. Word got out, and soon tour buses began filling the parking lot of Maranatha Baptist Church. A congregation of eighty to a hundred found themselves swamped with three hundred, five hundred, even a thousand visitors on Sundays. CNN donated some used cameras, and the Sunday School class now accommodates overflow crowds with a video hook-up in another room. Every other month he takes his turn cutting the grass outside the church while Rosalynn, his wife, cleans the bathrooms indoors.

Around town, I heard stories of how Carter wields his power. When Habitat for Humanity boasted about eliminating all substandard housing in Sumter County, Carter telephoned to tell them about Josephine, who lived in a house with holes in its siding plugged with rags. When a young woman in the church entered adulthood with a face badly deformed from a genetic defect, Carter called the head of Emory Hospital in Atlanta and arranged for plastic surgery.

Carter showed me paulownia trees he is raising on a plot in his back-yard—"the fastest-growing tree in the world," he claims—hoping they might solve the terrible problems of deforestation. He keeps cranking out books, hammering nails for Habitat, judging elections. Rosalynn champions the causes of childhood immunization and treatment for mental illness. Together, they seem the ideal small-town citizens, if you forget for a moment that they used to entertain kings and queens and slept next to a briefcase with nuclear codes that could destroy the planet.

Carter's reputation has recovered well. In 2002 he received perhaps the most prestigious honour on earth, the Nobel Peace Prize. He remains on a first-name basis with world leaders and commands respect and attention wherever he goes. In a stunning reversal, he now makes the list of most admired presidents, and if someone held a contest for best ex-president, he would win hands down. While others leave the White House to enjoy golf or to cash in on their celebrity status, the Carters have devoted themselves to service.

The Carters' story brings to mind Jesus' statement "For whoever wants to save his life will lose it, but whoever loses his life for me and for the gospel will save it." When asked to reflect on his life—engineer, naval officer, peanut farmer, governor, president—and name what phase he most enjoyed, Carter thought for a minute, then flashed that famous smile and said, "Now."

———————

If the world is sane, then Jesus is mad as a hatter and the Last Supper is the Mad Tea Party. The world says, Mind your own business, and Jesus says, There is no such thing as your own business. The world says, Follow the wisest course and be a success, and Jesus says, Follow me and be crucified. The world says, Drive carefully—the life you save may be your own—and Jesus says, Whoever would save his life will lose it, and whoever loses his life for my sake will find it. The world says, Law and order, and Jesus says, Love. The world says, Get, and Jesus says, Give. In terms of the world's sanity, Jesus is crazy as a coot, and anybody who thinks he can follow him without being a little crazy too is labouring less under the cross than under a delusion. "We are fools for Christ's sake," Paul says, faith says—the faith that ultimately the foolishness of God is wiser than the wisdom of men, the lunacy of Jesus saner than the grim sanity of the world.

FREDERICK BUECHNER

CHAPTER THIRTEEN

practising the existence of God

... for this was all thy care—
To stand approved in sight of God, though worlds
Judged thee perverse.

JOHN MILTON

Søren Kierkegaard once wrote a parody styled after the book of Ecclesiastes:

> I saw that the meaning of life was to secure a livelihood, and that its goal was to attain a high position; that love's rich dream was marriage with an heiress; that friendship's blessing was help in financial difficulties; that wisdom was what the majority assumed it to be; that enthusiasm consisted in making a speech; that it was courage to risk the loss of ten dollars; that kindness consisted in saying, "You are welcome," at the dinner table; that piety consisted in going to communion once a year. This I saw, and I laughed.

I find it easy to unmask similar values in the modern era. A few minutes watching television infomercials on thigh-reducers or instant-wealth schemes yields plenty of material. Or I thumb through popular magazines and read the ad slogans. Do people really believe that changing mouth-wash or beer brands will solve loneliness and satisfy a search for meaning?

I stop laughing, though, when I examine my own life in light of another world. I ask myself whether my actions more reflect the values of the visible or the invisible world. And how can I live out my belief in the unseen world in the midst of this one?

I have met monks who cloister themselves, unplugged from the surrounding culture, and organize their days around prayer and worship. They try to attune to God all day long. Most of us, though, need strong reminders just to stay aware of the invisible world and our particular role in its drama. The monk Brother Lawrence wrote about practising the presence of God—often it seems as if I barely practise God's existence, much less God's presence.

Richard Mouw of Fuller Seminary recalls a ditty sung in his Sunday School days:

> O be careful, little eyes, what you see,
> O be careful, little eyes, what you see,
> For the Father up above is looking down in love,
> O be careful, little eyes, what you see.

Other verses of the song admonish ears to be careful what they hear, feet to be careful where they go, and tongues to be careful what they say. In Mouw's childhood church, as in mine, the song served as a warning, pressing home the notion of God as an all-seeing judge looking down to catch us in some mistake.

Mouw suggests another way to sing that song. We can make it a positive reminder: *do* be careful to see what God sees, hear what God hears, and go where God goes. Set your mind on things above. In other words, absorb the priorities of the kingdom of heaven and put its reality into practise.

As a kind of checklist, I have chosen several ordinary things in the visible world—money, hardship, death, and moral failures—to examine in the light of God's kingdom. How can belief in another world change my response to these universal experiences?

Money. Jesus spoke more often on the topic of money than any other, and surely I must view it differently in light of another world. Money is, after all, the most sought-after value in the visible world.

Critics of Christianity have long accused the church of using the hope of rewards in the unseen world as a way of suppressing the poor, who are not succeeding in the visible world.* With the collapse of communism, though, fewer make that complaint. Countries with a Christian heritage tend to top the list of the wealthy—ironic, in view of their religion's founder's attitudes toward wealth.

At times Jesus showed an attitude approaching disdain toward money. He counselled a rich man to give away all that he had. He dismissed Solomon, the wealthiest man of Old Testament times, in a comparison with the common lily. He praised a woman who had just "wasted" expensive perfume by pouring it on his feet. His parables and pronouncements emphasize a fact about money that has become a truism: You can't take it with you.

When I lived in Chicago, the murder of Willie Stokes Jr, a young gambler on the south side, attracted local attention when the family had an auto-body shop outfit his coffin as a Cadillac Seville, complete with trunk and front grille, windshield and dashboard, silver spoke wheels, working headlights and tail lights, and Stokes's vanity licence plate. Newspaper photos showed the embalmed gambler, like a display in a wax museum, sitting at the steering wheel of his coffin-car in a hot-pink suit, with five hundred-dollar notes stuffed between his left thumb and forefinger. Flannery O'Connor wrote a short story with the title, "You Can't Be Any Poorer than Dead," and I imagine at some level even the Stokes family realized that inescapable truth as they lowered the well-appointed coffin into the ground.

Despite knowing this obvious fact about money and possessions, many people spend their lives in a frantic chase to accumulate more.

209

---

*As one of Richard Wright's African American characters insisted, "Nobody but poor folks get happy in church.... I ain't that poor. Happy in this world, not out of it."

Market economies, with their insatiable demands, press home a message that has become a yuppie bumper sticker: "The one who dies with the most toys wins." Wins what?

Money exerts a powerful and seductive force in the visible world. It can make a table mysteriously appear in a crowded restaurant and allow an insignificant and ugly man to purchase companionship and sex with a beautiful woman. Watch the women on TV bid to become the wife of a millionaire they've never met or the *Survivor* show contestants eat rats and cockroaches in their effort to gain a million-dollar reward.

Jesus saw money as something to guard against, not desire. "Where your treasure is, there your heart will be also," he said—an alarming thought to those of us who live in societies loaded with tangible treasure. He portrayed money as a negative spiritual force, a god named Mammon that pits itself against the kingdom of heaven. "You cannot serve both God and Money," he said bluntly.

As a defence, Jesus challenges us to do whatever it takes to break free of money's power, even to the extent of giving it all away. I remember reading *Money and Power,* Jacques Ellul's provocative book about money, and being shocked by some of his suggestions. We must find ways to profane money, he said, to demagnetize its spiritual force, even if that means handing wads of bills to strangers or throwing them into the air on a busy street. Such a notion seemed to me preposterous and almost obscene—which gave me a clue that I had succumbed to the spiritual force of Mammon. I considered its waste a form of desecration.

At the time, I thought I was using money to serve the kingdom of heaven. I came to see that I had missed the point of giving. I worried about exactly how much I should give, and to whom. I sought out the charities that offered the best return, the most result per dollar invested, and of course I expected a tax-deductible receipt and a thank you note for my efforts. That kind of uptight, calculated giving is the opposite of what the Bible teaches. The apostle Paul mentions a hilarious, or cheerful, giver, and the hilarity comes because the act of giving is at its core irrational. It destroys the aura of worth surrounding money. By instinct we hoard money in steel vaults and secret caches; giving flagrantly sets it free, turning grace loose in a world of competition and balance sheets.

Living in downtown Chicago, I became aware of needs around me that fit no rational giving scheme. My wife, who was working among the low-income elderly, often came home with heartrending stories of senior citizens who were about to be evicted or have their electricity turned off. A hundred dollars or so would see them through another month—but try to get a government bureaucracy or even a closely audited charity to respond quickly to such a need. We began putting fifty- and hundred-dollar bills in envelopes and slipping them under the door, with an anonymous note that said simply, "From someone who cares."

It seemed like sacrilege the first few times, to give with no assurance the money would be well used and with no tax receipt making it worth our while. Those feelings betrayed the real sacrilege, I soon realized. I had adopted a rational-economic viewpoint that exalted money as the supreme value, and I needed to profane it and break its hold over me, as Ellul had suggested. I needed to see money for what it is, a loan that God has entrusted to me for the purpose of investing in the kingdom of heaven, the only kingdom that pays eternal dividends. Give to the needy in secret, said Jesus. "Then your Father, who sees what is done in secret, will reward you."

I also needed to learn to laugh at the desperation of poor Willie Stokes Jr, who rode a Cadillac to the grave in the shape of a coffin, as well as at the somber actors on television who warn me what may happen if I don't choose the right mutual fund or buy the right insurance policy. I needed to treat *Fortune* magazine and the money programmes on CNN as if they were pornographic, for I recognized they had that effect on me. Money works on me much like lust and pride: it holds me in a pythonic grip and attracts me to fantasies it can never fulfil. And, like lust and pride, money presents an arena of personal struggle that I will never "get over." It is a force with a personality. It is, in truth, a god, and Jesus called it that.

Early communities of Jesus-followers formed a sort of army of resistance against the god Mammon. The book of Hebrews tells of believers who "joyfully accepted the confiscation of [their] property." No one in a right mind joyfully accepts the confiscation of property—unless, that is, they anticipate "better and lasting possessions" in an unseen world, unless they live for God and not for themselves. Likewise, Paul advised the Corinthians to drop their lawsuits and resign themselves to being cheated, as an example to unbelievers. Teresa of Ávila prayed that she would see the world's riches as dangerous, like a stroll among lions; when a rich patron showed her diamonds and precious stones, "I only laughed to myself, and felt sorry that people should value such things, when I remembered what the Lord has in store for us." In different ways, each of these found freedom by profaning the treasures of the visible world.

I would be woefully dishonest if I pretended to anything like the spirit of freedom shown by these giants of faith. Yet I have felt tremors of a gradual shift, even as my income has grown more than I anticipated. I have lived in poverty and in abundance, and money presents a powerful temptation in either situation. While a poor person battles envy, a rich person contends with greed. Money provides a ready battleground for a clash of two worlds.

"I know what it is to be in need, and I know what it is to have plenty," said the apostle Paul; "I have learned the secret of being content in any and every situation." He carried money lightly, using it to accomplish God's work but showing no signs of bondage to it. Christian saints throughout the centuries have reflected a similar holy indifference to money. John Wesley, informed that his house had just burned down, had this reaction: "The Lord's house burned. One less responsibility for me!"

Hardship. In my visits to churches overseas, one difference from North American Christians stands out sharply: their view of hardship and suffering. We who live in unprecedented comfort seem obsessed with the problem of pain. Sceptics mention it as a major roadblock to faith, and believers struggle to come to terms with it. Prayer meetings in the U.S. often focus on illnesses and requests for healing. Not so elsewhere.

I asked a man who visits unregistered house churches in China whether Christians there pray for a change in harsh government policies. After thinking for a moment, he replied that not once had he heard a Chinese Christian pray for relief. "They assume they'll face opposition," he said. "They can't imagine anything else." He then gave some examples. One pastor had served a term of twenty-seven years at hard labour for holding unauthorized church meetings. When he emerged from prison and returned to church, he thanked the congregation for praying. Assigned a dangerous prison job, he had managed to couple together one million railroad cars without an injury. "God answered your prayers for my safety!" he proudly announced. Another imprisoned pastor heard that his wife was going blind. Desperate to rejoin her, he informed the warden that he was renouncing his faith. He was released, but soon felt so guilty that he turned himself in again to the police. He spent the next thirty years in prison.

I found the same pattern in Myanmar (formerly Burma), a dictatorship with brutal policies against religious activities. The person who invited me to the country informed me, "When you speak to pastors, you should remember that probably all of them have spent time in jail because of their faith."

"Then should I talk about one of my book topics like *Where Is God When It Hurts?* or *Disappointment with God*?" I asked.

"Oh, no, that's not really a concern here," he said. "We assume we'll be persecuted for faith. We want you to speak on grace. We need help getting along with each other."

In preparation for the trip, I read several biographies of Adoniram Judson, one of the first missionaries from the United States and the one who first brought the Christian faith to Burma. Hardship stalked his life. When war broke out with England, the Burmese arrested Judson because, light-skinned and English-speaking, he looked and talked like the enemy. (Actually, the U.S. was still recovering from its own wars against England.)

Judson was force-marched barefoot for eight miles to a prison, where each night the guards passed a bamboo pole between his heavily shackled legs and hoisted the lower part of his body high off the ground. Blood rushed to his head, preventing sleep and causing fierce cramps in his shoulders and back. Clouds of mosquitoes feasted on the raw flesh of his feet and legs. Treatment like this went on for almost two years, and Judson managed to endure only because his devoted wife brought him food each day and pled with the guards for better treatment.

A few months after his release, Judson's wife, weakened by smallpox, died of fever, and shortly after that their baby daughter also died. Judson nearly had a breakdown. He would kneel by his wife's grave for hours each day, regardless of weather. He built a one-room hut in the jungle, morosely dug his own grave in case it might prove necessary, and worked in solitude on a translation of the Bible in the Burmese language. Only a handful of Burmese had showed any interest in the Christian message. Yet he stayed on, thirty-four years in all, and because of his faithfulness more than one million Burmese Christians today trace their spiritual roots to Adoniram Judson. The dictionary he compiled, now nearly two hundred years old, remains the official dictionary of Myanmar.

I have read enough such stories and interviewed enough saintly people so as to become impervious to any hint of a prosperity gospel that guarantees health and wealth. "If anyone would come after me, he must deny himself and take up his cross and follow me," said Jesus, who could never be accused of false advertising. "All men will hate you because of me," he told his disciples. But the trials would be worth enduring, for "he who stands firm to the end will be saved.... Do not be afraid of those who kill the body but cannot kill the soul."

Christians claim a loyalty to another world, and from the time of the Roman Empire on, that fact has aroused the suspicion and ire of governments and other religions alike.* In Hindu India, Buddhist Sri Lanka, athe-

*In one of his sermons, Augustine spoke of the spectators in Rome who screamed and shouted as the Christian martyrs fell to the beasts in the Colosseum. "But that bloodthirsty response in other people, under some circumstances, could and did indeed change into a spiritual one.... Oh they saw the bones broken, and they watched the blood flow, and they heard the heart-rending screams of the Martyrs. But then they came to see the unseen; that's to say, the faith of the Christians as they died the death on the arena sand. There was no sight at the games quite like this! A body being mauled while its soul remained unscratched. I know. I've been there."

istic China and Vietnam, and scores of Muslim countries, present-day Christians experience discrimination and outright persecution. As George Ladd wrote, "When God's people are called upon to pass through severe sufferings and tribulation, they should remember that God has not abandoned them, but that their sufferings are due to the fact that they no longer belong to This Age and therefore are the object of its hostility."

Even for those fortunate to live in societies that honour religious freedom, following Jesus complicates life, often inviting hardship. I know Christians who have adopted emotionally and physically damaged children, bringing a permanent disruption into their lives. I know a man who resigned his position as president of a Christian college in order to care for his wife afflicted with Alzheimer's disease. In the Philippines I met an ordinary middle-class couple who invited a few street orphans into their houses and ended up running both an orphanage and school.

As I write this, the rock star Bono, lead singer for the band U2, is travelling across America in a bus, speaking at colleges and churches in an attempt to awaken American Christians to the tragedy of AIDS in Africa.'* By instinct I do not want to hear about yet another tragedy, but down deep I know I have no option. I must care about that holocaust of human suffering because God cares.

Why, then? Why would anyone choose to follow a man who promises more hardship, not less? I will let the apostle Paul answer that question. Here are his qualifications:

> I have worked much harder, been in prison more frequently, been flogged more severely, and been exposed to death again and again. Five times I received from the Jews the forty lashes minus one. Three times I was beaten with rods, once I was stoned, three times I was shipwrecked, I spent a night and a day in the open sea, I have been constantly on the

---

*Bono told the students at Wheaton College, "When 2.5 million people die in Africa each year from AIDS, that's not a cause; it's an emergency.... There are those who think it will take a miracle [to fix the AIDS problem]. I think it much more likely that God is waiting for us to act. I think he is on his knees begging us to care as he does."

move. I have been in danger from rivers, in danger from bandits, in danger from my own countrymen, in danger from Gentiles; in danger in the city, in danger in the country, in danger at sea; and in danger from false brothers. I have laboured and toiled and have often gone without sleep; I have known hunger and thirst and have often gone without food; I have been cold and naked.

And this is Paul's answer to the question, Why?

Though outwardly we are wasting away, yet inwardly we are being renewed day by day. For our light and momentary troubles are achieving for us an eternal glory that far outweighs them all. So we fix our eyes not on what is seen, but on what is unseen. For what is seen is temporary, but what is unseen is eternal.

Paul had two pictures of himself. One image he could view in a mirror, and the insomnia, beatings, imprisonments, and deprivations must have left their mark in the gaunt and weary face that stared back at him from the crude Roman glass. The other image he could not see. Nevertheless he could sense his inward self being renewed and made more fit, tempered by hardship. Belief in another world cast hardship in such a different light that he could compile a list of his many personal calamities and call them "light and momentary troubles."

I get the overwhelming sense, reading Paul and the book of Acts, that the unseen world became for the apostles more real than the visible world around them. Jesus too had faced tribulation in this world but had returned from death with a promise of triumph and hope. They trusted him with their future.

Not long ago I picked up a dusty old book by Richard Baxter, *The Saints' Everlasting Rest,* which contains several chapters on how Christians should view affliction. The preface presented Baxter as an inadvertant expert on the subject. In his lifetime in the seventeenth century, his native London lost one-third of its inhabitants to the Great Plague and one-third of its buildings to the Great Fire. Civil war ravaged

the country, religious conflicts broke out, and in his seventies the physically frail Baxter spent two years in jail for his nonconformist beliefs. It
did not surprise me, though, to find Baxter's book void of whining or
complaining. The problem of pain seems to call forth an odd inversion:
the writers on the subject who suffer the most tend to complain the least
(the same pattern I note among contemporary Christians in countries
marked by hardship).

Baxter borrowed the title of his book from the book of Hebrews,
which promises a time of rest, everlasting rest, for the people of God.
Assume that as our ultimate goal, says Baxter, and affliction looks different. In ordinary activity we anticipate rest to follow a time of work
and toil. Should we expect eternity to be any different? Can there possibly be rest in another life without weariness in this one? Indeed, he continues, afflictions can serve a most useful purpose in keeping us from
mistaking this life as our time of rest. If we fall too much in love with the
world, afflictions rudely break the spell.

Baxter noted the difference between his own prayers in times of
health in contrast to sickness, in prosperity versus adversity. Hardship
quickened his pace and heightened his appetite for rest. He felt a kind of
homesickness for another world and sought God more urgently.

No one gets an exemption from hardship on planet Earth. How we
receive it hinges on whether we believe in an alternate reality that transcends the one we know so well. The Bible never minimizes hardship or
unfairness—witness books like Job, Psalms, and Lamentations. It simply
asks us to withhold final judgement until all the evidence is in.

"Do not be afraid" is the most frequent command in the Bible, which
seems wholly appropriate in an era when terrorists could strike at any
moment and a mailed envelope may carry a biological agent. We have a
thousand fears: mammograms and prostate tests, our children's future as
well as their present, retirement funds, job security, crime. We fear not
getting the job we want or the lover we desire, and if we have them we
fear their loss. In the face of such everyday fear, Jesus points to a lily, or
a sparrow, and calmly says, Trust. Seek first the kingdom of heaven.

Trust does not eliminate the bad things that may happen, whatever sparked our fear in the first place. Trust simply finds a new outlet for anxiety and a new grounding for confidence: God. Let God worry about the worrisome details of life, most of which are out of my control anyway. "Do not be anxious about anything, but in everything, by prayer and petition, with thanksgiving, present your requests to God," Paul wrote. "And the peace of God, which transcends all understanding, will guard your hearts and your minds in Christ Jesus."

When I question the practicality of those words in view of all the terrible things that have happened to Jesus' followers over the years, I remind myself that Paul wrote them from a Roman prison cell. God's peace indeed "transcends all understanding."

Death. What happens after death forms the deepest divide between those who believe in two worlds and those who do not. Psychiatrist Irvin Yalom, in his book *Love's Executioner,* tells of two *delusions,* or "fixed false beliefs," that help his cancer patients allay fears about death: the belief in personal specialness and belief in an ultimate rescuer. Like many modern thinkers, Yalom sees the afterlife as wishful thinking, an escapist way of denying the finality of death.

Death casts its shadow in advance. Not one of us has experienced death, yet no one doubts it will come. We live in constant awareness, from media reports of cancer agents to fears of war and terrorist attacks. When death strikes closer—someone we know, someone we love—the shadow deepens.

The Bible gives scant clues into the afterlife through most of the Old Testament, as though reluctant to disclose the secret that changes everything. With Jesus, however, the wraps came off. "I am the resurrection and the life. He who believes in me will live, even though he dies; and whoever lives and believes in me will never die," he told a friend grieving over her brother's death, and then proceeded to give a demonstration of what he meant. Death was not the end-mark for Jesus, but the change-mark.

It took several centuries for the church to "tame" death from the natural human fear response, but finally it happened. First in France, and then throughout Europe, churches stopped banishing dead bodies and brought them into the very churchyard in *cemeteries,* or sleeping places. The dead mingled with the living, and soon parishioners stood among tombs while they prayed and sang, a thin divide of a floor or wall separating the two states.

In Victorian times neighbours and friends would gather around a person who was approaching the gates of death. They would listen to any words of wisdom that might fall from cracked and swollen lips, contribute what strength they could through prayers and hymns, and try to learn from what they believed to be the most significant moment of life for a Christian. The dying themselves used the time to reflect on their lives, repent, and say goodbye. People of faith aspired to a "good death"—not one empty of grief, surely, but one that trusted God for what lay ahead. "Come sweetest death, come blessed rest, and take my hand and lead me gently on," wrote Bach in one of his cantatas.

In our own day, that tableau has been spoiled. Families live apart and often cannot gather as death approaches. Many people die alone or in intensive care rooms equipped with tubes and monitors and flashing lights, where hymns and prayers would not be welcome. Few regard any deaths as "good."

I have not yet faced death and do not know how I might respond. I know only its advance tremors in the earliest signs of ageing. Aching joints after a day's activity. Forgetfulness. An impatience in learning new technology. Difficulty concentrating at night. Sleeplessness. I turned fifty a few years back, and my body keeps finding new ways to remind me I'm on the downhill side. Ageing *unprepares* us for life in this visible world and gives opportunity to prepare for the next. No amount of vitamins and supplements can forestall my body's certain march toward death.

Henri Nouwen had much time to ponder death after being struck by a car and losing two-thirds of his blood due to internal injuries. His faith became more personal and more certain, he reports. Despite a lifetime of spiritual activity, he had always been pestered by fear, guilt, and shame. "But now, when I walked around the portal of death, all ambiguity and all uncertainty were gone.... Death lost its power and shrank away." He became convinced that dying is our most important act, for which life is a long journey of preparation. It puzzled him that when he returned to health, friends and relatives congratulated him on recovery, whereas he had grown willing to trust God's promises for the next life. "Theology means looking at the world from God's perspective," he concluded.

In a cold dungeon, his life nearing an end, Paul wrote his friend Timothy, "For I am already being poured out like a drink offering, and the time has come for my departure. I have fought the good fight, I have finished the race, I have kept the faith." He then spoke of anticipating rewards from "the Lord, the righteous Judge." My goal for growing older, for preparing to die, is to care less about how others view me and more about how God views me. We'll have much longer together, after all.

Albert Raboteau, a scholar of slave religion in the American South, gives an account of a secret prayer meeting among slaves in Virginia of 1847. Slaves gather surreptitiously in the swamp, following signs marked on the trees pointing them to the selected spot. They begin by asking each other how they feel, the state of their minds. Stories of beatings, lynchings, and other cruelties pour out. Then the prayer service begins. As one slave reports, "The slave forgets all his sufferings, except to remind others of the trials during the past week, exclaiming: 'Thank God, I shall not live here always!'"

Perhaps that cry of longing, of homesickness, provides the answer as to how the church tamed death, as well as why the best writers on affliction wrote in the worst times and why Christians in repressive countries expect hardship. "God is just," insisted the apostle Paul. "He will pay back trouble to those who trouble you and give relief to you who are troubled, and to us as well." The only way to believe in that cosmic justice is to believe in an alternate reality, an unseen world as real as the visible world around us, where life begins again and fairness reigns.*

---

*Raboteau quotes a white woman in slavery days in Georgia: "I never saw a negro a Universalist; for they all believe in a future retribution for their masters, from the hands of a just God."

Even secular educator Jonathan Kozol, after spending time among inner-city children in Chicago, began to entertain thoughts about heaven. "I want to believe that there is something for the children after this because this isn't good enough." Some see that hope as wishful thinking, some as thoughtful wishing.

Moral failures. While I was researching a book on Jesus, I could not help noticing the tenderness with which Jesus treated people with wounds caused by moral failure. A Samaritan woman with five failed marriages, a dishonest tax collector, an adulteress, a prostitute, a disciple who denied him—all these received from Jesus not the judgement they expected, but forgiveness and reinstatement.

We followers of Jesus sometimes do the opposite. A film made in 2002, *The Magdalene Sisters,* documented the sad tale of the "maggies" of Ireland. They got that nickname from Mary Magdalene, which makes for a revealing story in itself. The Gospels mention only one fact of Mary Magdalene's past, that Jesus drove seven demons from her. Nevertheless, a church authority centuries ago decided that Mary Magdalene must have been the same woman as the prostitute who washed Jesus' feet with her hair. Hence when a strict order of nuns agreed to take in young women who had got pregnant out of wedlock, they labelled the fallen girls "maggies."

The maggies came to public attention in the 1990s when a religious order sold their convent, which brought to light the existence of the graves of 133 women inside, women who had spent their lives working as virtual slaves in the convent laundry. The media scouted out a dozen such "Magdalen laundries" across Ireland—the last one closed in 1996—and soon relatives and survivors were spilling accounts of the slave-labour conditions inside. Thousands of young women spent time in the laundries, some put away just for being "a temptress," forced to work unpaid and in silence as a form of atonement for their sins. The church took away illegitimate children born to these women and raised them in other institutions.

Joni Mitchell wrote a song about the maggies, a public outcry erupted, and eventually campaigners raised money for a memorial bench

221

installed in St Stephen's Green, a park in downtown Dublin. Having learned the story of the maggies, I determined to visit the memorial on a trip to Ireland. It was a typical grey day in Dublin, with a sharp September wind and the threat of rain in the air. I asked a policeman and a park guide about the memorial to the maggies, and they both looked at me quizzically. "Dunno that one. Sorry." Finally, the park guide suggested I explore an area designated for monuments.

My wife and I examined, one by one, the bronze statues and impressive fountains, mostly honouring fighters for Irish independence. Only by accident did we stumble across a modest bench beside a magnolia tree. A gay couple was sitting on it, but behind their backs we could see small carved heads and brass-coloured lettering. We asked if they would mind moving temporarily so we could read the inscription and told them the story behind the bench they were sitting on. The plaque reads, "To the women who worked in the Magdalen laundry institutions and to the children born to some members of those communities—reflect here upon their lives."

Walking away from the humble memorial, I found myself reflecting not simply on their lives but also on the sharp contrast between how Jesus treated moral failures and how the church often does. Jesus elevated sinners. He appointed the Samaritan woman as his first missionary. He defended the woman who anointed him with expensive perfume: "She did what she could.... I tell you the truth, wherever the gospel is preached throughout the world, what she has done will also be told, in memory of her." He restored Peter to leadership. And Mary Magdalene, she of the seven demons, he honoured as the very first witness of the Resurrection— a testimony at first discounted by his status-conscious followers.

I reflected also on the greatest gift we have from the unseen world, the gift of grace. Grace means that no mistake we make in life disqualifies us from God's love. It means that no person is beyond redemption, no human stain beyond cleansing. We live in a world that judges people by their behaviour and requires criminals, debtors, and moral failures to live with the consequences. As the saga of the maggies demonstrates, even the church finds it difficult to forgive those who fall short.

Grace is irrational, unfair, unjust, and only makes sense if I believe in another world governed by a merciful God who always offers another chance. "Amazing Grace," a rare hymn that in recent times climbed the charts of popular music, holds out the promise that God judges people not for what they have been but what they could be, not by their past but by their future. John Newton, a gruff and bawdy slave trader, "a wretch like me," wrote that hymn after being transformed by the power of amazing grace.

When the world sees grace in action, it falls silent. Nelson Mandela taught the world a lesson in grace when, after emerging from prison after twenty-seven years and being elected president of South Africa, he asked his jailer to join him on the inauguration platform. He then appointed Archbishop Desmond Tutu to head an official government panel with a daunting name, the Truth and Reconciliation Commission. Mandela sought to defuse the natural pattern of revenge that he had seen in so many countries where one oppressed race or tribe took control from another.

For the next two-and-a-half years, South Africans listened to reports of atrocities coming out of the TRC hearings. The rules were simple: if a white policeman or army officer voluntarily faced his accusers, confessed his crime, and fully acknowledged his guilt, he could not be tried and punished for that crime. Hardliners grumbled about the obvious injustice of letting criminals go free, but Mandela insisted that the country needed healing even more than it needed justice.

At one hearing, a policeman named van de Broek recounted an incident when he and other officers shot an eighteen-year-old boy and burned the body, turning it on the fire like a piece of barbecue meat in order to destroy the evidence. Eight years later van de Broek returned to the same house and seized the boy's father. The wife was forced to watch as policemen bound her husband on a woodpile, poured gasoline over his body, and ignited it.

The courtroom grew hushed as the elderly woman who had lost first her son and then her husband was given a chance to respond. "What do

223

you want from Mr van de Broek?" the judge asked. She said she wanted van de Broek to go to the place where they burned her husband's body and gather up the dust so she could give him a decent burial. His head down, the policeman nodded agreement.

Then she added a further request, "Mr van de Broek took all my family away from me, and I still have a lot of love to give. Twice a month, I would like for him to come to the ghetto and spend a day with me so I can be a mother to him. And I would like Mr van de Broek to know that he is forgiven by God, and that I forgive him too. I would like to embrace him so he can know my forgiveness is real."

Spontaneously, some in the courtroom began singing "Amazing Grace" as the elderly woman made her way to the witness stand, but van de Broek did not hear the hymn. He had fainted, overwhelmed.

Justice was not done in South Africa that day, nor in the entire country during months of agonizing procedures by the TRC. Something beyond justice took place. "Do not be overcome by evil, but overcome evil with good," said Paul. Nelson Mandela and Desmond Tutu understood that when evil is done, one response alone can overcome the evil. Revenge perpetuates the evil. Justice punishes it. Evil is overcome by good only if the injured party absorbs it, refusing to allow it to go any further. And that is the pattern of otherworldly grace that Jesus showed in his life and death.

Nothing can save us that is possible:
We who must die demand a miracle.

W. H. AUDEN

stereoscopic vision

I don't know what your destiny will be, but one thing I know: the only ones
among you who will be really happy are those who will have sought and
found how to serve.

ALBERT SCHWEITZER

Standing by a series of concrete fish ladders in Seattle one raw day, I
learned a new word, *smoltification,* from a placard describing the life
stages of a young river salmon. After several months of solitary content-
ment as a bottom-dweller and jealous patroller of its modest territory, the
fish takes a sudden interest in the larger world. It bobs to the surface now
and then, explores surrounding rocks and pools, and then one day
embarks on a journey far downstream, where a vast new world awaits
it—the Pacific Ocean.

Scientists are just beginning to understand smoltification, a whole
complex of bodily changes that accompany this strange behaviour. The
fish becomes more streamlined, the colour of its scales changes to silver,
endocrine activity increases, and its gills adjust to allow for a greater tolerance of sodium and potassium. The salmon is preparing to do something exceedingly rare among freshwater creatures: switch to a saltwater

environment. Eventually, after spending several years dodging predators in the ocean, it will return to its home stream, flinging itself in great silvery arcs up the fish ladders and natural rapids, only to mate and die, no longer able to thrive in fresh water.

All through this book I have been circling around a process that occurs inside the person who connects to the unseen world, a kind of smoltification of identity. "But our citizenship is in heaven," insists the apostle Paul, contrasting believers with people whose "mind is on earthly things." At that point, the fish analogy breaks down. Unlike the salmon, we must live in two different worlds simultaneously, the equivalent of salt and fresh water both. Our citizenship may be in heaven, but we also occupy bodies of skin, bone, fat, and muscle on a material planet.

Living in a decadent Roman Empire 1,600 years ago, Augustine of Hippo famously borrowed an image from Hebrews 11, which tells of Abraham's faith in a "city with foundations, whose architect and builder is God." Actually, believers hold dual citizenship, Augustine said: in the city of God and the city of Man. We are *perigrini*, or resident aliens on earth—a state Augustine knew well from his wanderings—and we must carefully weigh whether loyalty to one world conflicts with loyalty to the other. He wrote the book *City of God* in part to defend Christians against the charge that their lack of concern for the cities of this world had opened the door for barbarians to sack Rome.

Others have also questioned Christians' loyalty to the visible world. In Henrik Ibsen's play *Emperor and Galilean,* the emperor Julian comments on Christian martyrs, "Does it not seem, Maximus, as though these men live but to die? The spirit of the Galilean is in this. If it be true that his father created the world, then the son despises the father's work." To this day some governments harass Christians on account of their dual allegiance, environmentalists blame them for callousness toward the planet, and social activists accuse them of "being so heavenly minded that they are of no earthly good."

Do Christians truly, in anticipation of eternal life, despise the Father's gift of life in this world? My own reading of church history, and my acquaintance with a few modern-day saints, convinces me they need not. I think of Francis of Assisi, who cherished earth's creation; of Mother Teresa, who honoured those rejected by the society around her; of Dietrich Bonhoeffer and Archbishop Oscar Romero, who risked their own lives to save others'; of Frank Laubach, who practised the presence of God while teaching multitudes to read; of Dorothy Day, who served up philosophy, gourmet coffee, and homemade soup to Manhattan's homeless; of Harriet Tubman, who taught escaping slaves to sing "Wade in the Water" both as a memory of their baptism and also as a practical reminder of how to foil the bounty hunters' bloodhounds. I tend to agree with C. S. Lewis, who said, "If you read history you will find out that the Christians who did most for the present world were precisely those who thought most of the next."

Visit the most dangerous and deprived parts of the planet and on the front lines you will find Christians establishing micro-credit banks, staffing hospitals and schools, drilling wells, and housing refugees. Those who invest their hope in an unseen world prove it by their actions in this world. They strive not to be so heavenly minded as to be of no earthly good and not to be so earthly minded as to be of no heavenly good. They live, in other words, as citizens of two different kingdoms, putting feet to Jesus' prayer that God's will be done on earth as it is in heaven.

The Bible portrays this world as a temporary home, yes, but one that will be refashioned to match God's original design. Jesus does not say, "My kingdom is not of this world, so therefore just sit around and wait for the next world." Rather, he says, in effect, "My kingdom is not of this world, so therefore go and fulfil the two greatest commandments, to love God and to love your neighbour as yourself, and in so doing point the way to that kingdom."

Christians can answer the sceptics' criticism by keeping both eternity and the present in view. When travelling overseas, I use a watch that displays two different time zones, so that a single glance brings to mind my normal life in Colorado as well as the current time in whatever country I am visiting. "Do all your work as if you had a thousand years to live, and as you would if you knew you must die tomorrow," advised the founder of the Shaker community. In other words, keep aware of two time *dimensions,* not mere zones. Live for God in the here and now. Live also in the future, storing up for yourselves eternal treasure—which you do by living in the here and now.

Whenever I do that, I sense a curious transformation at work inside me, a kind of smoltification of character. Keeping the unseen world in mind changes me in subtle ways so that I serve the kingdom of heaven even while living on earth. My point of view shifts, and I begin to see this planet as God's beloved work of art. From God's perspective, after all, there are not two worlds but one, and God's presence fills both.

St Ignatius of Loyola pulled the two dimensions together:

God freely created us so that we might know, love, and serve him in this life and be happy with him forever. God's purpose in creating us is to draw forth from us a response of love and service here on earth, so that we may attain our goal of everlasting happiness with him in heaven.

All the things in this world are gifts of God, created for us, to be the means by which we can come to know him better, love him more surely, and serve him more faithfully.

As a result, we ought to appreciate and use these gifts of God insofar as they help us toward our goal of loving service and union with God. But insofar as any created things hinder our progress toward our goal, we ought to let them go.

———

The British novelist and playwright David Lodge was watching one of his own creations, a satirical revue, the evening of November 22, 1963. The theatre audience chuckled as an actor in the play showed up for a job interview with a transistor radio clutched to his ear, demonstrating his character's blasé indifference. The actor then set down the radio and tuned to a station, letting its news, music, or commercials play in the background while the play went on. This night, however, a voice came on the radio with a live news bulletin: "Today, the American President John F. Kennedy was assassinated ..."

The audience gasped and the actor immediately switched off the radio, but too late. In one sentence, the reality of the outside world had shattered the artificial world of the theatre production. Suddenly, whatever action took place onstage seemed superficial and irrelevant.

The city of God and cities of this world exist in parallel universes (from our perspective, at least), with low-level signals transmitted back and forth between them. The risk is that we may feel completely at home on earth, unaware of another world. Like the people in the theatre, we live inside a reality so engaging that for a time we can forget about any other—until the outside world abruptly intrudes.

Death breaks the spell for me, even as it did for the theatre audience. In the very process of writing this chapter, I learned that my dear friend Lew Smedes, a man wise and good, a man full of grace and realism both, fell off a ladder while hanging Christmas decorations. He lay in a coma, with no brain activity, and the next day doctors removed the artificial life support that kept his body functioning. Lew was in the very act of planning for the future, Christmas with his family, when suddenly there was no future. Yet Lew, as well as anyone I know, oriented his life around an alternate world he could neither see nor fully understand. No doubt he departed this planet anticipating his most memorable Christmas ever.

It takes something disruptive—an assassination, a friend's fall off a ladder, a skyscraper's collapse in lower Manhattan—to jar me into alert awareness of the city of God. The city of this world bombards me with signals that are sensual and enticing. God's city, in contrast, is quiet, invisible, ephemeral. Does it even exist? I have to cultivate transmissions across the chasm: through prayer, through listening.

C. S. Lewis, who died the same day as John F. Kennedy, delivered a sermon in Oxford entitled "Learning in Wartime" as England was bracing itself for a prolonged war with Nazi Germany. He addressed a question that must have troubled all the students at Oxford in those days: How could they be expected to concentrate on subjects like classical Greek and mathematics and medieval English literature when the country, indeed the world, was facing such a crisis? "Is it not like fiddling while Rome burns?" he asked.

Gently, Professor Lewis reminded the students that a crisis such as war merely aggravates the situation in which we always find ourselves. For of course none of us knows when life will come to a sudden end; war merely increases the immediate odds. The question is not whether literature is worth studying in wartime but whether literature is worth studying at all. The wise person lives in awareness of time and eternity both, a dual citizen of the city of God and the city of this world.

A friend of mine, a publisher in England, began receiving postcards filled with spidery script from a nun in a contemplative order who seemed to know a lot about art. After checking with various curators, my friend learned that Sister Wendy Beckett was indeed an amateur art critic with remarkable insight. All the experts had corresponded with her, though none had met her. Further investigation revealed that Sister Wendy lived in a plywood trailer on the grounds of a Carmelite convent, a contemplative order. She spent most of each day in prayer, allowing herself only two hours for work, during which she would translate medieval Latin manuscripts or study art from postcard reproductions.

Someone at the BBC got the idea of sending Sister Wendy on a tour of great art museums and filming her as she encountered the original works for the first time. Wearing a full-length habit, a bit frumpy, with oversized glasses, protruding teeth, and a face not made for TV, this sixty-something nun hardly fit the mould of a star. Nevertheless, she became a media sensation, first in Britain and then on PBS in the United States. Her books about art hit the best-seller lists and she became one of the most recognizable faces in Great Britain.

Meanwhile, Sister Wendy continued to live in her tiny trailer, devoting eight to ten hours a day to contemplative prayer. Broadcasters were amazed to discover that she owned no television and read no newspapers. "They would interfere with my prayers," she explained. She preferred to spend her time focusing on God, not the outside world.

I have watched Sister Wendy's programmes, and it almost seems that she looks at art, especially religious art, with two different eyes. Her left eye sees the brush strokes on canvas, the stylistic arrangements, the use of colour and design. Her right eye sees further, to the aesthetic and spiritual meaning, the hidden intent of the artist. Untold hours of prayer have trained her to look beyond the surface. Angels, characters from the Bible, the Holy Trinity—she knows these subjects intimately, and their depiction in art is a gateway to another reality in which she feels equally at home.

I envy Sister Wendy's stereoscopic vision, for all too easily I revert to a false division between the "natural" and "spiritual." The religious art-work she illuminates brings those worlds together. Abraham expressed his faith by packing his bags and moving. David administered a king-dom. Jesus pounded nails on a carpenter's bench. Paul made friends, sewed tents, planned journeys, and raised funds for the poor in Jerusalem. Through such ordinary deeds the kingdom of God advanced. *What* they did mattered less than *why* and *for whom*. In creation, in incarnation, in all acts on earth, God hallows the ordinary.

Indeed, as C. S. Lewis reminded the students at Oxford, there are no "ordinary" acts. The time I spend arranging these words, Lew Smedes climbing a ladder to celebrate Christ's birth, Sister Wendy poring over the great masters—each of these can be offered up as an act of worship. As can the soup ladled out with a smile in the church kitchen, the tokens of love that hold the threads of a marriage together, the daily service to a disabled child or parent, the professional work done with honesty and integrity.

Every day the city of this world tempts us to lust, to consume, to exploit, to dominate. Every act of resistance is a victory for the city of God, affecting life in both worlds at once. "Let us not become weary in doing good," said Paul, who was likely writing to himself as much as to us, "for at the proper time we will reap a harvest if we do not give up."

———

In his memoir of civil rights days, *God's Long Summer,* Charles Marsh tells of a most unusual political encounter involving Fannie Lou Hamer and Hubert Humphrey, Lyndon Johnson's running mate in 1964. Hamer, known to locals as "the lady who know how to sing," grew up as one of twenty children of an illiterate cotton picker. She courageously signed on to register black voters in Sunflower County, Mississippi, and was beaten senseless by local sheriffs. She eventually died from her injuries, but not before leading an alternate delegation from Mississippi to replace the lily-white slate of delegates at the Democratic Convention.

President Johnson, wanting no negative media coverage to taint his nomination, sent Humphrey, the distinguished Senator from Minnesota and later a presidential candidate himself, to negotiate with Hamer. "What are you seeking?" he began, the opening gambit in any political negotiation. "The beginning of a New Kingdom right here on earth," replied Hamer, a devout Christian. Humphrey, taken aback, began to explain his predicament. He had impeccable civil rights credentials and would personally champion her cause in the White House, but an ugly scene at the convention could threaten the Democrats' chances in November. Couldn't she quietly withdraw her public demands and work with the party ticket behind the scenes until they got elected?

Having survived beatings in a Mississippi jail just for registering voters, Fannie Lou Hamer had little feeling for the nuances of national politics. She replied: "Senator Humphrey, I know lots of people in Mississippi who have lost their jobs for trying to register to vote. I had to leave the plantation where I worked in Sunflower County. Now if you lose this job of Vice President because you do what is right, because you help the Mississippi Freedom Democratic Party, everything will be all right. God will take care of you. But if you take [the nomination] this way, why, you will never be able to do any good for civil rights, for poor people, for peace or any of those things you talk about. Senator Humphrey, I'm gonna pray to Jesus for you."

Thus ended the negotiations between the Johnson administration and Fannie Lou Hamer. She could see no possible compromise between the city of God and the city of this world.

The struggle for freedom and civil rights in the American South marks a classic struggle between the two worlds. Fannie Lou Hamer drew courage from a belief that God wanted her to help further the New Kingdom right here on earth. In doing so, she was following the path laid out by her forebears a century before. Slaves first took solace in the hope of freedom in a future life "in the sweet by and by." Over time, the conviction grew that God wanted justice in this life, here and now.

A slave in South Carolina reported that slave owners forbade his church to sing, "One of these days I shall be free / When Christ the Lord shall set me free." In a wordless protest, the tune became a favourite for slaves to hum as they worked, especially as the prospect of freedom seemed more and more likely. Booker T. Washington recalled that as the day of emancipation grew near, music grew bolder and louder in the slave camps, reverberating late into the night. "True, they had sung those same verses before, but they had been careful to explain that the 'freedom' in these songs referred to the next world, and had no connection with life in this world. Now they gradually threw off the mask; and were not afraid to let it be known that the 'freedom' in their songs meant freedom of the body in this world."

On a visit to Ebenezer Baptist Church in Atlanta, home church of Martin Luther King Jr, I got a taste of the two-world approach to faith in the contemporary African American community. I grew up in Atlanta during the 1950s and 1960s, when most positions of influence were closed to people of colour. Jim Crow laws deliberately demeaned nonwhite people, making them drink at separate water fountains, use separate bathrooms, and sit in the back of buses. At church, though, men and women like Martin Luther King Jr and Fannie Lou Hamer stood tall and learned the leadership skills that would galvanize a movement. When I visited Ebenezer in the 1990s, it was still serving as a way station for faith and courage.

"Have a little talk with Jesus," the choir sang, swaying in rhythm to the music. "Tell him all about our troubles; / Hear our feeble cry, / Answer by and by." After four verses the minister stood up and began talking as the choir hummed in the background. He told about an elderly woman who had been frightened last week by a brick thrown through her window. Shaken, she went to the neighbour's house—a lovely member of their congregation—to await the police. "The two of them," he said ... and turned to the choir who picked up right on cue, "had a little talk with Jesus!"

Another woman had lost her husband that week to a drive-by shooting. He was "promoted to glory," said the pastor, and he said it like he meant it. Still, he continued, we've got to look after this new widow. That's what faith is, he reminded us—looking after widows and orphans. She's in need. She ... he looked at the choir again ... "had a little talk with Jesus"—this time sung in a subdued, solemn tone. "Just a little talk with Jesus makes it right."

I left Ebenezer Baptist with a new appreciation for what served as the moral centre of a great movement in my lifetime. Outside, African Americans in Atlanta faced humiliation, scorn, and often outright hostility and violence. On Sunday morning they recharged. Church gave them the words for the freedom songs and the faith to believe those words might soon be realized. It equipped them for life in two worlds at once.

———

A few hours down the road from Atlanta, off state highway 19, in the flat red-clay fields of Sumter County, a radical Baptist preacher mobilized a different kind of community for the civil rights struggle. Clarence Jordan freely admitted the source of all his troubles: he took the New Testament literally. Jesus said love your enemies, so he became a conscientious objector. Jesus denounced wealth, so he determined not to have any. Paul said in Christ there is no Jew or Gentile, male or female, slave or free, so Clarence founded a radical community, the Koinonia Farm, in which women and men from any race or economic background could live, sharing income and ownership of property.

Such ideals did not settle well in rural Georgia of the 1950s and 1960s. "Communists" and "nigger-lovers" were two of the mildest epithets hurled their way. When Jordan sponsored two black students to enrol in a state college in 1956, two years after the Supreme Court had ruled against segregated education, opposition to Koinonia began in earnest. The community periodically found their fences cut, garbage strewn on their land, sugar poured in vehicle gas tanks, and crops vandalized. Signs advertising the farm's roadside market disappeared from the highways.

Soon vandalism turned to violence. The Ku Klux Klan made explicit threats against "anybody who eats with niggers." Bombs badly damaged the roadside market, and bullets were fired at farmhouses. Then a local boycott took effect, making it impossible for the Koinonia Farm to get its cotton processed or its crops sold. With no market for its eggs and poultry, the community was forced to butcher four thousand laying hens. The farm could not obtain insurance, buy fertilizer, or open a chequeing account. Vandals destroyed beehives and chopped down nearly three hundred apple, peach, and pecan trees.

Friends and supporters urged the community to relocate, but Koinonia members voted to stay put, convinced that Jesus wanted them to follow his commands regardless of consequences. As Clarence's wife, Florence, expressed it, "We knew we wouldn't be the first Christians to die, and we wouldn't be the last." A mail-order business enabled the community to stay afloat financially. "Help us ship the nuts out of Georgia," a catalogue for pecan products urged sympathetic buyers.

Jordan believed that citizens of God's kingdom should act boldly, no matter what kind of response they provoked from society around them. It grieved him that the civil rights movement had achieved its main victories in the courts, not the churches:

> The thing that just burns my heart out is that the Supreme Court is making pagans be more Christian than the Bible is making Christians be Christians. I can hardly stand it sometimes when the whole integration struggle is being fought not in the household of God but in the buses, the depots, and around the Woolworth tables in arguments

about whether or not we can sit down and eat hamburgers and drink cokes together. We ought to be sitting around Jesus' table drinking wine and eating bread together. . . . The sit-ins never would have been necessary if Christians had been sitting down together in church and at Christ's table all these many years.

Citizens of God's kingdom have different weapons in their arsenal, Clarence Jordan had to keep reminding the Koinonia community. The Christian fights with weapons of love, peace, goodwill, and service, which at the time seemed impotent against bombs, bullets, and boycotts. He believed the best proof of the reality of the unseen world is the evidence of transformed lives in this world.

Jordan had a way of getting under people's skin. Commenting on the elaborate church facilities of the South, he said that churches should spend at least as much money "trying to house their brothers whom they have seen as they do trying to house God, whom they have never seen." When a pastor proudly pointed out a $10,000 cross erected atop his church, Jordan remarked, "Time was when Christians could get those crosses for free."

The Koinonia Farm never achieved the ideals of harmony that Clarence Jordan hoped for. It did survive, though, despite all the KKK attacks and local boycotts, and survives to this day. Jordan's understanding of the gospel found expression in *The Cotton Patch Version,* his colloquial paraphrase of the New Testament, which gave his beliefs a wider circulation than he had ever envisioned. He died before completing the translation, but a musical, *Cotton Patch Gospel,* found its way to Broadway, with Jordan's words set to music by Harry Chapin.

Jordan had a more personal influence on a nearby peanut farmer named Jimmy Carter, who went on to become governor of Georgia and then president of the United States. And Millard Fuller, one of Koinonia's members, at Jordan's urging sold his law practice, gave away his money, and founded Habitat for Humanity, which has since built more than 200,000 houses for needy people around the world. Mobilizing church people as a resource for free labour, Habitat has shown them a practical way to "house their brothers whom they have seen."

All of us are called to do ordinary things for God. Once in a while certain individuals—King the preacher's son, Hamer the sharecropper's daughter, Jordan the visionary seminarian—listen more intently and hear a call that leads them on to do extraordinary things. The Quaker Thomas Kelley wrote, "Only now and then comes a man or a woman who, like [abolitionist] John Woolman or Francis of Assisi, is willing to be utterly obedient, to go the other half, to follow God's faintest whisper. But when such a commitment comes in a human life, God breaks through, miracles are wrought, world-renewing divine forces are released, history changes."

William James, a natural sceptic, studied such people and concluded they were society's torchbearers:

> Like the single drops which sparkle in the sun as they are flung far ahead of the advancing edge of a wave-crest or of a flood, they show the way and are forerunners. The world is not yet with them, so they often seem in the midst of the world's affairs to be preposterous. Yet they are impregnators of the world, vivifiers and animaters of potentialities of goodness which but for them would lie forever dormant. It is not possible to be quite as mean as we naturally are, when they have passed before us.

———

Christians sometimes describe their faith as a force that runs counter to culture. I wonder if we have it backwards. Perhaps the city of God is the culture and the city of this world the counterculture. Perhaps Jesus the revolutionary was actually setting out a normal pattern for life on this planet as revealed by its Designer. That he appears radical and got murdered for his beliefs may say more about us than about him.

Martin Luther King Jr faced arrests, beatings, and finally assassination, but now the U.S. remembers him on the only national holiday dedicated to an individual citizen. Clarence Jordan also attracted persecution and now is viewed as a modern prophet. Fannie Lou Hamer rose from poverty and obscurity to help change national politics. Sister Wendy Beckett represents the opposite of the media ideal, yet millions tune in to listen to her wisdom. When John Woolman, Francis of Assisi, and Mother Teresa first appeared on the scene, they seemed like oddballs, cutting against the grain of society. Later, looking back, we recognize them, in William James's phrase, as torchbearers who cast a different light on familiar surroundings.

Several times a year I disengage from American culture, either on a visit to a foreign country or on a hiking trip into the wilderness. Each time, on return, I experience a jolt of re-entry, a psychic adjustment similar to what astronauts must go through physically upon return to earth. I turn on a television sitcom and listen to the innuendoes and sarcastic put-downs and the canned laughter that follows. I watch the commercials promising sexual conquests if I drink a certain beer and professional esteem if I rent from a certain car company. The first day back, modern culture betrays itself as a self-evident lie, a grotesque parody of the day-to-day life I know. The next day my reactions moderate. A few days later I am breathing the air of lust, consumerism, selfishness, and ambition, and it seems normal.

Saints stand out because they refuse to breathe the air, to accept the lie without protest. They seek to live according to rules of the invisible world even while living in the visible. Clarence Jordan shrugged off all "don't rock the boat" and "these changes will take generations" warnings and insisted on following Jesus' way. Thomas Merton, realizing that the whole direction of modern life was geared to flight from God, decided instead to flee toward God, moving from New York City to a Kentucky monastery that required a vow of silence.

To Merton's friends, the move seemed an act of great sacrifice: *Think of all he's giving up!* To Merton himself, it seemed a liberation. Mainly, he discovered, he was giving up neuroses. "Everything in modern city life is calculated to keep man from entering into himself and thinking about spiritual things. Even with the best of intentions a spiritual man finds himself exhausted and deadened and debased by the constant noise of machines and loudspeakers, the dead air and the glaring lights of offices and shops, the everlasting suggestions of advertising and propaganda." The Manhattan world from which he had come gradually receded into a distant frenzy of noise and agitation. As he sat under the trees of Gethsemani Abbey and gazed at the tranquil clouds and silent sky, a jet airplane passing overhead seemed almost profane.

I have learned that when I choose to follow Jesus, in ways large or small, what seems like a sacrifice actually turns into a benefit: *I* am the one who benefits. When I swallow my pride and apologize to someone I've wronged, I feel a flood of relief. When I give anonymously, as Jesus commanded, I experience more satisfaction. When I resist temptation and invest instead in the hard work of marriage, I gain. As Merton expressed it, "The gift of ourselves in total submission to God is a sacrifice in which, far from losing anything, we gain everything and recover, in a more perfect mode of possession, even what we seem to have lost. For at the very moment when we give ourselves to God, God gives Himself to us."

The Gospels repeat one statement by Jesus more than any other: Whoever wants to save his life will lose it, but whoever loses his life for Jesus' sake will find it. I ask myself how I "lose my life" for Jesus' sake. I do not live in a monastery and I experience no real persecution for my faith. I can only apply that principle in far less dramatic ways, in mundane acts of self-denial. For me, that has meant several hundred (should be thousand) incidents of willingly giving up my own desires for those of my wife. It has included uncomfortable acts, such as seeking out a sick, whining friend in a hospital. It has meant spending time with emotionally needy people who want to ramble while I want to get work done. It has meant a constant scrutiny of my use of money.

Even so, Jesus is not calling me to do these things with a resigned sense of duty. Rather, his statement contains the paradoxical suggestion that if we lose our lives for his sake we will find them *in the very process of losing them.* That is the pattern I see demonstrated on large scale by saints. The word *ecstasy* comes from the Greek *ek stasis,* meaning to stand apart from, to go outside of one's self; and the more I extend out from myself, the more

239

I gain. My spirit deepens, I become more fully human, I enlarge. An apparent sacrifice actually ends up serving my own self-interest. In contrast, when I choose for myself alone, I pull in, disconnect from others, shrink.

What works best in the city of God works best in the city of this world. The rule applies not only to individuals but also to overall society. I believe this in part because I have visited countries where a visitor has to bribe officials to get a passport stamped or a laptop computer through customs, where you have to fight every taxi driver to keep from being cheated, where you have to count the change after every transaction and then wade through a sea of beggars. Who doesn't want a society characterized by honesty, compassion for the needy, stable and loving families, respect, low crime, supportive neighbours, kindness, civility—the very qualities of the city of God?*

I believe it also because I have seen the impact in my own country of selfishness and greed, of rising divorce rates and their effect on children, of racism, of overweening reliance on military might, of callousness toward the poor and homeless. The city of God prescribes how best to live in the city of this world. Study after study in the U.S. has demonstrated a direct tie between religious commitment and improved physical and mental health. Both the Clinton (Democrat) and Bush (Republican) administrations lobbied hard for "charitable choice" legislation because statistics prove that faith-based organizations are more efficient and effective than government agencies at creating jobs, housing the homeless, treating addiction, and feeding the hungry.

There are times, of course, when the city of God clashes with the city of this world, when the church becomes a burr in the saddle of society.

---

*Of course, places like Northern Ireland prove that Christianity does not always live up to its ideals. Yet over time it can have a leavening effect. To mention one example, the nonpartisan organization Freedom House each year rates countries on a scale determined by criteria of overall freedom. Nearly 90 percent of the nations that earn the rating "free" are Christian countries, while others earning that rating, such as South Korea and Taiwan, have large Christian populations. Freedom, democracy, medical care, education, and charity tend to flourish in countries with a heritage of Christianity and its profound respect for the individual.

Some protest against wars and are judged unpatriotic. Early Christians caused Rome to shut down the gladiator games. Christians led the way in movements against slavery, segregation, and apartheid. In one dramatic clash of loyalties, King Baudouin of Belgium temporarily abdicated his throne in 1990 because he could not conscientiously sign an abortion bill passed by parliament. The highest authority in Belgium bowed to an even higher authority.

Perhaps the Christian's most important role in modern times is to insist on a divided loyalty, for as history shows, the city of this world greedily seeks a monopoly on loyalty. Or, to state it differently, perhaps the Christian's most important role is to disprove the claim that we are mere animals who obey our selfish genes, and point instead to something higher. We have a reason for such unnatural acts as avoiding sexual temptation, resisting the pull of greed and dishonesty, and loving enemies. In so doing, we serve God and God's kingdom. A person can only transcend the destiny of biology if something transcendent actually exists.

———

Jesus told a story about a man who built his house on sand. Rain fell, streams rose, the winds blew, and soon the house toppled with a crash. It lacked a foundation to support the fine superstructure. He told another story about a rich man with so many crops that he had nowhere to store them. Distributing the surplus to the needy didn't occur to him. Instead he decided to tear down his barns and build bigger ones so that he could live the good life for many years to come. God himself pronounced the judgement: "You fool! This very night your life will be demanded from you. Then who will get what you have prepared for yourself?"

Jesus added this solemn warning, "This is how it will be with anyone who stores up things for himself but is not rich toward God." In these and other stark stories Jesus underscored the central message of the Bible, that life consists in more than the years we spend on earth, and reality consists in more than we can see with telescopes and microscopes. We would better spend our time and energy being "rich toward God" than in a search for wealth and pleasure that will inescapably end in futility and death.

Jesus' formula for living seems naive and even foolhardy—unless you share his view of the world. Most of us see life as an arc beginning with birth, which we can't remember, and death, which we can't imagine. Jesus spoke of his role before birth and after death and his years on earth as a period of transition. That point of view changes everything. He established settlements of the city of God while living in the city of this world.

During the days of the Great Proletarian Cultural Revolution in China in the 1960s, Chairman Mao dismissed beauty as a bourgeois concept. Red Guards closed flower shops and ordered people to destroy their goldfish. Everyone dressed alike, in unisex, unicolour uniforms. China became a drab society, on the surface at least. What actually happened, as later became clear, was that beauty went underground. Women cultivated flowers in their homes and wore brightly coloured blouses under their grey Mao jackets. Children hid jars of goldfish under their beds. Until government policy changed, bringing it back into the open, beauty existed as a kind of dangerous, hidden secret—a rumour of another world.

In *The Gulag Archipelago,* Aleksandr Solzhenitsyn presents *truth* as the dangerous secret shared by inmates of the Soviet prison system. Inside prison they spoke freely of an alternate reality different from the lies their government promulgated on the outside. And in the slave plantations of the Caribbean, Africans lived in two alternate worlds: the white man's world of the daylight and the African world of the night. After dark the slaves reclaimed the culture of their homeland, carrying chiefs and kings about on a litter and keeping their heritage alive. Although slaveholders tolerated the night world as a kind of child's world, to the African it was the true world, re-establishing what plantation life tried to destroy.

Perhaps that kind of shared secret was what Jesus had in mind when he told his critics they could not pin down the kingdom of God: "The kingdom of God does not come with your careful observation, nor will people say, 'Here it is,' or 'There it is,' because the kingdom of God is within you." In prisons, in catacombs, and even in the corridors of power, his followers whispered the provocative secret that our planet, marked by violence, decay, and death, is not all there is. We will live again, in bodies made whole, in a world made whole.

The apostle Paul grasped the secret. "If only for this life we have hope in Christ, we are to be pitied more than all men," he admitted. In his letters he sought to convince the new community of a way to live based on the reality of another world. The people to whom he wrote those words had a penchant for wild living. Why deny yourself any pleasure at all? they wondered. Paul agreed with their argument—provided there is no life beyond this one.

A French cardinal said that saints live in such a way that their lives would not make sense if God did not exist. The reverse also applies: the true sceptic lives in such a way that life would not make sense if God does exist.

———

Blaise Pascal, a scientist and mathematician who lived at the dawn of the Age of Enlightenment, sympathized with those who had trouble believing in an unseen world. "The eternal silence of these infinite spaces frightens me," he said, contemplating the short duration of his life set against eternity and the tiny space he filled against the immensity of space. Nonetheless, he could not understand the attitude of glee with which sceptics proclaimed their disbelief in God and immortality, treating it as a kind of liberation, a shaking off the yoke. A brief life in a meaningless universe and then annihilation—can anyone truly welcome such a prospect? Is it not, rather, "a thing to say sadly, as the saddest thing in the world"?

Pascal saw faith as a cosmic wager. He faced uncertainty either way. If he cast his lot with God and was proved wrong, he would forgo certain pleasures and selfish rewards in this life and then, at death, fade into nothingness. On the other hand, if he chose against God and was proved wrong, he would face an eternity of regret. After weighing the odds, Pascal decided it is better in every way to believe in something that isn't than to disbelieve in something that is. The best course of all is to believe in something that is—the ultimate wager of faith.

In the life of faith, we no longer judge God and his kingdom through worldly eyes but, instead, view this visible world in the light of God. Vision will always be clouded and imperfect, at least until the day of unification promised in the book of Revelation. Then, "The kingdom of the world has become the kingdom of our Lord and of his Christ, and he will reign for ever and ever." Then rumours will cease, transposed into praise.

———————

So now, from this mad passion
    Which made me take art for an idol and a king
I have learnt the burden of error that it bore
    And what misfortune springs from man's desire ...
The world's frivolities have robbed me of the time
    That I was given for reflecting upon God.

MICHELANGELO

acknowledgements

I have been writing books for twenty-five years, and I find that the process gets harder, not easier. Partly that's because I have a clearer idea of what I'm doing wrong as I do it. In this book, I also struggled because I found myself caught in the borderlands, torn between scepticism, on the one hand, and unconvincing pieties on the other. A number of people helped me sort out my thoughts and "voice" in the process, and I am deeply grateful to them: David Graham, Chris Grindem, Klaus Issler, Ted and Connie Ning, Tim Ogden, Brenda Quinn, Tim Stafford.

Kathy Helmers and John Sloan went considerably further, helping to reshape the book in several successive stages. Bob Hudson prepared it for publication, and Melissa Nicholson assisted with many of the details, including the tedious task of tracking down the sources I cite. Truly, it takes a village to raise a book.

sources

Part 1

11. *Dostoyevsky:* Fyodor Dostoyevsky quoted by Jürgen Moltmann, "Science and Wisdom," in John Wilson, *The Best Christian Writing 2002* (San Francisco: HarperSanFrancisco, 2002), 170–71.

1. Life in Part

13. *Einstein:* Albert Einstein, "What I Believe," in *Forum* (Oct. 1930).
15. *Descartes:* René Descartes, quoted in Brian Easlea, *Liberation and the Aims of Science* (Totowa, N.J.: Rowman & Littlefield, 1973), 255.
15. *Crick:* Francis Crick, quoted in Malcolm Jeeves, "Brain, Mind, and Behavior," in *Whatever Happened to the Soul,* by Brown, Murphy, and H. Newton Malone (Minneapolis: Fortress, 1998), 87.
17. *Magellan's explorers:* Story cited by Robert Kirschner, *Divine Things* (New York: Crossroad, 2001), 40.
18. *Kierkegaard:* Søren Kierkegaard, *The Gospel of Suffering* (Minneapolis: Augsburg, 1948), 123.
19. *Dillard:* Annie Dillard, *Teaching a Stone to Talk* (New York: Harper & Row, 1982), 69.
20. *Monod:* Jacques Monod, *Chance and Necessity* (New York: Knopf, 1971), 172–73.
21. *Wilson:* Edward O. Wilson, *On Human Nature* (Cambridge: Harvard University Press, 1978), 155–56.
21. *de Waal:* Frans de Waal, *Good Natured* (Cambridge: Harvard University Press, 1996), 218.
22. *Darrow:* Clarence Darrow, quoted in Carol Iannore, "The Truth About *Inherit the Wind,*" in *First Things,* Vol. 70 (February, 1997), 28–33.

23. *Hitler:* Adolf Hitler, quoted in Christopher Nugent, *Masks of Satan* (London: Sheed and Ward, 1983), 170.

23. *Lenin:* Vladimir Lenin, quoted in *New York Times Book Review* (Oct. 27, 1996), review of *Censored by His Own Regime,* by Orlando Figes, 32.

23. *Darwin:* Charles Darwin, *The Autobiography of Charles Darwin* (New York: Harcourt, Brace & Co., 1959), 138–39.

24–25. *Muir:* John Muir, quoted in Frederick Turner, *Rediscovering America: John Muir in His Time and Ours* (San Francisco: Sierra Club, 1985), 139.

25. *Havel, "I believe":* Vaclav Havel, quoted in Colin E. Gunton, *The One, The Three and The Many* (London: Cambridge University Press, 1995), 71.

25. *Havel, "I come":* Vaclav Havel, quoted in "News and Comments," *The Chesterton Review,* Vol. XXII, No. 3, Aug. 1996, 388–90.

26. *Eliot:* T. S. Eliot, "Choruses from *The Rock*" in T. S. Eliot, *The Complete Poems and Plays, 1909–1950* (New York: Harcourt, Brace, 1952), 96.

2. Rumours

27. *Auden:* W. H. Auden, "Song of the Beggars No. VIII," *Collected Poems* (New York: Random House, 1976), 119.

29. *Lewis:* C. S. Lewis, *God in the Dock* (Grand Rapids, Mich.: Eerdmans, 1970), 35.

29. *"It is [God] who made us":* Psalm 100:3.

29. *"We all, like sheep":* Isaiah 53:6.

29. *Dyson:* Freeman Dyson, quoted in Karl W. Giberson, "The Goldilocks Universe," in *Books & Culture* (Jan/Feb. 2003), 30.

30. *Woolf:* Virginia Woolf, *Moments of Being* (New York: Harcourt Brace Jovanovich, 1985), 72.

30. *Milton:* John Milton, *Paradise Lost* (New York: New American Library, 1961), 160.

31. *Dillard:* Annie Dillard, *The Writing Life* (New York: Harper & Row, 1989), 18.

32. *Lewis:* C. S. Lewis, *Perelandra* (New York: Macmillan, 1944), 81.

32. *Krushchev:* Nikita Krushchev, quoted in Jacques Ellul, *The New Demons* (New York: Seabury, 1975), 64.

32. *Brezhnev:* Leonid Brezhnev, quoted in Jacques Ellul, *The New Demons* (New York: Seabury, 1975), 64.

32. *Wilson:* A. N. Wilson, *God's Funeral* (New York: W. W. Norton, 1999), 304.

33. *"my people . . . have forsaken me":* Jeremiah 2:13.

33. *Allen:* Woody Allen, "The Heart Wants What It Wants," *Time* (August 31, 1992), 61.

33. *Ryan:* Michael Ryan, *Secret Life: An Autobiography* (New York: Pantheon, 1995), 335.

34. *Dostoyevsky:* Fyodor Dostoyevsky, *The Possessed* (New York: Modern Library, 1963), 674–75.

34. *Weil:* Simone Weil, quoted in Robert Coles, *Simone Weil* (Reading, Mass.: Addison-Wesley, 1987), 148–49.

34. *Barron:* Robert Barron, *And Now I See* (New York: Crossroad, 1998), 145.

35–36. *Lewis:* C. S. Lewis, *The Weight of Glory* (Grand Rapids, Mich.: Eerdmans, 1949), 4–5.

36. *Augustine:* Augustine of Hippo, *"whole life of the good Christian"* quoted in Jürgen Moltmann, *The Spirit of Life* (Minneapolis: Fortress, 1992), 92.

36. *Augustine: "smiling face"* and *"wedding ring"* quoted in Peter Brown, *Civitas Peregrina* (Berkeley: University of California Press, 1969), 325–26.

37. *Augustine: "scattered longings"* from *The Confessions of St Augustine* (Garden City, N.Y.: Image, 1960), 272.

37. *Augustine: "I had my back,"* Ibid., 111.

37. *Merton:* Thomas Merton, *The Seven Storey Mountain* (New York: Harcourt, Brace, 1948), 108.

37. *Weil:* Simone Weil, *Selected Essays* (London: Oxford, 1962), 215.

37. *Herbert:* George Herbert, *The English Poems of George Herbert* (London: Rowman and Littlefield, 1974), 73.

38. *"eternity in our hearts":* Ecclesiastes 3:11.

38. *"burden of the gods":* Ecclesiastes 3:10.

38. *Lewis:* C. S. Lewis, *Miracles* (New York: Macmillan, 1947), 132.

39. *"temple":* 1 Corinthians 3:16–17.

41. *"eyes to see":* Matthew 13:16.

41. *Orwell:* George Orwell, *The Collected Essays: Journalism and Letters of George Orwell;* vol. 2, *My Country Right or Left* (New York: Penguin, 1970), 30.

3. Paying Attention

43. *Berryman:* John Berryman, "Eleven Addresses to the Lord," no. 2, in *Love & Fame* (New York: Farrar, Straus & Giroux, 1970), 85.

43. *Corde:* Carmen Corde, quoted in Henri Nouwen, *¡Gracias!* (Maryknoll, N.Y.: Orbis, 1983), 74.

43. *O'Connor:* Flannery O'Connor, *Mystery and Manners* (New York: Farrar, Straus & Giroux, 1969), 180.

44. *Eckhart:* Meister Eckhart, quoted in "Holy Fools," *Sojourners* (July 1994), 20.

44. *"God saw":* Genesis 1:31.

45. *Pascal:* Blaise Pascal, *Pascal's Pensées* (New York: E. P. Dutton, 1958), 182.

46. *Augustine:* Augustine of Hippo, *The Confessions of St Augustine* (Garden City, N.Y.: Image, 1960), 254.

48. *Mirandola:* Pico della Mirandola, "Oration on the Dignity of Man," available on numerous Internet sites including *http://history.hanover.edu/courses/excerpts/111pico.htm.*

48–49. *Fabre:* Jean Henri Fabre, *The Insect World of J. Henri Fabre* (Boston: Beacon, 1977), 326.

49. *Hopkins:* Gerard Manley Hopkins, "God's Grandeur," in *Poems and Prose of Gerard Manley Hopkins* (Baltimore: Penguin, 1953), 27.

49. *Pachomius:* Saint Pachomius, quoted in James Bryan Smith, *Embracing the Love of God* (San Francisco: HarperSanFrancisco, 1989), 138.

49. *Muir:* John Muir, *The Story of My Boyhood and Youth* (New York & Boston: Houghton Mifflin, 1913), 84.

49. *"Are not two sparrows":* Matthew 10:29.

50. *"Remember your creator":* Ecclesiastes 12:1.

50. *"Fear God":* Ecclesiastes 12:13.

51. *Calvin:* John Calvin, *Institutes, I, xiv* (Grand Rapids, Mich.: Eerdmans, 1964), 157.

51. *Kempis:* Thomas à Kempis, *The Imitation of Christ* (Nashville: Nelson, 1979), 70, 129.

53. *Dillard:* Annie Dillard, *Pilgrim at Tinker Creek* (New York: Harper's Magazine Press, 1974), 8.

54. *Celibidache:* Sergiu Celibidache, quoted in "Podium Paradox," in *Chicago Tribune* (April 16, 1989), Section 13, "Arts," 14–15.

55. *Weil:* Simone Weil, *Gravity & Grace* (New York: Routledge, 1995), 108, 105.

55–56. *Sacks:* Oliver Sacks, *Awakenings* (New York: Dutton, 1983), 67–79, 188–201.

56–57. *Chittister:* Joan Chittister, OSB, in James Martin, ed., *How Can I Find God?* (Liguori, Mo.: Triumph, 1997), 85–86.

57. *"There is nothing":* Romans 14:14 (KJV).

57. *"So whether":* 1 Cor. 10:31.

58. *Columba:* from Adamnan's *Life of Saint Columba,* quoted in Robert Hudson and Shelley Townsend-Hudson, *Companions for the Soul* (Grand Rapids, Mich.: Zondervan, 1995), June 6 entry.

58. *"fruit of the Spirit":* Galatians 5:22.

58. *Buechner:* Frederick Buechner, *A Room Called Remember* (San Francisco: HarperSanFrancisco, 1984), 152.

4. God Loveth Adverbs

59. *Keller:* Helen Keller, quoted on numerous Internet sites, including *www.csee.wvu.edu/~murphy/quotations.html.*

62. *"The thief comes":* John 10:10

62. *Agee:* James Agee, *Let Us Now Praise Famous Men* (Boston: Houghton Mifflin, 1969), 99.

63. *"Hypocritical liars":* 1 Timothy 4:2–4.

63. *Pascal:* Blaise Pascal, *The Mind On Fire* (Portland: Multnomah, 1989), 288.

63. *"God loveth adverbs":* Joseph Hall, Puritan quoted in Charles Taylor, *Sources of the Self* (Cambridge: Harvard University Press, 1989), 224.

63. *Merton:* Thomas Merton, quoted in Tom Stella, *The God Instinct* (Notre Dame, Ind.: Sorin, 2001), 124.

64. *Luther:* Martin Luther, *By Faith Alone* (Grand Rapids, Mich.: World, 1998), September 6 reading.

65. *Chittister:* Joan Chittister, OSB, *Wisdom Distilled from the Daily* (San Francisco: HarperSanFrancisco, 1990), 6, 179.

66. *Smedes:* Lewis B. Smedes, *My God and I* (Grand Rapids, Mich.: Eerdmans, 2003), 56.

67. *"We have the mind":* 1 Corinthians 2:16.

68. *"You did not choose":* John 15:16.

68. *"book on marriage":* Gary Thomas, *Sacred Marriage* (Grand Rapids, Mich.: Zondervan, 2000).

68. *"Regard no one":* 2 Corinthians 5:16 (RSV).

69. *Guyon:* Madame Guyon. Source unknown.

70. *"We are not trying":* 1 Thessalonians 2:4.

70. *"For none of us":* Romans 14:7–8.

70. *Balthasar:* Urs von Balthasar, quoted in Robert Barron, *And Now I See* (New York: Crossroad, 1998), 141.

71. *Paterson:* Evangeline Paterson, quoted in Mark Noll, *Scandal of the Evangelical Mind* (Grand Rapids, Mich.: Eerdmans, 1994), 245.

71. *Chardin:* Pierre Teilhard de Chardin, quoted in Richard Foster, *Prayer* (San Francisco: HarperSanFrancisco, 1992), 169.

5. Designer Sex

73. *Waugh:* Evelyn Waugh, *Brideshead Revisited* (Boston: Little, Brown, 1945), 303.

74. *Mill:* John Stuart Mill, *Autobiography,* John Jacob Cross, ed. (New York: Columbia University Press, 1924), 75.

75–76. *Rape:* Randy Thornhill and Craig T. Palmer, *A Natural History of Rape* (Boston: MIT Press, 2001).

78. *Lewis:* C. S. Lewis, *Mere Christianity* (New York: Macmillan, 1952), 89.

78. *Ellul:* Jacques Ellul, *What I Believe* (Grand Rapids, Mich.: Eerdmans, 1989), 68.

78. *Chesterton:* G. K. Chesterton, quoted in *Mars Hill Review,* Summer, 1997, 19.

79. *Shakespeare:* William Shakespeare, *The Tempest* (New Haven: Yale University Press, 1955), Act IV, Scene 1:51.

80. *Jerome:* Saint Jerome, *Select Letters of St Jerome* (Cambridge: Harvard University Press, 1933), 67–8; *"Hebrew":* 419; *"I praise wedlock":* 95.

80. *Jerome:* Saint Jerome. *"Anyone who is too passionate"* quoted in Steven Ozment, "Re-inventing Family Life," in *Christian History,* Issue 39 (Vol. XII, No. 3), 22.

81. *Sayers:* Dorothy L. Sayers, *Christian Letters to a Post-Christian World* (Grand Rapids, Mich.: Eerdmans, 1969), 138.

82. *Blake:* William Blake, *The Marriage of Heaven and Hell* (New York: Dutton, 1927), 8.

83. *"You have heard":* Matthew 5:27–28.

83–84. *Luther:* Martin Luther, *By Faith Alone* (Grand Rapids, Mich.: World, 1998), April 24 reading.

84. *Berryman:* John Berryman, "Eleven Addresses to the Lord," no. 3, in *Love & Fame* (New York: Farrar, Straus & Giroux, 1970), 88.

85. *O'Connor:* Flannery O'Connor, "A Temple of the Holy Ghost," in *Flannery O'Connor: The Complete Stories* (New York: Farrar, Straus & Giroux, 1983), 238.

85. *"Do you not know":* 1 Corinthians 6:15–16.

85–86. *"By faith Moses":* Hebrews 11:24–26.

86. *Vanier:* Jean Vanier, *Man and Woman He Made Them* (New York: Paulist Press, 1985), 102–4, 174.

87. *"Blessed are the pure":* Matthew 5:8.

87–88. *Bonhoeffer:* Dietrich Bonhoeffer, *The Cost of Discipleship* (New York: Macmillan, 1963), 119.

88. *Lewis:* C. S. Lewis, *The Four Loves* (London: Geoffrey Bles, 1960), 109.

88. *Lewis:* C. S. Lewis, quoted in Lyle W. Dorsett, *And God Came In* (Wheaton, Ill.: Crossway, 1991), 137.

89. *Williams:* Charles Williams, *Outlines of Romantic Theology* (Grand Rapids, Mich.: Eerdmans, 1990).

89. *Shakespeare:* William Shakespeare, *The Tempest* (New Haven: Yale University Press, 1955), Act I, Scene 2:445.

90. *Lewis:* C. S. Lewis, *The Four Loves* (London: Geoffrey Bles, 1960), 130–31.

90–91. *Dostoyevsky:* Fyodor Dostoyevsky, *Notes from the Underground,* in *Great Short Works of Fyodor Dostoyevsky* (New York: Harper & Row, 1968), 339ff.

91. *"After all":* Ephesians 5:29–32.

92–93. *ACLU:* Official letter from ACLU Spokeswoman Marjorie C. Swartz, dated May 26, 1988, to the California Assembly of Education Committee.

94. *Puritans:* Quoted by Bill Moyers in Joseph Campbell, *The Power of Myth* (New York: Doubleday, 1988), 201.

95. *Habits of the Heart:* Robert N. Bellah, et. al., *Habits of the Heart* (New York: Harper & Row, 1985).

95. *Ellul:* Jacques Ellul, *What I Believe* (Grand Rapids, Mich.: Eerdmans, 1989), 69.

95. *Sayers:* Dorothy L. Sayers in *Dorothy L. Sayers: Her Life and Soul,* quoted in *Christianity Today* (October 6, 1997), 70.

Part 2

97. *Eliot:* T. S. Eliot, "Murder in the Cathedral," *The Complete Poems and Plays, 1909–1950* (New York: Harcourt, Brace, 1952), 214.

6. Out of Order

99. *Weil:* Simone Weil, *Gravity & Grace* (New York: Routledge, 1995), 62–63.

99. *Waugh:* Evelyn Waugh, *Brideshead Revisited* (Boston: Little, Brown, 1945), 286.

100. *Milton:* John Milton, *Paradise Lost* (New York: New American Library, 1961), 157.

101. *Smedes:* Lewis Smedes, *Sex for Christians* (Grand Rapids, Mich.: Eerdmans, 1994), 27.

102. *Merton:* Thomas Merton, *Run to the Mountain* (San Francisco: HarperSanFrancisco, 1996), 452.

102. *Hunt:* Morton Hunt, *The Universe Within* (New York: Simon and Schuster, 1958), 358–59.

105. *"It is not the healthy":* Mark 2:17.

105. *"This son of mine":* Luke 15:24.

107–108. *Himmler:* Heinrich Himmler, quoted in Joaquim Fest, *The Face of the Third Reich,* translated by Michael Bullock (New York: Pantheon, 1970), 115.

108. *"Watch out!":* Luke 12:15.

108. *Chesterton:* G. K. Chesterton, quoted in Richard J. Foster, *Freedom of Simplicity* (San Francisco: Harper & Row, 1981), 110.

109–110. *Gilkey:* Langdon Gilkey, *Shantung Compound* (New York: Harper & Row, 1996), 96–105.

111. *Merton:* Thomas Merton, *Run to the Mountain* (San Francisco: HarperSanFrancisco, 1996), 63.

7. A Word Unsaid

113. *Chesterton:* G. K. Chesterton, *The Man Who Was Thursday* (New York: Putnam,1980), 176.

113. *Percy:* Walker Percy, *Lancelot* (New York: Farrar, Straus & Giroux, 1977), 52.

116. *Muir:* John Muir, quoted in Frederick Turner, *Rediscovering America* (San Francisco: Sierra Club, 1985), 23.

116. *"Lamb that was slain":* Revelation 13:8.

116. *"God is love":* 1 John 4:8.

116. *Menninger:* Karl Menninger, *Whatever Became of Sin?* (New York: Hawthorn, 1973).

118. *Glover:* Jonathan Glover, *Humanity: A Moral History of the Twentieth Century* (New Haven: Yale University Press, 2000).

118–119. *Lippmann:* Walter Lippmann, quoted in Jaroslav Pelikan, *Jesus Through the Centuries* (New Haven: Yale University Press, 1985), 76.

119. *New York Times:* Ron Rosenbaum, "Staring into the Heart of Darkness" *New York Times Magazine* (June 4, 1995), 36–72.

120. *Cheever:* John Cheever, quoted in Robert Coles, *The Call of Stories* (Boston: Houghton Mifflin, 1989), 151.

121. *Greene:* Graham Greene, *The Quiet American* (New York: Penguin, 1996), 189.

121. *"founders of Alcoholics Anonymous":* from Ernest Kurtz, *Not-God* (San Francisco: Harper & Row, 1979), 59.

122. *Wilson:* Bill Wilson, quoted in Ernest Kurtz, *Not-God* (San Francisco: Harper & Row, 1979), 61.

122–123. *James:* William James, *The Varieties of Religious Experience* (New York: Modern Library, 1929), 77–162.

123. *Spencer:* Herbert Spencer, quoted in D. R. Davies, *On to Orthodoxy* (London: Hodder and Stoughton, 1939), 12.

123–124. *Muggeridge:* Malcolm Muggeridge, *Paul, Envoy Extraordinaire* (New York: Harper & Row, 1972), 147–48.

124. *Lenin:* Vladimir Ilyich Lenin, *Letters on Modern Atheism*, quoted in *Sojourners* (December, 1981), 17.

125. *Berryman:* John Berryman, "Eleven Addresses to the Lord," no. 2, in *Love and Fame* (New York: Farrar, Straus and Giroux, 1970), 87.

8. The Good Life

127. *Auden:* W. H. Auden, "Thanksgiving for a Habitat," *Collected Poems*, Edward Mendelson, ed. (New York: Random House, 1976), 525.

129. *Franklin:* Benjamin Franklin, *The Autobiography of Benjamin Franklin* (New York: Buccaneer, 1984), 112.

132. *Dan Quayle:* Barbara DaFoe Whitehead, "Dan Quayle Was Right," in *Atlantic Monthly* (April 1993), 47–84.

133. *"a kingdom of priests":* Exodus 19:6.

133. *"The Sabbath was made":* Mark 2:27.

134. *Henry:* Matthew Henry, *The Secret of Communion with God* (London: Marshall, Morgan & Scott, 1963), 28.

134. *Stuntz:* William J. Stuntz, "Law and the Christian Story," in *First Things* (December 1997), 26–29.

135. *"The entire law":* Galatians 5:14.

135. *"We serve":* Romans 7:6.

135. *Augustine:* Augustine of Hippo, *Treatises on 1 John 7.8*, quoted in Dietrich von Hildebrand, *Transformation in Christ* (Manchester, N.H.: Sophia Institute, 1990), 496.

135. *"So if the Son":* John 8:36.

139. *Augustine:* Augustine of Hippo, *The Confessions of St Augustine* (Garden City, N.Y.: Image, 1960), 354.

139. *Auden:* W. H. Auden, "Herman Melville," in W. H. Auden, *Collected Poems* (New York: Random House, 1975), 200.

9. The Gift of Guilt

141. *Huxley:* Elspeth Huxley, *The Flame Trees of Thika* (New York: Penguin, 1959), 123.

142. *Moby Dick:* Herman Melville, *Moby Dick* (New York: Bantam, 1967), 493–516.

143. *Calvin:* John Calvin, *Institutes of the Christian Religion* (Philadelphia: Westminster, 1977), 3:3:10.

143. *Raskolnikov:* Fyodor Dostoyevsky, *Crime and Punishment*, translated by Jessie Coulson (New York: W. W. Norton, 1964), 67.

144. *Kierkegaard:* Søren Kierkegaard, in Thomas C. Oden, ed., *Parables of Kierkegaard* (Princeton, N.J.: Princeton University Press, 1978), 93.

144. *"Against you":* Psalm 51:4.

145. *Twain:* Mark Twain, "Pudd'nhead Wilson's New Calendar," in *Following the Equator* (New York: Collier, 1897), 238.

147. *Luther:* Martin Luther, quoted in Edith Simon, *Luther Alive* (Garden City, N.Y.: Doubleday, 1968), 36.

148. *Groeschel:* Benedict Groeschel, *Quiet Moments with Benedict Groeschel* (Ann Arbor, Mich.: Servant, 2000), 33.

149. *Miller:* J. Keith Miller, *Secret Life of the Soul* (Nashville: Broadman & Holman, 1997), 182.

150. *"And if any man":* 1 John 2:1 (KJV)

151. *Lewis:* C. S. Lewis, *Mere Christianity* (New York: Macmillan, 1952), 60.

153. *Wilde:* Oscar Wilde, *The Picture of Dorian Gray* (New York: Bantam, 1982).

154. *"a man after":* Acts 13:22.

155. *"God, I thank you":* Luke 18:11.

155. *"in the same way":* Luke 15:7.

155. *"God is love":* 1 John 4:8.

156. *"Adam, where are you":* Genesis 3:9.

156. *"You do not delight":* Psalm 51:16–17.

157. *Lewis:* C. S. Lewis, *Letters of C. S. Lewis* (New York: Harcourt, Brace & World, 1966), 199.

157. *Traherne:* Thomas Traherne, *Centuries* (New York: Harper & Brothers, 1960), 156.

Part 3

159. *Ionesco:* Eugene Ionesco, *Present Past Past Present* (New York: Grove Press, Inc., 1971), 158.

10. Why Believe?

161. *Kazantzakis:* Nikos Kazantzakis, *Report to Greco* (New York: Bantam, 1965), 451.

161. *Thurber:* James Thurber, *My Life and Hard Times* (New York: Harper & Row Publishers, 1973), 62.

162. *Thompson:* William Irwin Thompson, *Evil and World Order* (New York: Simon & Schuster, 1975), 81.

162. *"Where are you?":* Genesis 3:9

162. *Adams:* Henry Adams, *The Education of Henry Adams* (New York: Modern Library, 1996).

162–163. *King:* Larry King, quoted in Ravi Zacharias, "Questions I Would Like to Ask God," Ravi Zacharias International Ministries, *Just Thinking, www.gospelcom.net/rzim.*

163. *James:* William James, *The Varieties of Religious Experience* (New York: Modern Library, 1936), 475, 498, 506–7.

164. *"What good is it":* Mark 8:36.

165. *"So we fix our eyes":* 2 Corinthians 4:18.

165. *"The Creation waits":* Romans 8:19.

166. *Dostoyevsky:* Fyodor Dostoyevsky, *The Brothers Karamazov* (New York: Doubleday), 593, 656 (literal translation of the Russian, *esli Boga net—znachit, vsio pozvoleno*).

167. *Lewis:* C. S. Lewis, *Mere Christianity* (New York: Macmillan, 1968), 118.

168. *Powers:* J. F. Powers, *Wheat That Springeth Green* (New York: Pocket Books, 1988), 48.

169. *Ellul:* Jacques Ellul, *The Humiliation of the Word* (Grand Rapids, Mich.: Eerdmans, 1985), 1.

169–170. *Merton:* Thomas Merton, *The Seven Storey Mountain* (New York: Harcourt, Brace, 1948), 190–91.

170. *Blake: "To see a world":* William Blake, "Auguries of Innocence," quoted in George K. Anderson and William E. Buckler, eds., *The Literature of England* (Glenview, Ill.: Scott, Foresman and Company, 1966), 149.

170. "*Good advice for Satan's":* Malcolm Muggeridge, *A Third Testament* (Farmington, Penn.: Plough, 1976), 57.

170. *Merton:* Thomas Merton, *Run to the Mountain* (San Francisco: HarperSanFrancisco, 1996), 431.

170. *"They will not be convinced":* Luke 16:31.

170. *James:* William James, *The Varieties of Religious Experiences* (New York: Modern Library, 1936), viii.

171. *"Surely the Lord":* Genesis 28:16.

171. *"Love never fails":* 1 Corinthians 13:8, 7.

172. *"For God so loved":* John 3:16–17.

173–176. *Gordon:* Ernest Gordon, *To End All Wars* (Grand Rapids, Mich.: Zondervan, 1963), 105ff.

175. *"Greater love":* John 15:13 (KJV).

177. *Eliot:* T. S. Eliot, *Christian Register* (19 October 1933), quoted in Graham Martin, ed., *Eliot in Perspective, A Symposium* (London: Macmillan, 1970), 243.

11. Earth Matters

179. *Weil:* Simone Weil, *Gravity & Grace* (New York: Routledge, 1995), 119.

180. *"For in the same":* Matthew 7:2.

181. *Pagans and Christians:* Robin Lane Fox, *Pagans and Christians* (New York: Knopf, 1989).

182. *"certain of what we do not see":* Hebrews 11:1.

182. *"we fix our eyes":* 2 Corinthians 4:18.

182. *"For our struggle":* Ephesians 6:12.

184–185. *"By faith we understand":* Hebrews 11:3.

186. *de Chardin:* Pierre Teilhard de Chardin, quoted in Steven R. Covey, *The 7 Habits of Highly Effective People* (New York: Simon and Schuster, 1989), 319.

186. *"Now we see":* 1 Corinthians 13:12.

186. *"The body that is":* 1 Corinthians 15:42–44.

187. *"I saw Satan":* Luke 10:18.

187. *Herbert:* George Herbert, *English Poems of George Herbert* (Totowa, N.J.: Rowman and Littlefield, 1974), 142.

188. *"For by him":* Colossians 1:16–17.

189. *"Work out your salvation":* Philippians 2:12–13.

189. *"your will be done":* Matthew 6:10.

190. *Hesiod:* Hesiod, quoted in Russell Kirk, *The Roots of American Order* (Washington, D.C.: Regnery Gateway, 1991), 26.

190. *"I tell you the truth":* Matthew 18:18.

190. *More:* Thomas More, quoted in Robert Bolt, *A Man for All Seasons* (New York: Vintage, 1962), 81.

12. Eyes of Faith

191. *Law:* William Law, *A Serious Call to a Devout and Holy Life* (London: Macmillan, 1898), 246.

191–195. *Montagu:* Ashley Montagu, *The Elephant Man* (New York: Dutton, 1971), 1, 15, 24, 27.

195. *"imitation of grace":* Bernard Pomerance, *The Elephant Man* (New York: Grove, 1979), 38.

196. *Darwin:* Charles Darwin, quoted in Marilynne Robinson, *The Death of Adam* (Boston: Houghton Mifflin, 1998), 43, 35.

196. *Johnson:* Harriet McBryde Johnson, "Unspeakable Conversations," *The New York Times Magazine* (February 16, 2003), 50.

197. *Kierkegaard:* Søren Kierkegaard, *The Sickness Unto Death* (New York: Penguin, 1989), 33.

197. *Edwards:* Jonathan Edwards, quoted in Marilynne Robinson, *The Death of Adam* (Boston: Houghton Mifflin, 1998), 172.

198. *Spurgeon:* Charles Spurgeon, Sermon No. 897, "The First Cry from the Cross," delivered October 24, 1869, at the Metropolitan Tabernacle, Newington, London, England. *http://www.spurgeongems.org*

198. *"Not many of you":* 1 Corinthians 1:26–29.

198. *"The Lord does not look":* 1 Samuel 16:7.

199. *Body Project:* Joan Jacobs Brumberg, *The Body Project* (New York: Random House, 1997), xxi.

200. *Chrysostom:* John Chrysostom, quoted in Margaret Schatkin, "Culture Wars," *Christian History*, Issue 44 (Vol. XIII, No. 4), 34–35.

200. *"Set your minds":* Colossians 3:2.

201. *"came down from heaven":* John 6:58.

201. *"From now on":* 2 Corinthians 5:16.

202. *"as though God":* 2 Corinthians 5:20.

202. *Nouwen:* Henri Nouwen, *¡Gracias!* (Maryknoll, N.Y.: Orbis, 1993), 20.

202. *Treves:* Frederick Treves, quoted in Ashley Montagu, *The Elephant Man* (New York: Dutton, 1971), 79.

202–203. *Vanier:* Jean Vanier, *Man and Woman He Made Them* (Mahwah, N.J.: Paulist Press, 1985), 174.

205–206. *"For whoever wants":* Mark 8:35.

206. *Buechner:* Frederick Buechner, *The Faces of Jesus* (New York: Stearn/Harper & Row, 1989), 136.

13. Practising the Existence of God

207. *Milton:* John Milton, *Paradise Lost* (New York: New American Library, 1961), 171.

207. *Kierkegaard:* Søren Kierkegaard, *Either/Or,* quoted in Thomas C. Oden, ed., *Parables of Kierkegaard* (Princeton, N.J.: Princeton University Press, 1978), 20.

208. *Lawrence:* Brother Lawrence, *The Practice of the Presence of God* (Nashville: Nelson, 1981).

208. *Mouw:* Richard Mouw, *Uncommon Decency* (Downers Grove, Ill.: InterVarsity, 1992), 59.

209. *Wright:* Richard Wright, *Native Son* (New York: Harper Perennial, 1993), 412.

210. *"Where your treasure is":* Matthew 6:21.

210. *"You cannot serve":* Matthew 6:24.

210. *Ellul:* Jacques Ellul, *Money and Power* (Downers Grove, Ill.: InterVarsity Press, 1984).

211. *"Then your father":* Matthew 6:2–4.

212. *"joyfully accepted":* Hebrews 10:34.

212. *Teresa:* Teresa of Ávila, *The Life of Saint Teresa of Ávila by Herself* (New York: Penguin, 1957), 284.

212. *"I know what it is":* Philippians 4:12.

212. *Wesley:* John Wesley, quoted in Edward W. Bauman, *Where Your Treasure Is* (Arlington, Va.: Bauman, 1980), 73.

214. *"If anyone":* Matthew 16:24.

214. *"All men will hate":* Matthew 10:22, 28.

214. *Augustine:* Augustine of Hippo, *Sermons to the People,* translated by William Griffin (New York: Image/Doubleday, 2002), 6.

215. *Ladd:* George Eldon Ladd, *The Gospel of the Kingdom* (Grand Rapids, Mich.: Eerdmans, 1959), 39.

215. *Bono:* From a speech delivered at Wheaton College, December 4, 2002.

215–216. *"I have worked":* 2 Corinthians 11:23–27.

216. *"Though outwardly":* 2 Corinthians 4:16–18.

216. *Baxter:* Richard Baxter, *The Saints' Everlasting Rest* (New York: American Tract Society, 1758), 291–327.

218. *"Do not be anxious":* Philippians 4:6–7.

218. *Yalom:* Irvin Yalom, *Love's Executioner,* (New York: HarperCollins, 2000), 7.

218. *"I am the resurrection":* John 11:25–26.

219. *Bach:* Johannes Sebastian Bach, "Come Sweetest Death," or *Komm, süsser Tod,* Cantata in A minor, BWV 478.

219–220. *Nouwen:* Henri Nouwen, *Beyond the Mirror* (New York: Crossroad, 1990), 36, 66.

220. *"For I am already":* 2 Timothy 4:6–8.

220. *Raboteau:* Albert J. Raboteau, *Slave Religion* (New York: Oxford University Press, 1978), 217.

220. *"God is just":* 2 Thessalonians 1:6–7.

220. *Raboteau:* Albert J. Raboteau, *Slave Religion* (New York: Oxford University Press, 1978), 291.

221. *Kozol:* Jonathan Kozol, quoted in Klaus Issler, *Wasting Time with God* (Downers Grove, Ill.: InterVarsity, 2001), 108.

222. *"She did what she could":* Mark 14:8–9.

223–224. *van de Broek:* Stanley W. Green, *The Canadian Mennonite* (September 4, 2000), quoted in *Leadership* (Spring 2001), 71.

224. *"Do not be overcome":* Romans 12:21.

224. *Auden:* W. H. Auden, "For the Time Being: Advent," in *Collected Poems* (New York: Random House, 1976), 274.

14. Stereoscopic Vision

225. *Schweitzer:* Albert Schweitzer, quoted in John C. Maxwell, *The 21 Indispensable Qualities of a Leader* (Nashville: Nelson, 1999), 139.

226. *"But our citizenship":* Philippians 3:20, 19.

226. *"city with foundations":* Hebrews 11:10.

226. *Ibsen:* Henrik Ibsen, *Emperor and Galilean* (Lyme, N.H.: Smith and Kraus, 1873), 162–63.

227. *Lewis:* C. S. Lewis, *Mere Christianity* (New York: Macmillan, 1968), 118.

227–228. *"Do all your work":* Ann Lee, founder of the Shaker Community, quoted in Elizabeth O'Connor, *Cry Pain, Cry Hope* (Waco, Tex.: Word, 1987), 34.

228. *Ignatius:* Saint Ignatius of Loyola, quoted in David Fleming, *The Spiritual Exercises of St Ignatius: A Literal Translation and a Contemporary Reading* (St. Louis: The Institute of Jesuit Sources, 1978), 23.

228. *Lodge:* David Lodge, *The British Museum Is Falling Down* (New York: Penguin, 1981), xvii–xviii.

229–230. *Lewis:* C. S. Lewis, *The Weight of Glory* (Grand Rapids, Mich.: Eerdmans, 1949), 43.

231. *"Let us not become weary":* Galatians 6:9.

231–232. *Marsh:* Charles Marsh, *God's Long Summer* (Princeton, N.J.: Princeton University Press, 1997), 39–40.

233. *Booker T. Washington:* Albert J. Raboteau, *Slave Religion* (New York: Oxford University Press, 1978), 249.

234–236. *Jordan:* Clarence Jordan, quoted in Dallas Lee, *The Cotton Patch Evidence* (Americus, Ga.: Koinonia, 1971), 105–20, 190–95.

237. *Kelly:* Thomas Kelly, *A Testament of Devotion,* quoted in Robert Hudson and Shelley Townsend-Hudson, *Companions for the Soul* (Grand Rapids, Mich.: Zondervan, 1995), September 9 reading.

237. *James:* William James, *The Varieties of Religious Experience* (New York: Modern Library, 1936), 350.

238–239. *Merton:* Thomas Merton, *No Man Is an Island* (New York: Harcourt, Brace, 1955), 108–9.

239. *Merton:* Thomas Merton, *Ascent to Truth* (San Diego: Harcourt, Brace, Javonovich, 1951), 117.

241. *"You fool!":* Luke 12:16–21.

242. *"The kingdom of God":* Luke 17:20–21.

243. *"If only for this life":* 1 Corinthians 15:19.

243. *Pascal:* Blaise Pascal, *Pascal's Pensées* (New York: Dutton, 1958), 61, 57.

224. *"The kingdom of the world":* Revelation 11:15.

244. *Michelangelo:* Michelangelo Buonarroti, *The Complete Poems of Michelangelo* (Chicago: The University of Chicago Press, 1998).

We want to hear from you. Please send your comments about this
book to us in care of zreview@zondervan.com. Thank you.

ZONDERVAN™

GRAND RAPIDS, MICHIGAN 49530 USA

WWW.ZONDERVAN.COM